the
darkest
house

SECRETS OF THE HOUSE

The house invites you in.

The house hates you.

The house wishes to be left alone.

The house is lonely.

The house is in pain.

The house wants your pain.

The house hates you.

All houses in which men have lived and suffered and died are haunted houses.

~Mary Roberts Rinehart, The Red Lamp

INTRODUCTION

Haunted house.

The term conjures instant images of spooky, old, run-down houses with a ghost within. Creaking floorboards. Strange moaning sounds. Objects moving on their own. The ghost wants something, probably something that will put it to rest, leaving the house once again at peace. If that's what a haunted house is, then the Darkest House is not one.

Certainly, there are spirits of the unquiet dead here. There are old floorboards, strange sounds, and maybe even objects that move on their own. But the Darkest House isn't a house with a ghost in it. There aren't angry or evil spirits tainting an otherwise mundane location. The house *is* the haunting. If there are angry, pained spirits denied an eternal rest within the Darkest House, it's the house inflicting that upon them, not the ghosts affecting the house.

The house is the true villain of this story, not the things within it.

The house has an origin wrapped in pain, longing, and misery. You'll learn that story eventually, but know that even the story is a lie because the house has always existed. The house is older than most of the worlds it intrudes upon. Perhaps it is an infection that spreads throughout the worlds. Perhaps it is an entity constantly worming and seeping its way into new universes. Or maybe it is older than all worlds. Perhaps it is not some malady afflicting the many worlds, but rather the soil in which all worlds grow. Perhaps the worlds need the house somehow. Perhaps it is where they store away their own pain, emptiness, and misery.

All worlds touch the house. One way or another, the house exists in every conceivable existence. Whether it seeks out new worlds or the worlds seek out the house, the house can be entered—and perhaps exited—from any world.

I've come to loathe the words "realism" or "realistic" as applied to roleplaying games (RPGs). There simply is no such thing. RPGs, like virtually all fiction, always take liberties with what's real for the sake of story, or to facilitate an action. To really represent a battle between two small groups (some adventurers vs. some generic orcs, say), and take into account every move and countermove, every step and every stance, the weight of every object, the force of every blow, each thought of each participant, the chance of sweat from each combatant's brow blurring vision a bit at any given moment—it would take days, not minutes, and would likely be one of the least fun gaming experiences you could have.

Regardless, applying the idea of "realism" to an (unconventional) haunted house is probably doubly absurd. If you're of a mind to criticize "dungeons" because they're just rooms of danger waiting for PCs to come to them, stop and consider for a moment: that's *exactly* what haunted houses are. A haunted house waits for people to come to it, or is awakened by being disturbed. For the most part, the archetypal haunted house has no real meaning or existence without someone from outside of it coming in to experience it.

There's no ecology in the house. Yes, there are a bunch of cats in the Cat Menagerie room, but if you're worrying about what they eat, you're misunderstanding the Darkest House. If you need an explanation, you can rationalize something supernatural, like the house sustains them, or they're not real cats, or they're the ghosts of cats . . .

But honestly, the thing that strips the horror right out of horror is too much explanation.

That said, The Darkest House—like most horror tales—does have something to say. It's not just meaningless encounters. Rather than explanations, there are themes at play. The sections of the house have far more to do with the dark side of family and love than ecology or realism.

The house hates you. Does the house hate everyone? Maybe. But one thing we know for certain, it hates *you*. And of course, by you, we mean the player characters (PCs). It doesn't matter who they are.

This isn't necessarily some broad, sweeping statement about the house. It's a specific statement about the player characters. The house hates *them*.

It doesn't matter why. It would only matter if there was some way to assuage that hate. To change the house's mind.

There isn't. There is no way to make amends for some tangible wrongdoing in the past, because it isn't that simple.

It would be wrong to assume that the dangers and obstacles encountered in the house are necessarily there to harass or harm visitors. The house hates, and its existence is hateful, but it is not filled with traps set by some intelligence to be worrying or dangerous to intruders. That's simply too intentional. Too deliberate. While the house might sometimes take active steps to harm others, the interior of the house is what it is because that's the nature of the house. Belladonna isn't poisonous to ingest because of any kind of intention on the plant's part. It's just the nature of the plant (and the nature of creatures that consume it). This is similar to the house.

In fact, it's not wrong to think of the house as being a toxin, just simply one that afflicts the universe (or universes). Another way of thinking of it is as a virus. Or a cancer. In other words, the house has its own nature, regardless of and independent of the context and in particular the understanding and the expectations of those that encounter it.

If the house doesn't make sense, that's because it has no interest in doing so, at least from the point of view of some mortal beings. It's arrogance on the visitors' part to assume otherwise. Besides, it's a dangerous and difficult path to begin assigning too much in the way of conventional and comprehensible human goals to the house. The house is more akin to some unknowable entity conjured by Lovecraft's fevered imagination or dream (or both).

Except . . . except that a Lovecraftian being has no interest in you. You are beneath its notice like a bacterium in the dirt on its metaphorical shoe. But here, you don't even get the tiny modicum of comfort the anonymity of Lovecraftian nihilism might afford. Because the house is aware of you. It *does* have an interest in you.

And the house hates you.

Horror is a wide spectrum, so it's helpful to know what the intended mood of The Darkest House is, and what it is not (you can of course do whatever you want with this).

What The Darkest House is:
It's the descent into madness. It's old traumas and emotional scars. It's the fear of death and what we're afraid might come afterward. It's a bit of Clive Barker mixed with a little Shirley Jackson with a bit of *House of Leaves*. It's one's own inner demons given substance and life. It's slow, creeping horror that comes upon you with a lingering dread building slowly to a dark crescendo. It's the monster you can't see, but you strongly suspect is there, in the shadowy darkness. It's the implications of terrible, difficult choices.

What The Darkest House is not:
It's not skulls and gore, at least not as simply decor. It's not torture porn. It's not Stephen King. It's not Lovecraft. It's not tentacles. It's not classic medieval demons or ghosts. It's not kaiju monsters or zombie hordes. It's not action-packed, tactical battles.

In many ghost stories and haunted house tales, the story comes from learning the background of the ghost or the place and then "putting things right." The heroes attempt to put the ghost to rest by doing something they left undone. Those can make great stories; however, that's not this story. The most the PCs can hope to do is sever the Darkest House from their own home world.

Through the journal pages and other clues the PCs can find in the house, they can learn some of the story of Phillip Harlock, one of the owners—perhaps the original owner—of the house. These might provide some insight into some of the encounters, and perhaps into the nature of the house overall (and provide appropriate flavor), but they aren't meant to provide a way to "save" Phillip or "cleanse" the house. Things have gone way, way past that point (if they ever were there at all). The house is a force of nature (or unnature) unto itself at this point.

If you're reading this, you've entered the Darkest House already and it's too late to warn you off. So you might as well discover the house's secrets. The house hates you, but this book does not.

You're probably going to be the Game Master as you explore the house—if you're not, read the short Being a Player in the Darkest House section of this book book (page 8). The downloads referred to in this section are explicitly for players. The rest is for the GM.

Very well then, GM. Let's get started. Within these pages, you'll find the rooms of the Darkest House, a house that could be located in any (or every?) world. It's a house with a mind of its own, and a deep, dark hatred for anything and everything that has to do with people. But that's only a part of all the information and material it offers for you to make running the Darkest House adventure as easy and fun as possible.

Perhaps the first thing you should read is The House System, including The Truth and Lies We Bring With Us. These sections explain how the game will be played, including how to convert characters from other game systems, or how to convert the house to your game system of choice. After that, The Nature of the House is pretty much everything the GM needs to know—it's the behind-the-scenes secrets and overview of the house. The section Running Games Set in the Darkest House offers advice on how to set the right tone, troubleshooting issues that can arise, how to get a game started (including enumerating all four potential entrances) and so on.

There are also resources meant for the players, starting with the different character sheets (there are four different versions). You'll want to give them the *Crossing the Threshold* PDF (with player-relevant House System information) and the House System Reference for Players. All of these things are PDF downloads that you can get access to so that they can be used and referred to at the table, either as electronic files or as printed-out forms.

While you're downloading things, you'll also want to download the GM's Reference Sheet and the Key Guide. These form-fillable sheets serve as rules references, a house action tracker, and a means to track the keys that are important to the navigation through the house, as well as which keys the characters have found.

At the end of the book, you'll find an appendix that has all of the Remnants—handouts meant to be shown to the players at certain points.

Before you get to the meat of the book—The Rooms—take a look at the *Journal of Phillip Harlock* PDF (available for download at the link below). Players can find the scattered pages of the journal (included with all the other Remnants) to see Phillip's descent into madness within the house, but this section offers all the text of the journals in order, so you can get the clearest possible understanding of something that's not at all clear and beyond mortal understanding.

Download all the PDFs mentioned here, and Consent in Gaming, an informational resource for gaming safety here:

https://mymcg.info/tdh-Using-This-Book

There had stood a great house in the centre of the gardens, where now was left only that fragment of ruin. This house had been empty for a great while; years before his—the ancient man's—birth. It was a place shunned by the people of the village, as it had been shunned by their fathers before them. There were many things said about it, and all were of evil. No one ever went near it, either by day or night. In the village it was a synonym of all that is unholy and dreadful.

~William Hope Hodgson, *The House on the Borderland*

THE HOUSE SYSTEM

Rather than being designed for a specific game system, The Darkest House has its own internal system called the House System. The House System is easy to use and easy to understand, although likely quite different from the system(s) you use most of the time. This is intentional. Because the Darkest House experience isn't about stats and numbers, it's about mood and story (both dark). The characters will almost certainly leave the house with some permanent changes that are going to affect any ongoing campaigns.

Some gamers might balk at how simple the system is. They want more granularity and robust options in their game. I understand. But the House System does two things:

1. It allows both players and GM to really focus on the story and the mood.
2. It tells the players in a very overt way, "Things are different here." It makes that statement in a language all players will understand, in a tone they will all hear: via game mechanics that govern how their character works. Thus, if the game's mechanics are the laws of physics for your game, the laws of physics work differently in the Darkest House.

I know many of you will say, "I don't want to change. My group likes the system we're used to." And if that's your desire, well, okay. Games are meant to be enjoyed and you should do what you want. Use your system as normal. But all the inhabitants and challenges in this product have House System Ratings. The great thing is, the rules for conversion work both ways. The simple stats you'll get in the Darkest House will be enough for you to convert to your group's favorite game system.

Thus, your 5e characters can tromp around in the Darkest House using the stats they're used to, and the challenges they face will have familiar resolution mechanics. And you can *still* convert PCs and NPCs from other campaigns into the Darkest House using the simple conversion methods and then into your current system, using the Darkest House internal system as a sort of "Rosetta Stone" of game mechanics.

If this is the case, the GM should figure a way to at least incorporate the **House Die** (page 22) and characters acquiring **Dooms** (page 24) into their system of choice.

Imagine everything in the world was rated on a scale of 1 to 10. 1 is the worst, and 10 is the best. The worst door in the world is maybe a light curtain, while the best door in the world is a titanium vault door. All other doors fall somewhere in between, so that an interior door you have in your house is a 3, while an exterior door on your house is probably more like a 5. A really sturdy iron door might be an 8.

And when I say everything, I mean *everything*. Not just objects, but actions, characters, creatures, and entities.

Usually, if an object has a Rating, that Rating is used to determine the difficulty of an action. In other words, the difficulty of doing something to the object. If you're trying to break something with your hands, breaking a piece of dry spaghetti is a Rating 1, while breaking a vault door is a Rating 10. In this case, you're not really rating the objects, you're rating the action of breaking them, and judging how hard it would be. A lock with a Rating of 5 is harder to pick (or jimmy, or force) than a lock with a Rating of 3. The object determines the Rating of a task involved in overcoming it.

And of course, creatures, inhabitants, and entities in the house have Ratings too. When engaging with creatures, inhabitants, and entities in the house, their Rating determines the Rating of the task involved in opposing it. Attacking a foe with a Rating of 3 is a Rating 3 task.

While 5 is the median Rating, it is not necessarily the average. Most things a character will encounter are likely Rating 3 or 4. When in doubt, you could just say the Rating is 4 and move along with the story. Something with a Rating of 4 is challenging to average characters but practically ignorable by powerful ones.

In general, higher-rated characters are more likely to succeed, but higher-rated tasks are harder to accomplish.

But here, you need to make a decision on your own, based on your play style. I'm going to advocate that you take Ratings as absolutes. In other words, a door with a Rating of 3 is always going to have a Rating of 3, no matter who the PCs are or what their Rating is.

Some groups, however, will want to make the Ratings based more on the Ratings of the PCs. So in effect, the challenges meet the characters on sort of an "even ground." In this case, you might want to say that **target numbers** (page 20) are always about 3 or 4 higher than the Rating of the PCs. You might improve your story that way, with the characters always being challenged, but not *too* challenged.

Doing it the other ("absolute") way probably makes the Darkest House more challenging and frightening overall, and creates an interesting possibility of the "return to" story, where the PCs go to the house, have to run from most encounters, and just barely escape with their lives, but return later after they have gained greater skills and powers, to combat the forces within the house directly. That's what I recommend, but everyone's style is different.

When PCs enter the Darkest House, they also get converted to this simplistic, light system. Think of it like this: the Darkest House has its own laws of reality, and characters in the house must work within those laws, even if they're a bit different from what they're accustomed to. You can—and should—use PCs from all your favorite RPG systems in the Darkest House. Notice that I didn't say "any"; I said "all." That's because The Darkest House offers you an opportunity to introduce a strange setting into your campaign and then pull it out again and use it in a different campaign, even if the second one uses an entirely different game system.

In fact, we'll go one further. You could also introduce an NPC from your old campaign (again, using a different system) as someone trapped in the Darkest House. In other words, your 5e group could run into that Call of Cthulhu villain they used to hate. Or your Cypher System players could encounter their own Pathfinder characters, this time as NPCs.

You could even have PCs from different campaigns (and different systems) join up within the halls of the Darkest House. Imagine a couple of PCs from the Shadow of the Demon Lord game you play on Saturdays joining together with a pair of Numenera PCs from the game you play every other Thursday. The possibilities are endless.

To make it possible to convert any character to the House System, we don't deal with the specifics of every system. I'm not going to tell you how to convert 5e hit points to Fate stress boxes or try to tell you how to convert Cypher System Effort to something else. Instead, we're going to convert mechanics and characters conceptually. It's a narrative conversion rather than a purely mechanical one.

Essentially, the philosophy behind the conversions is this: rather than trying to create a formula that converts this aspect of a 5e character to be the equivalent of an aspect of a Cypher System character as well as an aspect of a Fate character and a Vampire character and so on, we convert the character as a whole, *proportionally*. In other words, we measure a 5e character as compared to all other possible 5e characters, and a Cypher System character as compared to all other possible Cypher System characters so that we can then compare the 5e character and the Cypher System character proportionally. We say, on a scale of 1 to 10 of the entire 5e system, this 5th-level half-orc fighter with all his various aspects is about a 3. Or, we say, this tier 2 Numenera Glaive with all her various aspects is also a 3 on a scale of 1 to 10. And thus, in the House System, those two characters are very close in terms of power and capability, and are both a Rating 3 character (we'll get to what that means shortly).

Why not do a more formulaic conversion? Well, first off, I have serious doubts whether such a thing is even possible. There are just too many systems to take into account. But even if it were, you'd end up with something that might be technically "correct" but it would feel all wrong. It's like the difference between language translation and language localization. Translation just goes through word by word and converts each to its equivalent. Localization takes the text and makes it seem as though it was originally written in the new language by converting cultural differences, phrasing, slang, idiom, and so on. We're aiming for localization here, not a direct translation.

Hopefully, the result will be characters that feel similar to their old selves but will function quite differently. A Pathfinder paladin will still effectively hit things with their sword, a Shadowrun adept will still wield magical powers, and a Call of Cthulhu character will still, well, be really quite fragile and should probably run from most dangers encountered in the house.

Let's begin.

CHARACTER RATINGS

Here's where the conversion part of all of this comes in. Because you can insert existing characters into the House System, and if they enter the Darkest House, you should.

Most RPG systems have some kind of ability scores, various skill scores, offensive and defensive values, and so on. As mentioned earlier, the House System simplifies all of that into a single Rating, on a scale of 1 to 10.

Fortunately, many games already have a numerical rating in the form of levels or ranks or what have you. This is handy because you can measure the character's level to the maximum level attainable to figure out where they might fall on a 1–10 rating scale. So if your system rates characters on a scale of 1 to 20 levels, just cut the level in half and you have the Rating.

The following chart can help with this process. If the original system has numerical levels or tiers, use the most appropriate column to approximate this level to a House System Rating. If the original system has numerical skill ratings but not levels (or anything similar to levels), take the general average of the character's skill scores on the scale similar to one of the columns to approximate a House System Rating. So, if the system has percentile scores for skills, take a general average of the truly useful skills and look at the 1–100 column to get an approximate Rating.

House System	1–20	1–4	1–6	1–100
1	1–2	1	1	1–10
2	3–4	1	2	11–20
3	5–6	2	2	21–30
4	7–8	2	3	31–40
5	9–10	2	3	41–50
6	11–12	3	4	51–60
7	13–14	3	4	61–70
8	15–16	3	5	71–80
9	17–18	4	5	81–90
10	19–20	4	6	91–100

If the original system uses points of some kind to build a character, use the number of points a player would need to build the current character and compare it to the number of starting points and a maximum (or a high but realistic number). For example, if characters start with 150 points, and could get as high as, say, 500 points, but the character in question was probably built with about 200 points (about 40% of 500), we would call that a Rating of 3 or 4.

No matter what system you're using, if you're not sure which number to use between two different conversion results, use the lower one. When in doubt, round down, not up.

If the original system doesn't have anything like these numerical values, you'll have to just approximate like you would with anything else. On a scale of 1 to 10, where does the character fall in terms of ability, skill, prowess, toughness, and so on? If you're still unsure, make them Rating 4 and just keep going.

All of this requires a hefty dose of attention and logic. Because evaluating Call of Cthulhu characters by comparing them to all characters in that game and evaluating all 5e characters by comparing them to all characters in that game are two very different processes. The toughest Call of Cthulhu character is likely not the equivalent of even a moderately tough 5e character. And yet, a really tough 5e character is not the equivalent of a moderately tough Champions character.

So, sometimes you'll want to compare the character to the broad range of the world they come from. A highly skilled cybernetic-enhanced street samurai from Shadowrun might be the equivalent of a vampire from Vampire, but exist in a very different context than a Gumshoe investigator (on one end of the spectrum) or a Mutants and Masterminds character (on the other end).

Consider these rules of thumb:

✦ If the character is basically a "real world" human, or very close, their *maximum* Rating is 4.

✦ If the character is basically a superhero or the equivalent, their *minimum* Rating is 5.

✦ If the character is a heroic fantasy character, an enhanced science-fiction character, or has any sort of paranormal abilities, their Rating can be anywhere from 1 to 10.

✦ No matter what system you're using, if you're not sure which number to use between two different conversion results, use the lower one. When in doubt, round down, not up.

SMALL MODIFICATIONS

Now, a single Rating might not fully model a character. A character might be Rating 3 but they're so good at stealth that they're a Rating 4 when sneaking quietly. A character who has vast mental powers but is relatively frail might be Rating 5, but only a Rating 4 when it comes to physical activities. Feel free to make as many such exceptions like this as it seems like the character needs, but you'll rarely want to give them an adjusted Rating that is more than one away from their main Rating.

WHAT ABOUT CHARACTERS' STUFF?

A sword is a sword is a sword. A laser pistol is a laser pistol is . . . you get the idea. A character entering the Darkest House brings whatever they have with them at the time.

Armor and defensive equipment can modify a character's defense Rating or confer Boons to defense rolls. In the case of a physical attack, the target's Rating can be increased by armor: +1 for light armor like leather or something that offers only partial covering, or +2 for most other armors.

They might find a way to make use of some lockpicks, a bag of tools, or a handheld scanner, but that's really all narratively driven. This character conversion is much more interested in the character, not their belongings. In the end, the weapon doesn't matter as much as the warrior wielding it.

Do keep in mind that there's **no contact with areas outside the Darkest House** (page 55), so radios, communicators, cellphones, netlinks, etc. don't work. In fact, they are pretty dangerous.

WHAT ABOUT CHARACTERS' SPELLS, MAGIC ITEMS, AND SPECIAL ABILITIES?

At the discretion of the GM, abilities, spells, and magic items may be represented in the House System mechanically and/or narratively. Any ability that allows a character to do something special, like fly, turn invisible, see through walls, or control minds works just as it usually would. Those kinds of things are more narrative than mechanical.

Some special abilities may increase a character's specific Rating. For example, a character may have a supernatural defense acting as quasi-mental armor, increasing their Rating by 1 or 2 when avoiding mental attacks or shock.

Any ability that makes a task easier is a **Boon** (page 23). So if you have a strength-enhancing ring and you try to tip over a heavy bookcase, you have a Boon on that action.

Abilities that inflict damage or unwanted conditions on an opponent are handled like any other attack. In the House System, a character rolls to affect a target or targets just like they would a typical attack—regardless of their original system's having the defender roll saving throws, resistance, or what have you.

If spells or special abilities normally have some limitation on usage, such as "Use three times per day," they keep that limitation. If they have a cost in terms of stats, power points, or something of that kind, either just bring those points (or whatever) over to the House System or simply assign them a reasonable number of uses. If they cost the user something in terms of stamina or mental well-being, treat the cost as a minor **wound** (page 29).

You're going to be doing a lot of adjudication here. Remember that this is a narrative conversion more than a mechanical one. Narratively, the character should be able to do what they could do before, and their powers should work like they did before (unless the house is altering them—we'll get to that later too). Do what seems reasonable at the time and don't dwell on it too long. In a narrative conversion, the overall feel is far more important than the particulars.

You might be tempted to grant someone a modification to their Rating rather than giving them a Boon. Changes to a character's Rating should only come when you are initially converting the character. Circumstances should always result in **Boons or Banes** (page 23).

OKAY, BUT WHAT ABOUT HIT POINTS, ATTRIBUTES, SAN SCORE, SPEED, MOVES . . .

Obviously, every game system is going to have its own way of doing things, but the House System already tracks how you **make attacks** (page 36), how you **suffer damage** (page 29)—both physical and mental—how you **resolve tasks** (page 25), and so forth, so any mechanics dealing with such things don't need to be brought over. It means you don't need health or hit points, Armor Class, and a lot of other things that the original system uses.

If something happens that is stat-related or task-resolution related (including combat), use the House System.

MONEY

Some characters in some rules systems won't care about money. Others will care about it a lot. In the Darkest House, you won't find any currency, but the value of important things is given in dollars should the PCs try to loot the place. In another system, 1 U.S. dollar might equal 1 silver piece, 1 gold piece, 1 credit, .83 Euros, or whatever you want.

LANGUAGE

All characters can understand and be understood in the Darkest House. Don't worry what language anyone speaks or what language the journal pages found in the house are written in.

PC RATINGS AND THE DARKEST HOUSE

If the PCs are mostly Rating 1 or 2, they should be prepared to move stealthily through the Darkest House, and run when most of the dangers reveal themselves.

PCs of Rating 3 to 6 will be greatly challenged in the house, but stand a decent chance to make it out alive.

PCs of Rating 7 or higher are powerful enough to take on the Darkest House head-on.

CONVERTING CHARACTERS BACK

Once the PCs leave the Darkest House, you'll want to convert them back to your system of choice. More than likely, players can just pull out their old character sheets. The only things that might have changed would be:

+ Character has wounds. While you can try to convert this to hit points, stress, or whatever damage mechanic the game has, it might be easiest to just say that the character should rest a week or so to recover from the whole harrowing experience.
+ Character has some kind of lingering curse, trauma, or similar affliction—including the effects of Dooms—upon leaving the house. These are very likely more narrative than mechanical. Convert them to your system if need be, but the effects should be more meaningful to the story than to a character's stats.
+ Character gear has changed. Maybe they lost some things, or used some expendable supplies. Just cross them off the original character sheet. Simple. And if they gained some things, like treasures or whatnot, add those to the character's original sheet. Most of the magical treasures in the Darkest House were designed so that they don't really have mechanical effects, but instead narrative ones. There are a few that add a Boon, and this should just be converted to some minor bonus (+1 on a d20, for example).
+ Characters gained experience. If your game uses some kind of experience system to track character advancement, consider escaping the Darkest House to be a major accomplishment. Advancement toward the next level, rank, tier, etc. (if applicable) should be significant. If characters advance by improving their skills or increasing abilities in some other measurement, this advancement should also be significant. Let the characters (and the players) be proud of what they have survived.

Whenever PCs do anything significant where the outcome is in question—attack with a knife, shoot a gun, persuade an NPC to help, try to bash down a door, leap over a pit, figure out the historical significance of an item—the action is resolved with a roll.

To resolve an action, the player rolls two six-sided dice (2d6), adds the dice together, and then adds their character's Rating. In order to succeed, they need to beat the given target number, which is always 7 plus the Rating of the task.

Let's look at an example: let's say a task has a Rating of 3, which means the target number is 10. If the PC has a Rating of 3, then they need to roll a 7 or higher on their 2d6 roll in order to succeed. This means the character—or in fact, any character facing a challenge with a Rating equal to their own—has just over a 50% chance to succeed. If the same character tries something with a Rating of 5, the target number is 12 and they're still just adding their Rating (in this case 3). So now they need to roll a 9 or higher. That's a much lower chance to succeed (just over 25%, actually).

If a task is rated 6 or more above a character's Rating, it is impossible. For example, if the aforementioned Rating 3 character attempts a task with a Rating of 9, they need to reach 16 (9 + 7), and that would mean they would need to roll a 13 on 2d6, which isn't possible. The player might have a chance if they called upon the house for help and used a **House Die** (page 22), but they should know that the task would normally be impossible before they even try.

Likewise, any task rated 6 or more lower than the character is impossible to fail. A Rating 9 character attempting a Rating 3 task can't fail, because the lowest they can possibly roll is a 2. The idea here is that characters can routinely handle tasks well below them in Rating, but some tasks are too difficult for them to even have a chance of success.

THE PLAYER ALWAYS ROLLS

In the House System, players do all the dice rolling. That means that when a player wants to affect an object or an NPC (pick a lock, punch an enemy, sneak past a monster), they roll with the target number determined by the Rating of the object or the NPC.

If something is trying to affect a PC, the player also rolls. So if a foe casts a spell on a PC, attacks them physically, or tries to fool them with an illusion, the GM doesn't roll to see if the NPC succeeds. The player rolls to see if the PC resists, dodges, or sees through the deception. The PC is always the active character, never the passive one. If the PC leaps over a pit, the player rolls for the jump, but if a boulder tumbles down the hill, the player rolls to get out of the way.

This is important because of the **House Die** (page 22) mechanic. The GM should never roll to determine the actions of the house—the players should. The players in the Darkest House need to engineer their own doom.

Of course, that means that if an NPC has a **Boon** (page 23) affecting their action, the player rolls as if the PC has a Bane. Likewise, if a NPC has a Bane affecting their action directed against a PC, the player rolls for their character with an additional die as a Boon.

This method of playing also leaves the GM to focus more on the story.

Should two NPCs act against each other, or an NPC attempt an action not opposed by a PC, simply look at the NPC Ratings. Highest Rating always succeeds. A Rating 7 NPC always breaks open a barrier with a Rating of lower than 7. Ties (equal ratings) always go to the defender.

WHEN DO YOU ASK FOR A ROLL?

Players roll whenever the outcome is in question, and the action is significant. Don't have players make a lot of inconsequential rolls. Attacks, resisting effects, jumping over a wide pit, trying to bash down a door . . . these all call for the dice to come into play.

Do players roll to talk to the NPC, or do they just play out the conversation? That's really up to you and your group's preferred way of playing. Do they roll when the PCs search an area for secrets, or do you just let them narrate where they search, and if they look in the right spot, they find the hidden thing? Again, that's more of a group preference.

However, I will say that I always reward narrative play and stress it over mechanics. So if a character says just the right thing to persuade an NPC to do something, I don't then make the player roll to see if they succeed. Likewise with searching or listening. If there's something to find or something to hear, and the player specifically says their character is looking or listening, I'm probably going to just tell them what they perceive. Usually—particularly in the case of searching for secrets or clues—finding something is almost always more fun, more interesting, and more likely to move the story forward than finding nothing.

DICE ROLLING HACKS

Gamers that want to spice up the die rolling of the system could try one or both of these hacks.

Special Success: If a character rolls equal to or higher than the target number on *a single die* plus their Rating, this is a special success. The player gets to decide generally what the special success entails. Perhaps the task goes faster, a thrown object goes farther, a jump is particularly graceful, and so on. A special success in combat inflicts double damage or, if the player wishes, some effect specific to the situation, such as stunning the foe so it loses its next turn.

Obviously, it's only possible to get a special success if the target number is fairly low (less than 6 + the character's Rating).

Partial Success: If the roll fails to hit the target number but the player rolled doubles (the same number on both dice), this indicates a partial success. Partial success might mean that the full desired result isn't achieved but it's not a complete failure, it takes longer, and so on. So a character attempting to climb over a wall gets halfway to their goal, perhaps.

THE HOUSE DIE

But wait. The house watches everything that happens within it. The house hates you. It resents your success. This means that every time a player rolls the dice for an action (not damage), they also roll an additional, special die. This is called the House Die. If the House Die is the highest die rolled, regardless of whether the character succeeds, **the house acts** (page 67). It's definitely not good.

Usually, the House Die has no effect on whether or not the character succeeds. It only determines if the house acts.

There is one exception, however. If a character is desperate, they can "call upon the house" for aid, either consciously or subconsciously. If a character does this, the House Die is *added* to their normal result. There is no limit to how many times a player can do this, but when they use this option, two things happen.

1. The house acts. It's bad.

2. The character gains a **Doom** (page 24). Dooms always come back to haunt a character.

The two regular dice can be the same color or not, size or not, etc., but the House Die should be significantly different from the other dice. The most obvious choice would be to roll a die darker in color for the House Die, like a dark blue or a black.

BOONS AND BANES

Sometimes, circumstances make accomplishing things easier. Sometimes, they make them harder. These circumstances are called Boons and Banes, respectively.

Boons can come from getting help from a friend, having a particularly good tool, fighting a distracted opponent, and so on. Anything that helps or makes things easier for the PC to succeed is a Boon. Having a Boon means you roll an additional d6 and discard the lowest die.

Banes are anything that makes actions or tasks more difficult, like thick fog, a serious injury, a creature clinging to your arm, and so on. A Bane means you roll an additional d6 and discard the highest roll.

The Boon or Bane die doesn't need to be distinguishable from the normal dice, but it does need to be distinct from the House Die.

You never roll more than three dice (not counting the House Die) when taking an action. Thus, multiple Boons or Banes do not give more than one additional die. But, it's still important to keep track of how many Boons and Banes a character has for any given action, because Boons and Banes cancel out. If a character faces a Bane due to circumstances, but wields a sword that grants a Boon, the player just rolls their regular 2d6 when attacking with the sword. However, if in addition to the Boon from the sword, the character has a Boon from a magic spell, the player rolls an additional die, because the Bane cancels only one of the two Boons that is affecting them.

As an example, consider **Arduk and his magical warhammer** (page 27). Let's say he has a Boon for all attacks. If he is fighting in thick fog, it's hard to see, so he also has a Bane. The Boon and the Bane cancel out, meaning he'll roll 2d6 and the House Die to attack in this scenario.

If Arduk has a magic spell cast upon him to improve his attack with that warhammer, he now has two Boons. Boons do not stack so this doesn't have any additional effect normally, but when he is in thick fog (or affected by any other type of Bane), he still has a Boon, because the Bane cancels one of the Boons, but not both. So he rolls an additional d6 and discards the lowest result.

Because the players always roll, that means that Boons and Banes applied to NPC actions reflect that the player rolls an additional die when resisting the NPC's action. However, in this case, an NPC Boon means the player rolls the extra die and discards the highest die, because the NPC has an advantage. An NPC Boon is essentially a PC Bane. Similarly, an NPC with a Bane means the player discards the lowest die, acting just like a Boon. Since Boons and Banes cancel each other out, that means that if an NPC with a Boon (a PC Bane) acts against a player with a Boon, they cancel out.

While it might be tempting to grant someone a modification to their Rating rather than giving them an extra die and discarding the high or low roll, circumstances should always result in Boons or Banes. Changes to Rating should typically be made only when you are initially creating/converting the character.

DOOMS

When a character gains a Doom, the GM should make a clear and obvious note of it. If possible, the player's online screen should show their ongoing Doom tally, perhaps next to the character's name. (Or, a player could write it on a pad or dry erase board visible to their camera, so that all can see it.) The feeling of increasing danger as Doom tallies rise should become palpable during the game.

When a wounded character **falls unconscious** (page 56) and then checks to see if they **eventually die from a wound** (page 33), they must subtract their Doom total from the roll. Fortunately, each time the character's Doom tally affects them in this way, they can remove one Doom from their total.

Players can also choose to lower their character's Doom total by 1 by spending a Doom. In this situation, they give the GM permission to do something terrible.

Finally, characters **leaving the house with Dooms** (see below) are not in the clear.

Spending a Doom

Players can choose to lower their PC's Doom total by 1, essentially "spending a Doom," as it were. In this situation, they give the GM "permission" to do something terrible. This could be a horrific vision (that inflicts a mental wound), an attack by a ghost or other inhabitant of the house, a vital piece of equipment breaks at an inopportune time, some beneficial magical effect ends early or malfunctions, and so on.

The only guidelines are: it must be significant, bad for the character, and the GM can "inflict" this upon the character or characters whenever they wish. In other words, the GM doesn't need to use the spent Doom right then. The GM can even accumulate a few of them for some truly awful set of circumstances to befall the group.

Leaving the House With Dooms

Use the following table to find the appropriate lasting Doom effect, or make up something new that is of equal significance. These Doom effects are cumulative, so someone with a lingering haunting might also have horrific dreams. Once a Doom effect is determined, a character loses all their Dooms.

LASTING DOOM EFFECTS

Dooms	Effect
1–2	Terrible nightmares and night terrors
3–4	A lingering haunting, with some spirit or spirits plaguing the character's life until they are somehow exorcised
5–6	A physical malady, such as a limp that impedes quick movement, a back injury that flares up at the worst times, or a prominent—perhaps even animate—and disturbing scar, OR a mental malady, such as post-traumatic stress syndrome that incapacitates in moments of stress, a terrible paranoia, or a serious and lengthy bout of depression
7+	A wasting disease that slowly but inexorably rots and withers the character's body into a horrific, almost impossible living corpse (and then they eventually die). Only serious and prolonged medical attention can save them, and there will likely be lasting effects even after that.

EVERYTHING IN TURN

When PCs act, if time matters, they all act in turn, along with the NPCs. The Darkest House room descriptions state whether the NPC acts first. Otherwise, assume the PCs act first. In this case, on their turn, the characters can each perform one action—make an attack, move about 30 feet, go through the door and close it behind them, use a special power, grab an item, hide behind a couch, and so on. Anything that could be done in about 10 seconds or so can be done on a turn, but don't worry about keeping careful track of time. Just make sure everyone gets a turn.

TASK RESOLUTION SUMMARY

When a character attempts any task, they compare their Rating with the task Rating.

+ If the task's Rating is 6 or more lower than the character's Rating, they automatically succeed.
+ If the task's Rating is 6 or more higher than the character's Rating, they automatically fail.
+ In all other cases, the player rolls 2d6 and adds their Rating. Their goal is to roll equal to or above 7 plus the Rating of the task, as determined by their opponent or the obstacle they are attempting to overcome.
+ If a character has a **Boon or a Bane** (page 23), they roll an additional die (so 3d6 in total). If the Boon is in effect, they use the two highest rolls. If a Bane is in effect, they use the two lowest rolls.
+ Anytime dice are rolled for an action, the **House Die** (page 22) must be rolled. The House Die has no effect on success or failure, but if the House Die is higher than either of the success dice, regardless of any other outcome, the **house acts** (page 67).

So in effect, a character is always rolling three dice (with the exception of damage rolls), and four if there is a Boon or Bane in effect.

Let's take a Cypher System character and convert them. We'll use Tacha, a Swift Explorer who Works Miracles. If you're not familiar with the Cypher System, that means pretty much just what it sounds like—she's swift, she's capable, and she can miraculously heal people. Tacha is tier 2 (out of 6). She comes from a modern fantasy setting.

Right off the bat, we look at the 1–6 column of the **Character Rating Conversion Table** (page 16) and see that as a tier 2 character she's either Rating 2 or 3. Let's start with Rating 2.

Now let's see if there are things we need to know other than her Rating (we certainly expect that answer to be yes). Her Might and Intellect Pools are mostly in the normal range (nothing extremely high or low) so we'll ignore those. She's Swift, so that gives her better initiative and running abilities, and it's right there in her character sentence, so we'll give her a Rating of 3 for all things having to do with speed. Further, as an Explorer, she's trained in swimming and climbing. We'll give her a Rating of 3 for both of those things as well. She's also skilled in geography, but frankly, that's never going to come up in the Darkest House, so we don't care. (We can give her a Rating of 3 for geography if it's important to the player.)

Tacha has some special defensive and offensive abilities that make her better at combat. Rather than figure in all these rather involved abilities, we'll just lump them all together and say she's a Rating 3 for attacks and defense. She also wears **light armor** (page 17), so we'll give her Rating 3 for resisting damage too.

She can heal people with her touch and alleviate unwanted conditions such as diseases. Since the House System is all about Ratings and—hey, what do you know—**wounds and conditions** (page 29) have Ratings just like characters do, we'll say that for every wound or unwanted effect that is on a creature, Tacha can **use her action** (page 20) to try to get rid of it. She'll just make a roll, using her Rating and the Rating of the wound or effect. These things normally cost her Intellect points to use, but that's a stat we're not converting, so instead, we'll say she can only try to use her power once per wound or effect. That puts a nice manageable limit on it without having to track points or anything.

Tacha's got a couple of special items, one that allows her to see through solid matter for a limited time and one that creates an area with reduced friction, making it really slippery. We'll just keep those as-is, and refer to the descriptions of those items when we need them, as neither really involves game mechanics much—they're both actually pretty narrative.

So now we have Tacha, who is Rating 2, Rating 3 for swimming and climbing, swiftness, attacks, defense, and resisting damage. She can heal and remove unwanted conditions. Done.

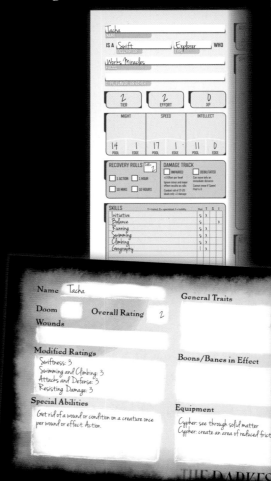

This time, we'll use Arduk, a dwarf fighter from 5e. He's 5th level. He comes from a traditional fantasy setting.

Level 5 in a system that goes from 1 to 20 converts to a Rating 3. That's our baseline.

His Constitution score suggests that like lots of dwarves, he's tough. We'll give him Rating 4 for resisting wounds. He's also got low Dexterity and very low Charisma, so we'll say he's only Rating 2 when it comes to things requiring nimble hands or acrobatics, as well as anything having to do with interacting with others. His skills suggest he should also be Rating 4 for perception and athletics. (There are some very minor bonuses he has to fairly inconsequential skills, so we're going to ignore those—they're all just wrapped up in him being Rating 3, basically.)

In addition to his high Constitution (which, as mentioned earlier, gives him a Rating 4 for resisting wounds), Arduk **wears plate armor** (page 17), which adds 2 more to his Rating. It means that for **resisting wounds** (page 29) he's actually Rating 6 (wow!).

He's got some abilities that give him a bonus to his Armor Class (that's defensive), and add to some combat maneuvers, so like with Tacha before, we'll lump all these together and decide he's Rating 4 for attacks and defense. He can see in the dark, too, but that doesn't require any conversion. It just works the same. Also, he's got a shield and his warhammer is magical, so both attacks and defense will get a **Boon** (page 23) when the player rolls.

In all, Arduk is Rating 3, Rating 2 for anything involving dexterity or charm, Rating 4 for perception, athletics, attacks, and defense (and attacks and defense have a Boon), and Rating 6 for resisting damage. Done.

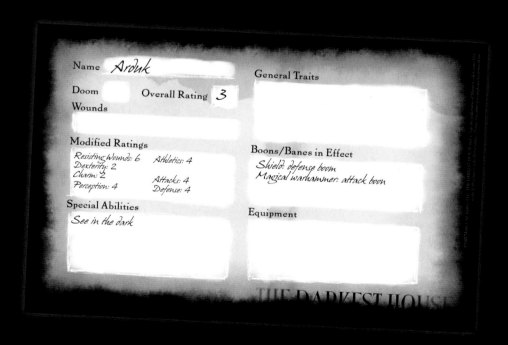

Name *Arduk*

Doom

Overall Rating *3*

Wounds

General Traits

Modified Ratings
Resisting Wounds: 6 Athletics: 4
Dexterity: 2
Charm: 2   Attacks: 4
Perception: 4   Defense: 4

Boons/Banes in Effect
Shield: defense boon
Magical warhammer: attack boon

Special Abilities
See in the dark

Equipment

THE DARKEST HOUSE

Now, what about Arduk's companion, Stevin, a 5th-level half-elf sorcerer?

Well, looking at the **Character Rating Conversion Table** (page 16), they also have a baseline Rating of 3. They're great at interacting with people (20 Charisma and similarly high scores in related skills). We'll say they have a Rating of 4 for social actions. They've also got a +7 stealth score, so let's give them Rating 4 for that as well. Of course, their hit points and physical attacks are fairly low, so we probably should make them Rating 2 when resisting damage and avoiding physical attacks.

As a sorcerer, they've got spells and spell slots. Regarding spell slots, we should just use the system as-is. They can cast each level's spells in the House System as often as they could in 5e. But let's go through them all and see how the House System would handle them.

Witch bolt: This is a magical attack that uses the base Rating of 3 when cast. If it hits, Stevin can continue to use their following actions to continue inflicting the same damage.

Magic missile: This is a magical attack (using their Rating of 3) that doesn't miss. They just roll the damage die against the target when it's cast.

Shield: Since this is a very short-lived but potent defense, I would say Stevin gets a Boon to defense rolls and their Rating is increased by 1 on the turn it's cast.

Invisibility: Works as written.

Levitate: Works as written.

Fireball: This is an attack (using their Rating 3) that can affect a bunch of targets in an area. Since this is a potent attack spell, I'd also say that the attack and damage rolls get a Boon.

Dispel magic: Casting this is a **significant action** (page 20) and is resolved as a task using their Rating and the Rating of the magic they're trying to dispel.

So that's Stevin: Rating 3, Rating 2 for resisting damage and evading physical attacks, Rating 4 for social tasks and stealth. And they can cast their listed spells as described. Done.

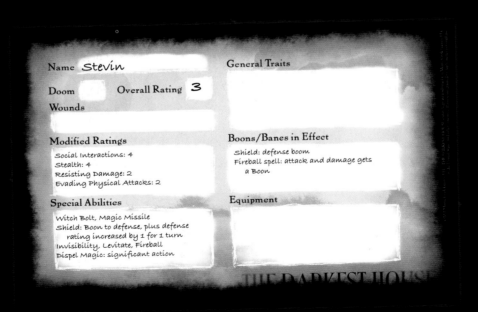

Name: **Stevin**

Doom:

Overall Rating: **3**

Wounds:

General Traits

Modified Ratings

Social Interactions: 4
Stealth: 4
Resisting Damage: 2
Evading Physical Attacks: 2

Boons/Banes in Effect

Shield: defense boom
Fireball spell: attack and damage gets
 a Boon

Special Abilities

Witch Bolt, Magic Missile
Shield: Boon to defense, plus defense
 rating increased by 1 for 1 turn
Invisibility, Levitate, Fireball
Dispel Magic: significant action

Equipment

THE DARKEST HOUSE

Rating even determines health and toughness, both mentally and physically. This is another way in which the House System might deviate from what you're used to. Because of the house's nature, it distinguishes between **physical harm** (page 30) and **mental harm** (page 32). Mental harm could be spiritual, emotional, or intellectual in the same way that physical harm could be a bleeding wound, a concussion, or a broken bone. It's all grouped together and abstracted.

That said, even though all damage is abstracted mechanically, narratively the GM is encouraged to describe the wounds—physical and mental—with as much detail as seems appropriate.

CALCULATING DAMAGE

To calculate damage, you roll 1d6. This is called the damage die. You add the attack's Rating to the result. Then, you subtract the Rating of the victim, with modifications (like **armor**, page 17).

If the result is a positive number, the victim suffers a wound with a Rating equal to the result.

If the result is 0 or less, the victim suffers a scratch, a glancing blow, a graze or something similar—but this has no mechanical effect. They're more or less unharmed.

Thus, Wound Rating = 1d6 + attack Rating – defense Rating

You never roll the House Die when rolling damage, but damage can have a Boon or a Bane.

Because players always roll the dice, this means that not only does a player roll the damage die when they make a successful attack, *they also roll the damage die when they fail to dodge or resist an attack made against them.*

In this case, they roll a damage die, add their foe's attack Rating, and then subtract their own Rating for resisting attacks to see if they get hurt.

Again, in the Darkest House, players bring upon their own downfall.

Mental damage works exactly the same way. Obviously, such wounds aren't about being scratched or hurt, but being affected by shock, fear, trauma, or instability (and eventually, unconsciousness or even catatonia).

PHYSICAL DAMAGE

When a PC or NPC is struck in combat, falls from a height, is burned with fire, or anything else that would cause bodily harm, calculate physical damage.

Out of combat, there might not be an attack roll if the danger is something like a fall, choking fumes, and so on. The player just rolls the damage die and adds the attack Rating and then subtracts their own Rating to see if their character is affected. If it seems like an attack, though, such as a falling rock, treat it like an attack and confirm a hit before determining damage. Either way, the GM determines the Rating of the attack. A fire might have a Rating of 4, for example, while a particularly hot or raging fire would have a Rating of 6.

A Few Sample Ratings for Physical Dangers

DANGER	RATING
Fire	4
Raging fire/lava	6
Fall	1 per 5 feet
Falling heavy object	4
Falling massive object	8
Intense cold	3

Some game systems give more powerful characters the ability to withstand more damage, while others grant them the ability to avoid damage instead. (And some give them either or both.) A "tough" character's Rating is higher for comparing to a damage die. A character skilled at dodging attacks might instead have a modifier to their Rating for defending against attacks. So you can tweak these Ratings to give the feel to which you are accustomed.

WEAPONS AND DAMAGE

A character's Rating is the dominant factor in their accuracy and damage in combat. However, in some cases, the weapon used should affect this as well. Some weapons are inherently more accurate (like a quick, small knife or a magical sword) and may add a Boon, and some are less accurate (like a very heavy axe), which might give the attacker a Bane.

HACKING DAMAGE

Mathematically—on the damage die—granting a Boon is pretty close to the same as increasing the Rating of the character's damage by 1, while granting a Bane is quite close to decreasing the Rating by 1. This means that if a character has a magical heavy axe, the GM could say that the magic increases the Rating by 1 and grant it a Boon, and that would be fine. However, if the character had a magical small knife, the GM could just have it do regular damage for the character, because +1 for the Boon and −1 for the size cancel out.

Note that a modification to Rating affects the maximum and minimum result in a way that a Boon or Bane does not. Thus, if a character's Rating is 3, the biggest wound they can inflict is 9 minus their foe's Rating, whether or not they've got a Boon. The extra die still rolls no more than 6. If you add +1 to the Rating, though, now the biggest wound the character can inflict is 10 minus their foe's Rating. That's going to matter, particularly against **really powerful opponents** (page 34).

If you're curious, a Boon or a Bane means more than a modification of Rating of +/−1 on a standard roll, where you're rolling two dice. A Boon or Bane is closer to +/−1.5 in that case. My advice is to never allow more than a modification of +/−1 to the Rating as it becomes cumbersome to manage within the range of dice and numbers the House System assumes.

MENTAL DAMAGE

Damage to one's mind or soul is less straightforward to envision, but it's handled in exactly the same way as damage to one's body. A terrible shock, a blast of psychic energy, or a horrific experience can all inflict mental damage.

The supernatural inhabitants of the house routinely use powers to affect and attack the minds of others. That's pretty straightforward.

Shock and horror depend on context. If the PCs come from a realistic setting where ghosts and monsters are rare, encountering even the minor spirit in the Boundless Room, for example, might be a terrible shock. But if the characters hail from a world where spirits and the supernatural are common, the shock might be nil.

The encounters presented in the Darkest House have shock/dismay value target numbers already provided for you; however, the values presume the PCs have some experience with the supernatural. For PCs with little to no knowledge of the supernatural, it makes sense to increase the Rating of the mental attacks related to shock/dismay, at least at first, as those characters are more likely to be affected by the experience. Even with those provided, the GM can rule whether the danger presented by the shock/dismay is appropriate to the PCs' original context.

Obviously, mental "armor" is far less common than **physical armor** (page 17), but some characters might have some kind of supernatural defense adding +1 or +2 to the character's Rating to avoid mental attacks or shock.

A Few Sample Ratings for Mental Dangers

DANGER	RATING
Experiencing something creepy	2
Experiencing something terrifying	4
Witnessing a friend's death	6
Experiencing something utterly impossible	7

ACCUMULATING DAMAGE

A wounded character always has a **Bane** (page 23) for each **wound** (page 29) sustained. But remember that Banes do not stack and their effects are not cumulative. Having multiple Banes only matters when it comes to canceling the effect of one or more Boons.

Players should keep track of wounds sustained, and the Ratings of each wound. Every time a wounded character sustains a new wound, they must roll as they would with any task, against the Rating of their most grievous wound (regardless of when it was sustained). If they fail, they fall unconscious or are otherwise completely unable to act due to their injuries.

An unconscious (or similarly debilitated) character with a wound rated higher than the character must, a minute or so later, roll against the wound with the highest Rating. The player must also subtract the number of Dooms the character has gained up to that point. If they fail the roll, they bleed out and die. As a rule of thumb, the amount of time before they must make that roll should be "about a minute." In truth, the GM should call for that roll when it feels most dramatic. And if the unconscious character receives any medical attention before that moment, they don't need to make the roll. The unconscious character need only make this roll once, and loses 1 Doom if they survive.

Both physical and mental attacks are handled this way. However, mental wounds are tracked separately from physical wounds. Mental and physical wounds don't relate to each other in any way. A character doesn't die from mental injuries, but instead becomes catatonic or some other, equally utterly debilitating state.

While the characters are in the Darkest House, the GM should pay attention to when they get wounded, as that accumulated damage can trigger Pain and Wounds.

Normally, the house mentally attacks anyone who **sleeps** (page 56) or is unconscious within it, but to keep things simple, this doesn't happen when a character is knocked unconscious from wounds. The house only attacks when a character is rendered unconscious in a different manner, such as from a magical effect, a drug, etc., or choosing to go to sleep.

PAIN AND WOUNDS

There is a special event that occurs if all of the PCs ever have a physical wound equal to or greater than their own Ratings at the same time. So, if all the characters have a Rating of 4 and they each have wounds rated as 4 or higher, the event is immediately triggered and they all disappear from where they are and reappear in a special room called the Fountain of Pain in the **Amator** (page 77) section of the house.

NPCs AND DAMAGE

Rather than handling damage to NPCs as you would with PCs, simply add up all the Ratings of the wounds inflicted upon an NPC, and once that total reaches three times the NPC's Rating, they are defeated (slain, unconscious, or destroyed). So, an NPC with a Rating of 4 needs wounds with Ratings that total at least 12 before they're defeated, such as a Rating 6 wound, a Rating 4 wound, and a Rating 2 wound. This makes things a bit easier to track, but it also likely makes NPCs a bit more fragile. Of course, the GM is free to use a threshold of four times (or more) the NPC's Rating for all NPCs or only for the particularly tough, powerful foes.

If an NPC ever suffers a wound with a Rating that is 3 (or more) higher than their own Rating, the NPC is immediately dead, destroyed, or perhaps knocked unconscious, depending on the circumstances. This means an NPC with a Rating of 3 can withstand multiple wounds (up until the total of all the wound Ratings is 9), but a single wound with a Rating of 6 will kill them outright.

NPCs can heal a single wound with a Rating less than their own Rating after a minute or so of rest, but a wound with a Rating higher than their own might take one or more days (depending on how the GM wishes to handle the situation). Magical NPCs might be able to heal even faster.

HEALING

Hurt characters should rest. When a character takes no actions, sits or lies down (or leans on a wall or something), and is in no immediate danger for at least a few minutes, this is considered resting. There is no limit to how many times a character can rest.

When a character rests, they roll for each wound they currently bear, with the Rating of each task equal to the Rating of that particular wound. Success means that the character recovers from that wound and can now ignore it. Failure means the wound remains, and the character cannot try to recover from that wound again by resting until 24 hours have passed. So, if a character fails to recover from a wound, they'll have to note when they can try again. Hopefully for the character's sake, this won't happen too often because not only does this increase the danger of future combats (where that wound will come into play again), it also means that's a Bane they won't soon be rid of.

Medical attention, such as aid from a character with some sort of skill and appropriate equipment like bandages, allows a wounded character to attempt to recover from a wound that they failed to heal without having to wait 24 hours. Further, the healer can use their Rating to roll to overcome the wound's Rating rather than that of the wounded character (if the wounded character is unconscious, you must use the healer's Rating).

Magical healing often just works, completely erasing one wound, usually starting with the lowest-rated wound a character has. In this case, highly advanced tech devices, such as a tissue knitter or something like that, are no different than magical healing.

The House System is likely more deadly or dangerous than many systems (and perhaps less deadly than a few) because it has such a high degree of randomness. A powerful character might drop unconscious after just two hits with a bad roll. Likewise, a character might shrug off many wounds. A tough character may find the effects of one truly debilitating wound just won't ever go away. It is not as predictable as a linear, arithmetic progression like a hit point tally. This is intentional.

BUT THAT'S NOT HOW IT WORKED BEFORE!

When you encounter a situation that is obviously unfair to a PC because of the conversion, you should change things right there on the spot to correct the problem. While the House System makes things simpler and in some ways more dangerous or difficult for the characters, it isn't the intention to take away the fun or hurt a character concept. There are many game systems out there, and unexpected things can happen when converting one to another. The GM will have to handle this on a case-by-case basis, but remember that, for example, the House System might make a character more fragile than normal, or more susceptible to harm from mental attacks, and this is intentional.

PC Attacking

✦ When a player makes an attack, they roll 2d6 and add their Rating. Their goal is to roll equal to or above 7 plus the Rating of the opponent. **Boons and Banes** (page 23) may mean rolling an extra die, and players must also roll the **House Die** (page 22).

✦ If successful, the player then rolls the **damage die** (1d6, see page 29) and adds their Rating. Then, they subtract their opponent's Rating. The result (if positive) is the Rating of the wound the NPC sustains.

✦ If the wound sustained has a Rating of more than 3 above the NPC's own Rating, they die immediately. Otherwise, they die when they have sustained wounds with Ratings totalling at least 3 times the NPC's Rating.

NPC Attacking

✦ When a player is attacked by an NPC, they roll 2d6 and add their Rating, hoping to roll equal to or above 7 plus the Rating of the opponent to avoid the attack. Just like before, Boons and Banes may come into play, and players must also roll the House Die.

✦ If not successful, the player then rolls the **damage die** (1d6) and subtracts their Rating. Then, they add their opponent's Rating. The result (if positive) is the Rating of the wound the PC sustains.

✦ If the PC is already wounded and they sustain a new wound, the player must roll against the Rating of their most grievous wound. If they fail, they fall unconscious or are otherwise completely unable to act due to their injuries.

EXAMPLE OF ATTACKING IN PLAY

While exploring the Darkest House, **Stevin the half-elf sorcerer** (page 28) (Rating 3) uses a *witch bolt* spell to attack a horrific fleshy thing crawling out of a small hole in the wall. Stevin's player **rolls 2d6** (page 20) and gets a 6. They add their Rating of 3 to get a 9. The target number for the attack is 7 plus the horrific thing's Rating of 2, for a total of 9. Stevin hits! (Of course, Stevin's player is rolling the House Die as well, but let's not worry about that right now.) Then they roll the **damage die** (page 29), and get a 4, and add their Rating to get a 7, and then subtract the creature's Rating to get a 5 (4 plus 3 minus 2 equals 5). The thing gains a Rating 5 wound—a devastating blast!

So devastating, in fact, that the wound is 3 higher than the target's Rating of 2, which means that it is an automatic kill so it explodes into a disgusting, bloody mess.

However, what poor Stevin doesn't realize is that another of the creatures has squirmed out of a hole in the ceiling. It attacks by dropping down on Stevin's neck with a **Boon** (page 23) from the surprise. Now Stevin's player has to roll for defense. They roll 2d6, but because the attacking fleshy thing has a Boon, the player rolls with a **Bane** (page 23). That means they roll 3d6, discarding the highest die. They roll a 4, a 1, and a 6. Discarding the 6, they get a 5 total and add their Rating of 3 to get 8. Because the creature's Rating is 2, its target number is 9.

That's not good enough to defend, so now the player must roll to determine damage. They roll 1d6, and get a 3. They add the fleshy thing's Rating of 2 and the total is 5. They're not good at resisting damage (they're a bit frail), so their defense Rating for this action is only 2. 5 minus 2 is 3, so Stevin sustains a Rating 3 wound on their neck. Ouch!

If that same creature had dropped down on the neck of Stevin's dwarven friend **Arduk** (page 27), who's tough and wears plate armor (Rating 6 for resisting damage), he would have shrugged off the damage as nothing but a minor irritant—the creature just couldn't significantly pierce that armor.

watches," he added suddenly.

e house. It watches every move

u make.

~Shirley Jackson,
The Haunting of Hill House

THE TRUTH AND LIES WE BRING WITH US

Every character coming into the Darkest House brings a truth or a lie with them, whether they realize it at first or not. Even if a player doesn't typically do much in the way of character development, their character has *something* they believe in. Their truth or lie is an idea that is fundamental to their being, and it's very basically stated. It could be as basic as "Brute force is always the best way to deal with a problem," or "Gold is good," or as deep as "Everyone other than your family members will eventually betray you, so you must watch them closely." Some characters may have more than one, but it doesn't matter—we only need concern ourselves with the one for now. A truth or lie that is quite specific and personal is the best kind. Something that involves a specific PC or NPC would be perfect. For example, "[another PC in the group] always has my back" or "My father was the worst person to have ever lived." But it's not required.

Ideally, what you want to make sure is that a character's truth or lie answers one of the following questions for the character:

- ✦ What's the key to success?
- ✦ How important are my friends?
- ✦ What's my ultimate goal?
- ✦ What's my most important principle or value?

It doesn't matter much whether this is framed as a truth or a lie. It is important, however, that at some point before entering the house, or very soon thereafter, you establish the truth or lie overtly and explicitly with the player. Don't just choose for them, even if you know the character well. It's important that the player knows that you're interested in that specific aspect of the character, because then they will be as well. The distinction very likely comes down to this:

- ✦ A truth is something the character believes is true, and so does the player.
- ✦ A lie is something the character believes is true, but the player does not.

The GM should find out one way or another what each character's core truth or lie is. The easiest way is to just ask. It might be best to just call it a truth, because from a character's point of view, at the start, they believe it to be true. Or perhaps when talking to players, call it a core ideal so as not to use weighted words like truth and lie at all. Further, it doesn't matter if every character has a different truth or lie from everyone else. It might even be that two people have the same ideal but for one it's truth and for the other it's a lie.

The Darkest House isn't merely a frightening locale. It changes those who go in, at least to a degree. No one coming back out is ever truly the same (and of course, some never come back out). We manage this by introducing a character arc that is specific to the character and to the events they experience in the Darkest House. This almost always involves the truth or lie they come in with.

Darkest House arcs fall into five likely types:

Positive Change: Character believes lie — discovers truth — accepts truth

Flat: Character knows truth — faith in truth is tested — character hangs onto truth

Fall: Character believes lie — discovers truth — rejects truth

Disillusionment: Character believes lie — discovers truth — truth is tragic

Corruption: Character knows truth — discovers lie — accepts lie

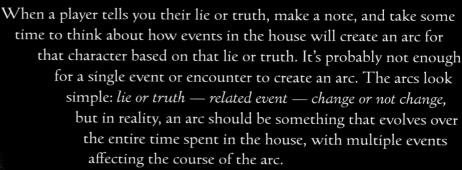

When a player tells you their lie or truth, make a note, and take some time to think about how events in the house will create an arc for that character based on that lie or truth. It's probably not enough for a single event or encounter to create an arc. The arcs look simple: *lie or truth — related event — change or not change*, but in reality, an arc should be something that evolves over the entire time spent in the house, with multiple events affecting the course of the arc.

You might need to tweak encounters here or there to make them pertain to the specific arcs of the characters exploring. For example, if a wizard character's truth is that their magic will always get them out of a jam, it's worth ensuring that the truth is tested. Fortunately, that's probably going to happen without any tweaking at all. At some point, a spellcasting character is going to cast some spells, and it might work out for them or it might not. A character whose lie is that money is the source of all success and happiness, however, might require some tweaking to the text. For example, the wax effigy in the Dripping Room might appear to be a bejeweled crown worth tens of thousands, and the money-loving character must choose between money and their friends.

The point is that in the Darkest House, we're shining a proverbial spotlight on what is important to the characters and creating situations where that idea is challenged, and then shining that same light on however that progression turns out. It might be that the character in question's faith is strengthened, or that they discover a potent and positive truth.

But that's not what the house actually wants. The house wants to shake the characters' faith. It wants to challenge their understanding of the world. It wants to bring on failure, fear, despair, disenchantment, distress, cynicism, and confusion.

The house hates you.

Thus, when possible, if there's only one character affected by something in a given room, the GM shouldn't choose the character randomly. They should choose the one whose truth or lie will be confirmed or denied. For example, if you have a character whose truth involves their faith in their friends in the Studio, have a different character—one of the first character's friends—potentially fall victim to the duplicate. That way, it's bad not only for the affected character, but for the character who had faith in the affected character.

The house is going to use its awful resources against the most vulnerable characters. That doesn't mean we're ensuring that characters will always have their shiny outlooks twisted and all their hopes dashed. That's up to the players. What we're ensuring is that the arc is real and meaningful.

You can, potentially, think of an arc as a test. In the end, it doesn't matter if the test is passed or failed, or whether passing or failing is good or bad for the character. What matters is that the test has an outcome of some kind. Regardless of the results, completed arcs potentially enable characters to **escape from the house** (page 70).

When the PCs first enter the house, you should determine how many arcs need to be completed to achieve closure and escape from the house. Ideally, that answer is, "Each character has to complete their arc," but recognize that this is a lever you can use to determine how long an expedition into the Darkest House might last. The more arcs that need completion, the longer the PCs will stay. Once enough arcs are complete, the characters just find a door to the outside, a window that opens, or some other egress. The house is done with them. For now. (As the GM, you can overrule this. If you want the PCs to escape the house using one of the other methods, that's fine. But be very aware of the desires of the whole group.)

Beyond enabling escape from the house, arcs are entertaining for their own sake. They lead to interesting character development and players thinking about their characters in a new way. You might also want to extend the benefits of completing an arc to a mechanical level. The most obvious way is through experience points or whatever your non-Darkest House system of choice uses to convey how characters advance. Completing an arc should be as significant as some major event or victory in a character's career in terms of reward.

"Essentially," he went on slowly, "the evil is the house itself, I think. It has enchained and destroyed its people and their lives, it is a place of contained ill will."

~Shirley Jackson, *The Haunting of Hill House*

THE NATURE OF THE HOUSE

The house is, in a very real sense, its own world. It has its own rules, and for the most part, those rules are absolute. No character that comes into the Darkest House is greater than the house itself.

INTRUSIONS INTO REALITY

The Darkest House seeps into every world and every reality. When it does, these intrusions take on a form that appears appropriate to the context. An intrusion into Medieval Japan will look appropriate to a house of that place and era. Intrusions into 1930s Chicago or a fantasy town built by elves will look appropriate to those contexts as well. And all these examples will appear very different from each other.

Once truly inside the Darkest House, however, any veneer of context disappears and the house has its own look, its own tone, and its own mood, which we'll get to shortly.

The Darkest House is sometimes called the House That Hungers. This is because once within a particular setting, it can absorb and retain locations (rooms, chambers, or the entirety of a building) into itself. If this happens, that room or building just disappears and becomes a part of the house, at least for a while. That is why sometimes an explorer will find a portion of the house that seems quite different from the rest. It might even be familiar, a place they've been to before. When a location is absorbed, or rather, devoured, by the house, it can bring whatever—or whomever—is within the location with it. This is, in fact, how some people end up unwillingly inside the house (such as the NPC in the Tea Room).

The Darkest House has a complicated history. Its origin might be tied to a man named Phillip Harlock. It might be tied to something far older, perhaps even something primal in the multiverse. Or it might be a combination of all such things.

We sometimes think that when two people spend extended periods of time together, one begins to take on qualities of the other. After years, they truly share everything, including a mental state, and perhaps even a mental space. We even begin to think that they physically resemble each other. It's more than just finishing each others' sentences; they share thoughts and dreams and emotions.

But what if one of those people isn't a person at all? What if it is a place? A house. What happens when someone spends the greater part of their life alone in a single house, and thus the house knows only one person? The person and the house begin to share their mental space as surely as two people would. The person discovers whole new aspects of the house—perhaps some invisible to any other, because surely, like people, houses have secrets. Some might have whole rooms or corridors that they don't reveal to just anyone, in the same way that people keep certain aspects of themselves private.

And as time passes, as the person learns more about the house, the house in turn takes from the person. It develops a consciousness that mirrors their mind. Or at least, as best as a house can.

One thing is certain: if such a thing were to happen, by all means let us hope that the person is stable and of good character. Because if that were not the case, who could predict what shape the house might take? A child can be scarred by poor parenting, but at least parent and child are the same types of being, and in theory, their roles are mostly predefined. But with a person and a house, who is the parent and who is the child? Can such disparate entities ever fully understand each other?

Or stranger still, what if it is the house that is not stable?

What if neither is?

Eventually, people die. (In theory, so do houses, but their lifespans can be much, much longer.) Ponder for a moment as to what happens once the person who has been the house's entire focus and experience for so long is suddenly gone. Being alone can be just as powerful a shaping force as being with someone else. What thoughts does the house think when left on its own?

And lastly, what if there are fundamental forces of the universe—the multiverse—representing particular concepts? Such a thing might be so integral to all of existence that we could think of them as pillars. Pillars that hold up the universe. What if someone or something, say for example a house scarred by its experiences and exposures and then left entirely alone, could somehow tap into such a force? What if it latched onto a specific pillar keyed to its own emotional state, one unique to itself that a human could never hope to fully understand? Infused with this essence, the house could likely do things and think thoughts that we could hardly comprehend. Clinging to a fundamental pillar of the multiverse, it could become not just a house, but the very idea of a house. One that extended into all worlds. A particular type of house.

A haunted house.

Ultimately, we just don't know the answers to all these questions, and perhaps if we did know, we wouldn't truly understand. And that only contributes to the mystery and the horror of the Darkest House. What we need to know is what happens when someone dares cross the threshold and walk its halls.

And what we know is that the house hates you.

PHILLIP HARLOCK'S STORY

A man named Phillip Harlock lived in the house for a very long time. That much is undisputed.

Even the origin of Phillip and the house, however, gets muddy. The characters may learn:

+ Phillip was the first owner of the house.
+ Phillip grew up in the house, so technically his parents were the first owners of the house.
+ There were other owners before Phillip. And the house may be far older than Phillip.
+ Phillip moved the house to its current location.

Phillip was an occultist. Now, if the setting's context is such that wizards and magic exist, then he was a well-known wizard. At least, in the sense of knowledge and understanding, if not accomplishments. Otherwise, he was someone who studied the occult and practiced magick, perhaps thought of as a "kook" by others. Either way, he was a recluse who, by his late twenties, rarely saw his friends, and by his thirties, never left his house. Very likely a severe agoraphobe, he had everything he needed delivered to him. By his late thirties, he stopped allowing even the rare visitor into the house. It's believed that he disappeared under mysterious circumstances some thirty years after that, but the timing is unclear.

Phillip spent a good deal of his life in the house, rarely leaving. It's possible that in so doing, he transposed the house he grew up in with this house. While there are many suggestions of Phillip's family's existence in the house, the PCs never find any records outside the house indicating that they ever lived there. (It's also possible that the Darkest House—also known as the House That Hungers—consumed and assimilated the house he grew up in, perhaps with Phillip's intentional or unintentional help.)

At some point, for some reason, the house tapped into something dark and fundamental to the multiverse. This may be because of Phillip—intentionally? Unintentionally?—but it's also worth considering that the house already had that sort of connection long before Phillip. Did the house inflict itself upon the man, or did the man inflict himself upon the house? We don't know.

And why was it darkness that the house found and attached itself to? Again, we don't know.

It's very likely that Phillip suffered some mental issues, and that they worsened as he got older. Some of these might be traced back to what seems like a potentially abusive childhood, but there is nothing in the public record to suggest abuse when he was young. It's not even clear if he actually had any siblings, despite what the house may suggest.

The family members endemic of the house now might be deeper and older than Phillip's childhood. It's possible that, as Phillip's mind deteriorated and as the house took a stronger and deeper hold upon him, the house imposed the dark archetypes of mother, father, sister, and brother upon him. It is questionable whether he even had a brother and a sister, for example.

Eventually, Phillip set out to learn what he could about the mysteries of the house. He disappeared into the so-called Backrooms of the house, which eventually led to a series of impossible caves, which themselves led to a vast subterranean ocean. Phillip attempted to cross that ocean and was never heard from again.

Since then, the house has only grown further, and the entities representing the dark aspects of family members—Mother, Father, Brother, and Sister, as well as a Lover—have grown stronger. Regardless of whether these entities were ever a real part of Phillip's past, we can be certain that there are beings in the Darkest House that were not. The Host, the Curator, the Gatekeeper, the Smiling Man, and others came from Outside. Outside the house, and outside reality as we understand it. Their presence in the house has far more to do with the darkness now inextricably woven into the fabric of the place than anything having to do with Phillip. Once the house began seeping in between the cracks and spaces of the multiverse, extruding itself into all different worlds, it opened itself to these Outsiders, and for reasons likely inexplicable to mortal minds, they accepted the invitation.

Again, these major players within the house are not ghosts with tragic pasts that the PCs can learn and understand. Because then it becomes the story of those ghosts. The Darkest House is all about the PCs' story. Ultimately, the only past, the only emotions, the only relationships important here are theirs, not Phillip Harlock's.

WHY NOT JUST SPELL OUT THE BACKGROUND OF THE HOUSE?

I already know that a lot of readers and potential GMs will be sad that the background of the house, of Phillip Harlock (and his final fate), and the actual nature of everything within isn't perfectly laid out and explained. Instead, I've left a lot of questions.

Did the house make Phillip go insane?

Did Phillip make the house go insane?

Are all the entities of the house, such as the Host and the Curator, all just aspects of Phillip's shattered mind?

Did Phillip conjure the Enemy of Light, turning the house into the Darkest House?

Did the Enemy of Light come to the house because it was the Darkest House?

Did Phillip create the aeolotropic structure? And if so, did he do it after he first discovered it, due to disjointed time?

Whose family—if anyone's—are Father, Mother, Sister, and Brother?

*Why did the Smiling Man scatter Phillip's **journal pages** (page 272) throughout the house?*

These are fun questions. And I'll go to my grave insisting that they're more fun because we don't know the definitive answers.

The thing is, the answers to these questions aren't going to help a GM run the house well. In fact, I'd argue they might make the experience a little bit worse. Because as you read through the room descriptions and the remnants, a story will emerge. Probably more than one. And as the players begin to explore, they'll start to develop their own theories. They'll put pieces together, and they'll make wild leaps of logic. They'll make the story of the Darkest House into what scares *them*, specifically.

And it doesn't serve your—or their—fun if I tell you that you're wrong.

Whether you want to think of these as adventure hooks or lures or story seeds, PCs need some motivation to go into a creepy old house. Here are a few ideas to get you started. Tailor them, of course, to the player characters themselves.

1. Treasure. Characters are always interested in loot, right? Well, lots of them, anyway. Rare relics, magical artifacts, or just lots of buried jewels hidden away by a previous owner of the house might entice plenty of PCs. The promise of this reward can be real or not. For example, the characters might learn of the very valuable Familial Diamond in the Attic. That's a real treasure, and it's actually in the house. Or, they might hear of some chest of priceless gems secreted away under the floorboards of the master bedroom, or a magical artifact in the cellar that kills demons. Those are not actually there.

2. Lore. Information and knowledge are their own variations on treasure. Perhaps a PC is looking for the word that will activate a magical staff they have found, the final line of an important prophecy, or the secret passphrase that will open an ancient vault found elsewhere. Or perhaps they want to know more about the fundamental forces that the house may very well have somehow tapped into.

3. Curiosity. Perhaps one or more of the characters learned of the existence of an anomalous house and heard some strange stories of unexplained disappearances and just decide to go check it out for themselves.

4. Pursuit. Someone or something important to the PCs goes into (or disappeared into) the Darkest House. A wraith has been harrowing some poor victim at night, and the characters follow it as it returns to its lair—a suitably creepy old house (clearly, it has access to a painting in the Gallery—you'll likely have to add one). A desperate criminal the PCs seek takes refuge unknowingly in the old abandoned house that everyone avoids. Investigating the disappearance of a child, the characters find that the trail leads to a mysterious, run-down house the neighbors claim is haunted.

STORIES WITHIN THE HOUSE

When we play RPGs, we're basically all telling a story as a group. Going in, the characters probably won't have much of a story regarding the house. It's likely that they're just exploring a strange place. And that's fine, but there's more to the Darkest House than simply a spooky funhouse carnival ride if the group wants there to be. However, in the end, the house is not the story. The characters and what they do are the story. There is no "big climax" set up within the rooms of the house. No linear, narrative progression that must be followed through its encounters. The story is what happens as your group experiences it all.

Here are some stories that you can discover in the house:

✦ **Get Buddy out of the house.** In the bedroom labeled simply The Dog, the PCs will encounter an innocent animal that they can befriend and perhaps rescue.

✦ **Locate and rescue the loved one.** This is an NPC close to, and important to, one of the PCs, now trapped in the house. They are in the Tea Room. (Not to be confused with the Lover, who is the entity that haunts the Amator section of the house.)

✦ **Find and restore the aeolotropic structure, also known as the Lacuna.** Somewhere along the line, someone (Phillip Harlock? The Enemy of Light? Father? Someone else?) built a device that allows one to step outside both time and space. It's currently located in the basement of the **Original House** (page 77) and it's currently damaged. But it could be repaired and used for some cosmic purpose having to do with spacetime on a fundamental level.

✦ **Find all the Mystic Tools.** Throughout the house, often hidden, there lie eight tools. Together, they form a set that can be used to build a door that can let characters leave the house, in effect, creating a new entrance—one that can be used as an exit as well.

If the characters find all eight Mystic Tools, they'll discover that one of the eight is a blueprint. This blueprint allows the tools to be used to construct a door in any room of the house, once. This **Mystic Door** (page 71) is permanent and immovable, and leads to the outside of the house. This process requires wood and metal, but that can be obtained by dismantling furniture or even walls or doors inside the house (such things will eventually reset, but that doesn't affect the Mystic Door). It takes about ten total hours of work, assuming at least three people are working. Two people would require fifteen hours, and only one person would take twenty hours. More than three people don't effectively make things go faster.

Once finished, the Mystic Tools disappear, lost within the house again (hidden in different places—because the house hates you), but the characters are free to use the door as often as they wish to enter or exit.

Mystic Tools Locations

Tool	Location
Saw	Cellar
Pliers	Secret Room
Hammer	Spirit of Destruction
Wrench	Mannequin Room
Plane	Dripping Room
Chisel	Music Room
Screwdriver	Secret Chapel
Blueprint	Private Study

Learned characters wise in the way of magic might ascertain that the Mystic Tools could be used to build something else—perhaps an extremely potent magical item or something similar—but the catch is that the Mystic Tools cannot be taken from the Darkest House. Learning that the only way to make a specific item is with the Mystic Tools in the Darkest House might be an interesting hook to get the PCs to go there, but keep in mind that the tools disappear after using them, so building whatever the PCs seek to build precludes doing so and then building the Mystic Door. Unless they go searching for the tools a second time . . .

✦ **Locate Phillip Harlock or at least find out what actually happened to him.** Good luck with this one. It's a twisty, contradictory tale involving time out of sync and memories lost (often more than once) and false memories gained. This would probably involve making it all the way through the Backrooms and across the dark ocean, which is really out of the bounds of this adventure, but it would be an epic and surreal journey and the vast majority of it would be in the Darkest House.

✦ **Sever the house from the rest of their world forever.** This is the big one. Remember when I said there's no inherent big climax to the stories of the house? Yeah, that wasn't entirely true. It's just that it's not my intention to say that PCs should go into the house to rid their world of it.

Severing the house would involve going to the Original House, possible only through the **Amator** section (page 77), and manipulating the recursive dollhouse found there. This would be quite difficult, but an epic quest to be certain. It would also mean that the characters could never return to the Darkest House, but by that point, they'll likely be grateful for that.

RESEARCHING THE HOUSE

Sometimes, wise characters will research a location before busting right in. They might comb the local library, county records office, or the local newspaper archives. If they do so, share the following text with the characters, revealing the fruit of their labors:

You find two references to the house, both quite contradictory.

One is about the supposed original owner of the house, a man named Phillip Harlock. Apparently, long ago, he went a bit mad and would never leave the house, telling friends—all of whom he eventually pushed away, one by one, over the course of a year or two—that there were "always more rooms in the house to see. Always more halls to walk." Eventually, he disappeared altogether. Other owners took possession and moved in over the years. All reported that the house was haunted. Various exorcists and experts were called in. The first three failed. The fourth died. The last owner claimed "it's not even a house anymore," before disappearing mysteriously. No one has lived there in a very long time, and it's been cordoned off for years. Occasionally, foolish thrill-seekers manage to get inside. Some report terrifying stories. Most won't talk about it or are never seen again. People began referring to it as the Darkest House.

The other, more esoteric, source says that the house has always existed, stretching between every layer of reality (whatever that means), filling in the cracks and seeping into whatever metaphysical pits it can find. This reference also mentions Phillip Harlock, but seems to suggest that he wasn't the first owner at all and that he inherited it from a distant relative and moved it to its current location somehow. But mostly this source just goes on about how the house is more a dark, fundamental force of the universe that takes on the appearance of a house than an actual house, like an animal that uses a part of its own body to lure in prey (it specifically references the spider-tailed horned viper). It also says that the house's outward appearance looks different in the other locations that it extends into, fitting in with local context. To top it all off, someone has written in that section of the book, scrawled over the print itself, "THE HOUSE HATES YOU."

See page 290 for a downloadable version you can share with your players.

RUMORS ABOUT THE HOUSE

PCs might talk to people in the neighborhood or others in the know about the house. They will likely hear many of the following rumors, amid warnings not to go inside, expressions of incredulity, or simply doors closed in their faces.

False Rumors

+ *No one has ever gone in and come back out alive.*
+ *The original owner was named Peter Wainwright, and he was married with three children.*
+ *The ghost of the original owner still haunts that place, and you'll meet him if you ever go inside.*
+ *The original owner was a vampire and preyed upon the people in the surrounding neighborhood in the dark of night.*
+ *Once each year, at the summer solstice, the house lights up from within and strange chanting can be heard.*

True Rumors

+ *A man named Phillip Harlock lived there his entire adult life and didn't come out for most of that time.*
+ *Phillip Harlock studied arcane secrets and occult lore for most of his life.*
+ *The interior of the house is confusing and doesn't match at all the way it appears on the outside.*
+ *The house is haunted by many ghosts. And things much worse than ghosts.*
+ *A priest attempted to exorcise the spirits in the house many years ago and died in the attempt.*
+ *There are powerful entities within the house that are neither living people nor truly ghosts, but something else.*
+ *There's something in the house that violates spacetime.*
+ *It's possible to close off the house forever, but no one knows how.*

Once characters enter the house, there are some things unique to its nature they will quickly realize. First and foremost, they will discover that leaving the house is neither straightforward nor simple. Doors won't open, and windows show only endless darkness. We'll discuss **escaping the house** shortly (page 70).

In addition, they'll discover the following:

THERE ARE ANACHRONISMS INSIDE

It might be that some of what the PCs will find inside is anachronistic or inappropriate to their home setting's technology or science. For example, there is a telephone, a radio, and a (seemingly) mechanical elevator. For PCs hailing from a medieval fantasy world, these things are unknown. Embrace that. Don't describe the telephone as "a telephone," but rather "a strangely shaped idol of unknown material. A shrill cry comes forth from it, and if the top portion is removed, distant voices can be heard echoing within."

If the contents of the house seem out of sync with the setting, particularly if they are something the players understand, even if the characters do not, that simply adds to the mystery of the place.

THERE IS MAGIC INSIDE

Characters from a setting where magic does not (or at least, should not) exist are going to be thrown for a loop in the house. Supernatural powers and entities are everywhere. They might try to explain them through a scientific or technological lens. That's fine. Alternatively, the group as a whole might simply think of the Darkest House as a place where the unexplained goes on. If it's accessed in context as if it were some private quarters on a space station, then it's just "that really weird place on the space station."

But even if you adopt a "what happens in the Darkest House, stays in the Darkest House" philosophy when it comes to such things, consider what happens when the PCs leave. They might bring with them magical "treasures" they've found. Or they might come out cursed, or sporting the unique **Dooms** (page 24) found in the house. It is highly recommended that these magical effects persist (somehow) even in a nonmagical setting. The lasting impressions given by the house should be . . . lasting.

TIME GETS STRANGE INSIDE

Space gets warped inside the house. So too does time. There aren't rules for this; it's far more ephemeral (dare I say, *timey-wimey*) than that. Or to put it another way, it's far too strange for mortal minds to fully comprehend.

This essentially means that time works exactly how you, the GM, want it to. If you don't want to pay attention to the passage of time and then suddenly say, "It's been a long time since you have eaten anything. Your stomach is growling," that's fine. If you want to keep closer track than that, that's fine too.

Same goes for sleep. Looking out any window in the house reveals that it's always night here—if you can see out the window at all. So who's to say how often the characters actually have to sleep? Let it just happen when the needs of the story suggest it should happen. This might make things inconsistent, but it's not only okay, it's the spirit of the house.

The only time (no pun intended) you really need to pay attention to the passage of time is if a character is wounded and needs to recover. But rather than track it, just let time flow along. "Oh," you might suddenly say, "you can check to see if you recover from your wound again." If the players start to get the idea time occasionally passes faster or more slowly, that's not a bad thing. It's great because it's true. Sometimes it may seem like a wound heals very quickly. Other times, it seemingly takes forever. The deeper into the house they go—and deep into the **Backrooms** even moreso—the truer this becomes.

There are perhaps other time-related activities in the house, like building the **Mystic Door** (page 71), but you can handle such things just the same way.

PC ABILITIES AFFECTED WITHIN THE HOUSE

Conversion issues aside, not all of the PCs' abilities are going to function the way they're used to. Certain things can't be done within the house, due to its nature.

Having something work differently is better than preventing it from working. This can be turning a beneficial effect into another (potentially) beneficial effect, such as a psychic ability to tell what is on the other side of a wall revealing a brief glimpse of a possible future instead. It can also be turning a beneficial effect into a detrimental one. Perhaps best of all is having a beneficial effect become a different and *potentially* beneficial effect, but also with the implications of detriment, such as having a teleportation spell cause the affected targets to only "half" teleport away and become temporarily insubstantial or invisible instead.

The point here isn't to frustrate, annoy, or punish the players for having these abilities, but to showcase that being in the house isn't like being anywhere else and to keep the flavor and mood consistent within.

House actions—when the **House Die** (page 22) indicates them—could certainly involve screwing with a player's abilities. And that might be frustrating or annoying, but the players will see that this is a force working against them, and not just the GM/scenario preventing them from doing what they wish.

There are two absolutes when it comes to the house trumping PC abilities: communicating by magical or technological means, and leaving the house.

No Contact With the Outside. There is no contact with the outside world once you're inside the house. Or, to put it more precisely, most attempts at contacting the outside world contact the house instead. And you don't want this. Coming into contact with the house itself is always a disturbing experience.

This includes magical communication (including with deities) and technological as well—radios, phones, and internet connections. Once inside the house, you can't even get a connected device to tell you the date or time. The moratorium also includes magical divination pertaining to anything outside the house, and perhaps most significantly it includes magical summoning and conjuration.

This even includes communication within the house between characters, but this almost always simply results in the house imitating or deceiving the characters, as described below.

All of these actions put one in contact with the house rather than the desired result. Additionally, anything that would reveal the paranormal nature of the house—from a handheld scanner to a spell that detects magic or the presence of evil in the house—puts one in contact with the house.

Being in contact with the house results in one of three things:

✦ **Deception.** The house impersonates whomever the PC was attempting to communicate with or even an entity they were attempting to conjure. The house uses this opportunity to toy with the character, feeding them false information that ultimately will be harmful.

✦ **Direct mental feedback that threatens to overwhelm the character.** This is a Rating 5 attack that inflicts mental damage.

✦ **Possession.** The house sends a spirit to possess the character. This is a Rating 5 spirit, and if it succeeds in its attack, the player loses control of their character. Begin feeding the PC instructions through Direct Messages, having them say and do what the spirit wishes. At first, the spirit's actions are relatively benign, and the spirit allows the character to act normally, although they cannot reveal the possession. Eventually, it will cause the character to attempt to deal harm to one of their companions, either through inaction or through a subtle action (not an outright attack). Every hour or so, the character can attempt an action to free themselves of the Rating 5 possession.

No Easy Exit. Only the most powerful effect is going to **get one out of the house** (page 70, other than using the "proper" exits. You cannot simply smash a window and get out. The outer walls (and windows) are immune to such attempts. You cannot walk through the walls or teleport out, even if such resources are normally available. You cannot damage the outer walls, doors, or windows of the house. You cannot force a door open.

Most of the time, there is no change to movement within the house, including supernatural movement. So characters can teleport from one room to another, or move intangibly through a wall from one room to another (assuming the connection even exists). Even when this happens, though, the character using the ability can tell that the environment they are interacting with is not normal, and the process is mentally taxing, although not enough to warrant mental damage.

SLEEPING IN THE HOUSE

Sleeping in the house is dangerous. Characters who sleep (or are rendered unconscious) face a Rating 5 attack from the house that inflicts mental damage in the form of horrific nightmares. The nightmares are always very personal, involving the character's loved ones, past stressful situations, and so on. This doesn't apply to characters knocked unconscious due to suffering damage, only sleeping characters or those unconscious due to a magical effect, a drug, or something of that nature.

DAMAGING THE HOUSE

For the most part, the interior of the house is not unlike a living body. Damage a portion and, given a little time, it will heal. Even moving the furniture around or making a mark on a doorway is considered damage. And this then heals as well. Essentially, it's as if any given area of the house resets to its original state when left alone for a time. Almost all objects and creatures heal in this way, with a few exceptions. The following house inhabitants never return if destroyed:

- The Host (in the Great Hall)
- The Curator (in the Gallery)
- The Gatekeeper (in the Gatekeeper's room)
- The Doorman (in the Gatekeeper's room or the Cellar)
- The Lurker (in the Foyer)
- The Barman (in the Ballroom)
- The Arbiter (in the Parlor)
- The Red Figure (in the Red Room)
- The Cenotaph (in the Prisoner)
- The Smiling Man (in the Storeroom or the Backrooms)
- The Antinomy (in the Original House)
- Buddy (in The Dog)
- Any actual people known to the PCs, such as those encountered in the Tea Room, the Prisoner, or a Familiar Room.

The entities known as Mother, Father, Sister, Brother, and the Lover do all reset, appearing again even if slain, should the **House Die indicate it** (page 22).

Likewise, beneficial treasures do not reset. Once they are destroyed, used, or taken, they do not return to their resting place. It is entirely possible, given a lot of time, that the house will produce all new treasures—or even inhabitants to replace those listed above.

Keys and objects of specific importance to the house, like the Eyes of the Child, do reset, but probably not until the characters leave or die.

Some houses just reject humanity.

~Jacob Geller

RUNNING GAMES SET IN THE DARKEST HOUSE

You may have run a "haunted house"-style adventure before. Even if you haven't, you've probably run a game with a "dungeon"-style location, with dangers keyed to various rooms that the characters explore. The Darkest House is similar to such adventures, but it has some truly unique aspects as well.

Consent in Gaming is a free PDF that we recommend to all GMs (see page 10). It's worth a read before you run an adventure like The Darkest House. You can use the checklist provided to make sure that everyone in your group is on board with the kinds of (hopefully challenging and entertaining) horrors involved. There are many troubling things, either overtly depicted or strongly suggested, in The Darkest House. Using the checklist can help you learn where people's boundaries are so that you can significantly downplay or delete problematic elements.

Overt Depictions:

✦ Gory violence

✦ Scary bugs and spiders

✦ Death

✦ Body horror

✦ Captivity

✦ Mental illness

✦ Addiction

✦ Deception/gaslighting

✦ Possible animal endangerment

✦ Possible child endangerment

Strong Suggestions (but not direct portrayals):

✦ Child abuse

✦ Consensual sex

There are many ways to cultivate a safe, supportive, and inclusive group at the gaming table. Do your research and use any safety tools that are appropriate for your group.

The Darkest House is designed to be inserted into an ongoing campaign (of any game).

Of course, many will want to use it as a "one-shot" adventure. That is, create new characters or dust off old ones, and have the game begin and end with just the Darkest House. It works well for that. The conversion opportunities of the **House System** (page 13) mean that you can bring a few players you haven't gamed with in years together with a couple of your more recent gaming friends and use the Darkest House to tie their experience together, even if their familiarities involve different game systems.

But The Darkest House is really meant for an ongoing campaign: there are long-term implications of things that happen in the house, such as **Dooms** (page 24). Character background information and character development can also emerge in the course of play. Further, the Darkest House is perhaps most fun when the PCs know it's still *there,* even long after they leave. They may eventually find the need to go back. In that way, the Darkest House can become a recurring villain in your ongoing campaign.

Ideally, it would go like this: the PCs **enter the house** (page 48) without a lot of foreknowledge. Maybe even by accident. They spend a session or two in the house and barely escape. They swear never to go back in. Then something happens and they discover that they have to go back in, to save someone trapped there, to recover an important item, and so on. So they go back in, accomplishing what they set out to do, encountering mostly new rooms, and finding a different way out.

Now, the third time's the charm: the house itself contacts one or more of them in their dreams, and dares them to return. It haunts them with frequent nightmares, always trying to draw them back in. This time, they find their way to the **Original House** (page 77) and find a way to sever the house's connection to their setting forever. They haven't destroyed the house, but they have made *their world* safe from it.

For the really long-term-thinking GM, you could introduce the Darkest House in one campaign and then incorporate it into a completely different campaign later on. The players will enjoy the literary irony of having all sorts of memories of what the Darkest House is, even if their characters don't. And what's more, who's to say that their old characters aren't still in there, somehow, having returned once again or, worse, having become spiritual echoes ringing around the house like so many others?

The **House System** (page 13) is fairly simple, so that at no time will it get in the way. Roll some dice and add your Rating. That's how you do everything. Except that in truth, even that simple mechanic isn't really the crux of the experience. Perhaps more than in many other games, the focus is on things that happen to and can affect the characters *without mechanics*.

The Darkest House is about character, not character sheets. By the time the PCs escape the house, they'll likely have been forced to recall the darker moments of their past, their loyalties to each other will be put in question, and they might even have lost some or all control over their actions at some point. In short, the truly significant challenges the PCs will face—and the true wounds they take—have little to do with dice. This means you don't have to concern yourself with how any lasting effects (and potentially any useful treasures the PCs find and take with them) will translate into the campaign's original system.

Use this approach to your advantage, and get the players into the spirit of it all. Encourage character development and the fleshing out of characters' pasts as you go along. Discovering a character's greatest love, their deepest fear, and more about their past are things that will make this adventure one they will always remember.

Running a scenario that's a bit different from the norm poses challenges. Running a game online poses challenges. Running a game high on mood and atmosphere poses challenges. The Darkest House does all these things at once. While we'll enumerate some of those challenges here, the big takeaway is this: talk to the players. Be up front with **what kind of scenario this is** (page 8), and the **kind of mood** (page 9) you're trying to establish. At the same time, be aware of what the players (not the characters) need and desire. Remember that this is a game, and it's supposed to be fun. A roller coaster ride is terrifying, yes, but it's ultimately something we do to entertain ourselves. So too with a horror adventure like The Darkest House.

Players struggling to get into the spirit of the house. The Darkest House is a horror scenario, and that implies a certain kind of dark mood and atmosphere—like you'd see in a horror film. Players making lots of jokes and making light of events is a part of almost every RPG session. While it's part of the fun of the game, if the jokes go too far or come too often, they're going to detract from, rather than add to, the session.

Worse, if some of the players are trying to adopt the proper mood and one or two aren't, it can be as bad as if you're watching an atmospheric film and the people behind you are cracking jokes the whole time. It detracts from the experience. Don't hesitate to talk to the players about this. If they're going to be in the Darkest House for multiple sessions, you might need to preface each session with a bit about the mood you're hoping to achieve.

On top of that, bad things are going to happen to the characters entering into a horror scenario like The Darkest House. Characters might get traumatized, scarred, maimed, doomed, cursed, possessed, or even killed. While getting everyone to fill out the **Consent Checklist** (page 60) helps get an idea of where people stand on the various elements, the PCs will inevitably experience that terrible place where everything repeatedly goes wrong and is bad. Make it crystal clear that you're not doing these things *to the players*. You're not getting some kind of perverse glee from this. You're not punishing the players. This is just the kind of scenario The Darkest House is, and sometimes victories that come at such a great cost are all the sweeter. Plus, just think of the stories they'll have if—I mean when—they get out.

Players resisting the character-building parts of the scenario. In The Darkest House, players are going to be asked to develop their characters perhaps more deeply or in ways they haven't before. We all know the player who just wants to have their character smash things with their axe. That's why they play RPGs. They might not like to think about their character's background, let alone come up with some nightmare the character had recently or how they felt about their parents. (Sometimes it's a victory to get these folks to even give their character a name. . .)

Encourage them to think outside the box they've created for themselves. Tell them this isn't just for story reasons and it actually affects the outcome of the encounter or the scenario as a whole (which is true). They might find they actually like it. And if they just don't, well, at least they tried.

There's another kind of player that might not want to fully participate in this part of the game: the shy or introverted player. They might very well know what their character's greatest fear is, or some deeply important event in their childhood. They just don't want to expound upon it in front of the whole group. That's okay. Use direct messages. Talk to them about it one-on-one before or after the game if that's more comfortable for them.

In the end, though, as hard as it might be to see it happen, players need to be able to opt out of any portion of a game, and that includes this kind of character building. That's why it's so important to talk about this before the game. Use the **Consent Checklist** (page 60). Let people know on a meta-level what kind of things are coming their way. (That's in part why the **whole character arc topic** (page 39) is right up front in converting characters to the Darkest House—it helps ready people for the kind of things they're going to encounter here.)

Players or characters nervous about exploring. Exploring is key to The Darkest House experience: characters delving into places the players believe to be dangerous and awful. But if you've got a player character just staying by the exit door, trying to get it open, no one's going to have much fun.

Just as bad is if you've used one of the **story hooks** (page 48) to get the characters into the house, and all the players do is focus on that single goal. There are **stories** (page 70) within The Darkest House (the biggest one being survive and get out) that should sweep up the characters. Sure, they might have come here hunting down a fugitive, but it should become clear early on that while they can keep that task in the back of their mind, finding the fugitive should not be their primary objective. If they race from room to room, ignoring anything that doesn't clearly have anything to do with the fugitive, they're not only missing out on vital details—they're probably missing out on the fun, too.

Players feeling frustrated. You really have to be good at reading your players. While you want the characters to be terrified or exasperated at being trapped in the house, you don't want the players to be having a similar experience. Now a little player frustration, while not necessarily desirable, can't always be avoided. If a player seems quite frustrated, try to subtly insert something that you know will interest them. If they like combat, have a fight break out. If they want treasure, hint that there's something really good not too far away.

The real goal here is to make the characters quite unhappy while the players are having a great time. And in the end, if you just need to provide a bunch of grumpy, frustrated players with an exit, do so. Don't let a difficult scenario wreck your whole game.

Players disliking the conversion. Everyone's allowed their opinion, and everyone plays the game(s) they love the most, so converting characters to the **House System** (page 13) might chafe some players. As stated in the conversion rules, if you think this is going to be a problem (or if it's going to be an issue *for you*), convert the house, don't convert the characters.

If a player insists that some sort of bad thing that's just happened to their character would never have happened if the group was using the system they converted from, give them the benefit of the doubt. Don't necessarily always reward the complainer with success, though; just change the nature of the bad thing. If someone's mind is controlled and they're certain that it wouldn't have happened if they were playing the Cypher System because they would have used Effort on their Intellect defense roll, tell them, okay, you break free from the mind control, but the cost of doing so is a Rating 3 mental wound (which is a lot like spending Intellect points to use Effort in the Cypher System).

The house can be difficult and deadly. Depending on the Ratings of the characters, a lot of the encounters within the house will be challenging on a mechanical basis. You can gently lead players to run from an overwhelming encounter. Perhaps more importantly, you can encourage them to call upon the house to help them succeed when they roll dice. This is a significant mechanic in the game and an important one to remember, though the concept is likely as new to you as it is to the players. At first, players might be afraid to **call upon the house** (page 22) because it's pretty scary, but it's actually something that gives them a fair bit of agency in challenging situations, just at a cost. The system assumes that they'll do it a fair bit because it's better to get a **Doom** (page 24) than to die.

Most of these techniques exist only in the metagame, but that's the point. You're creating and maintaining a mood. Obviously, if you have players who will be personally really bothered by such things, don't do them. The techniques are meant to be good fun, and enhance the experience, like when you're playing a video game and the controller vibrates.

Dim the lights. Consider putting up a virtual or physical background behind you, even if it's just a sheet hanging from the ceiling. Your unmade bed and your messy bedroom aren't scary (I hope). Better to see a blank sheet behind you than something that will hurt the mood. If you want to take this to an extreme level, dim the lights and then set up mundane objects (a trophy, a cup full of pens, whatever you have nearby) in front of a light source off-camera. If you do it right, you'll cast strange, unidentifiable shadows behind you.

Read aloud. The **Remnants** (page 272) are there for you to share with your players in a chat or DM or what have you, and you should do that, so that everyone can read and reference them. But they also should be read aloud, either by you or by a player with a good reading voice. They carry a lot more impact that way.

Describe. Words have power to evoke imaginations. Even though there are a lot of art pieces to show the players, don't let them take the place of your verbal descriptions. Art shouldn't do all your work for you. Use the illustrations to enhance your descriptions, not replace them.

Whisper. Gradually lower the volume of your voice, talking softer and softer, until the mic is right up to your mouth and you're whispering. Whispering sets off all kinds of subconscious feelings and behaviors in the listener, all of which help create a creepy atmosphere.

Vary your voice. If you use the whispering technique, you can then add in a sudden, loud pronouncement about something that happens suddenly and instantly set everyone on edge. "Suddenly, the bookcase falls toward you!" Except you don't have to say "suddenly" when you do this; unexpectedly raising your voice does that work for you.

Use the players' environment against them. While The Darkest House is all about having the environment working against the characters, you can instill a little unease in the players by doing the same thing. "Hey, Annie," you might say, "what's that thing behind the chair there?" Annie looks, and says, "You mean the lamp?" "No," you respond. "Never mind. It just looked weird there for a second. Must be the light." Done subtly a few different times during a session, you'll start to make your players feel uneasy (even if they don't know why) and that'll help put them in the right mood for the game.

When the **House Die** (page 22) indicates it, as discussed earlier, the house acts. There are many actions that the house can take, and keep in mind that its motivations ultimately cannot be parsed. But the house hates the PCs, and that likely explains most of its actions while they are present.

Use these actions in order. They escalate in severity and implication. If one is inapplicable (such as there being no inhabitants wounded for #2), skip it and move to the next. If you reach the end of the list, start over, but try to vary your description of it.

HOUSE ACTIONS

1. Creaking sounds, footsteps, or similar noises can be heard. The entity tied to that section of the house is coming closer.
2. A wounded inhabitant of the house is fully healed.
3. A cold draft blows. If the characters are using torches or candles for light, they go out. One or more beneficial ongoing effects (spells, powered items, etc.) inexplicably ends.
4. Whispering can be heard. A character's name is mentioned amid some indecipherable words. That character is subject to a Rating 2 attack that inflicts mental damage from the creepiness.
5. Every character fails their next action. Everyone can somehow sense that something horrible is getting close. (This is the entity tied to that section of the house.)
6. Unseen, icy fingers seem to run up one character's spine and they are subject to a Rating 5 attack that inflicts mental damage (in the form of unreasonable terror).
7. A translucent image appears, and the characters see a scene that they cannot interact with. For example, they see a scene of a man in that very room watching his family suddenly transform into monstrous, hungry creatures that attack him. Or they see the scene of a brutal murder. Or the looming presence of a monstrous being. Or anything that seems horrible and appropriate to the house. The vision fades, but it is a Rating 4 attack that inflicts mental damage on all the PCs.
8. An object in a character's possession grows a fanged mouth, hisses horribly, and attacks like a snake with a Rating of 4. Alternatively, it grows spider legs and scuttles away into the darkness. Or begins screaming with a humanlike mouth. Regardless of what happens, the object is no longer usable.
9. The entity of that section of the house arrives. There is a section of text in each room devoted to what happens if this occurs.
10. An object important to a character is now cursed. Whenever the character uses it, they fail the next roll they make immediately after (or in conjunction with it).

There are four ways into the house. It is possible for all four to exist in the same world, but that isn't always the case, and depends on the outward appearance of the house as it appears in the context. For example, if the house lies in a neighborhood where the houses have large yards or gardens, and some of these are enclosed with private fences, all the entrances are likely viable. If the house manifests as an apartment in a high-rise building, it's likely only the front door entrance exists. In other words, use the entrances that work best for your setting.

FRONT DOOR

If the house is there, the front door is there. If at all appropriate to the context, the front door has a dilapidated front porch before it, with rotten wooden boards and probably some kind of animals or creatures nesting underneath it.

Again, depending on the context, there is likely to be some kind of warning sign on the outside. Perhaps there's an old "CONDEMNED" sign tacked to a post holding up an overhang above the porch. Or in a magical context, there's a secret, magical sigil upon the door itself indicating "Dangerous Magic Inside."

It's quite reasonable to assume, in a fairly orderly setting, that the local authorities (police or the like) patrol the area routinely, mostly to keep away curious kids or rowdy teenagers, due to past mysterious disappearances in the neighborhood.

The front door is almost always locked, but the lock was probably pitifully inadequate even when it was new, and now it's quite old (Rating 1). Peering through windows reveals the **Living Room** (page 82) and going through the front door takes the PCs there. The door slams shut behind them, and then vanishes.

Going through a window (by breaking it or forcing it open) also takes a character into the Living Room.

BACK DOOR

PCs leery of the front door and seeking a back way in might just find one. This is a weird entrance, though, because if the house has a backyard with a wall around it, PCs will have to go **Over the Wall** (page 69) and through the **Walled Garden** (page 194) first.

If it doesn't have that feature, and the back of the house just opens into an alleyway or something similar, then the back door presents itself there, with no windows in it or nearby. It leads into the **Foyer** (page 162).

Note, however, that if the PCs go through the back door into the Foyer without first going through the backyard (because in the current context, there is no backyard), the door doesn't look the same from within the Foyer. Stranger still, if anyone in the Foyer opens the door to look out or to try to escape the house, they will instead see the Walled Garden, regardless of whether it was there when they entered the back door.

OVER THE WALL

Rarest of the three conventional entrances, going over the wall presumes that there is a wall to go over. A wall requires some kind of backyard or garden space. Obviously, this requires the context to allow for such a thing.

If there is a backyard, then the yard is within the Darkest House, not outside it. That is to say, all the restrictions (including those about the difficulty of leaving) involved with being in the house are immediately in effect.

There is no garden gate—no door in the outer wall. One must climb, jump, or fly over it.

Going over the wall puts a character in the Walled Garden.

DEVOURED ROOM

Using a devoured room as an entrance is dictated purely by random chance. In other words, just simply bad luck. The House That Hungers devours (and eventually digests) rooms in other buildings, along with their contents and sometimes even their occupants. Those within a devoured room are just suddenly in the Darkest House, at a random location adjoining another room (the GM could place the room into one of the Familiar Room spots, or just simply append it onto the existing layout, adjoining one existing room, anywhere other than in the **Original House**, page 77). Basically, the PCs are literally anywhere in their normal campaign setting and they open the door out of the room they are in and instead of leading where they thought it would, it leads into some room of the Darkest House. Once a room is devoured, there's no escape other than those methods listed below.

There are basically six ways to escape the confines of the house, once the characters are inside. None of them are straightforward. The most important thing to remember is that escape should also carry a significant price for one or more of the characters.

1. Powerful Supernatural/Technological Effect. Because we don't want to *entirely* take away the agency of the PCs, particularly well-prepared and capable PCs, if they have access to a powerful supernatural or technological effect that should overcome most situations in their standard game, it can grant exit from the house. The basic rule of thumb is, if an effect is very likely the most powerful in the game (or is one of them), it will work, but not if it is less than that. A super-powerful alien artifact crafted by the ancients themselves—or whatever would be the equivalent in the campaign you're running—can return the PCs home.

For example, a *teleport* spell from a 5e game won't work, but a *wish* spell would. Characters from an Invisible Sun game will find that a typical spell doesn't provide exit, but a wicked key does. And so on.

Keeping with the cost that should be involved in the escape, however, use of the supernatural or technological effect should very likely result in the loss of that effect, at least for a time. If the effect comes from an item, the item is lost. If it is knowledge or an ability that comes directly from a character, access to it is lost for at least a while.

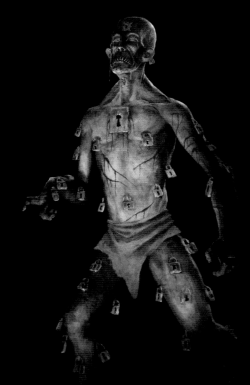

Alternatively, the price to pay could mean the character using the effect gains some sort of minor curse, such as that to ever use that power again, they must sacrifice something of value, only use it at night, anoint the object (or themselves) with their own blood each time, or something similar.

Lastly, the price might be story-based. Each time a power is used by a character to escape the Darkest House, some terrible tragedy affects them or their life. Their house burns down, their mother gets ill, and so on. The house hates you.

2. Find the Doorman. The primary door out of the house isn't an object—it's an entity. The Doorman can be found in two different locations (in the Cellar or with the Gatekeeper). Both appearances of the Doorman have different requirements for finding or reaching him, but both require keys to open his locks.

3. Some Number of Characters Complete an Arc. Every character entering the house begins with a lie or a truth that they bring with them. **That lie or truth is challenged, reinforced, or denied** (page 39) while in the house, very likely multiple times. The GM should—based on their group—decide how many characters need to progress all the way through their arc before the house is done with them. A heavy, in-depth roleplaying group might need all of the characters to complete their arc. A much more casual, beer-and-pretzels group might need just one. Most groups fall somewhere in between.

When this number is reached, the GM should provide ways out. An open window. A hole in the roof. A secret door. A magical treasure. This exit cannot be used again, nor can it be used as an entrance to return to the house. Either way, it's simply gone.

4. Create a Painting for the Gallery. Perhaps using the paint and canvas in the Studio, a painting of one or more characters can be created and hung in the Gallery, providing a two-way door that can indeed be reused, but each time takes a serious mental toll on the characters. More information can be found in the Gallery.

5. Build the Mystic Door. By collecting all eight **Mystic Tools** (page 49), the PCs can build the Mystic Door and create their own exit.

This Mystic Door is permanent and immovable, and leads to the side of the house (if applicable). This process requires wood and metal, but that can be obtained by dismantling furniture or even walls or doors inside the house (such things will eventually reset, but that doesn't affect the Mystic Door). It takes about ten total hours of work, assuming at least three people are working. Two people would require fifteen hours, and only one person would take twenty hours. More than three people don't effectively make things go faster.

Once finished, the Mystic Tools disappear, lost within the house again (hidden in different places—because the house hates you), but the characters are free to use the door as often as they wish to enter or exit.

6. Close Off the House From the PCs' World. If the PCs manage to take the correct puzzle piece found in the Happy Family puzzle in the closet of the Bedroom With a Secret Passage and place it in the recursive dollhouse in the Original House, they will not only escape the Darkest House, but they will also shut it off from their world forever. But just *their* world . . .

ESCAPING, BUT NOT HOME

Since the Darkest House **worms its way into all worlds** (page 44), it's very possible that when the PCs leave, they don't go back to their own world, but another. This could be intentional on their part—the house could be a way to travel between worlds. In a campaign where traveling to other worlds is unheard of, this could be another story reason to go inside the house. In a setting where travel between worlds is more common, perhaps there is some campaign reason why a particular world is hard to reach and the Darkest House is the only way. (Otherwise, *surely* there are easier ways to travel to other worlds . . .)

Alternatively, the PCs might travel to another world in their escape unintentionally. This should be used to enhance the overall story, not as a final gotcha. If the PCs really earned their escape and are truly desperate to get home, sending them to another world seems like it would just be frustrating, and not in a good way. Perhaps the best solution of all is to make it clear just as they escape that they have the option not just to go home, but to go anywhere. In that case, it's almost like an extra potential reward for surviving and getting out.

ESCAPING WITH DOOM

Characters leaving the house with Dooms are not in the clear. There are **long-term implications** (page 24) that will affect them long after they escape. Most of these will need some very potent, very specific remedies—magic of the highest order, alien or far-future tech, psychic therapy, and so on. The GM might rule that no remedy exists and the character must live with the consequences permanently. Acquiring the remedy should, at the very least, be a significant adventure on its own.

When a house is both hungry and awake, every room becomes a mouth.

~Kitty Horrorshow, Anatomy

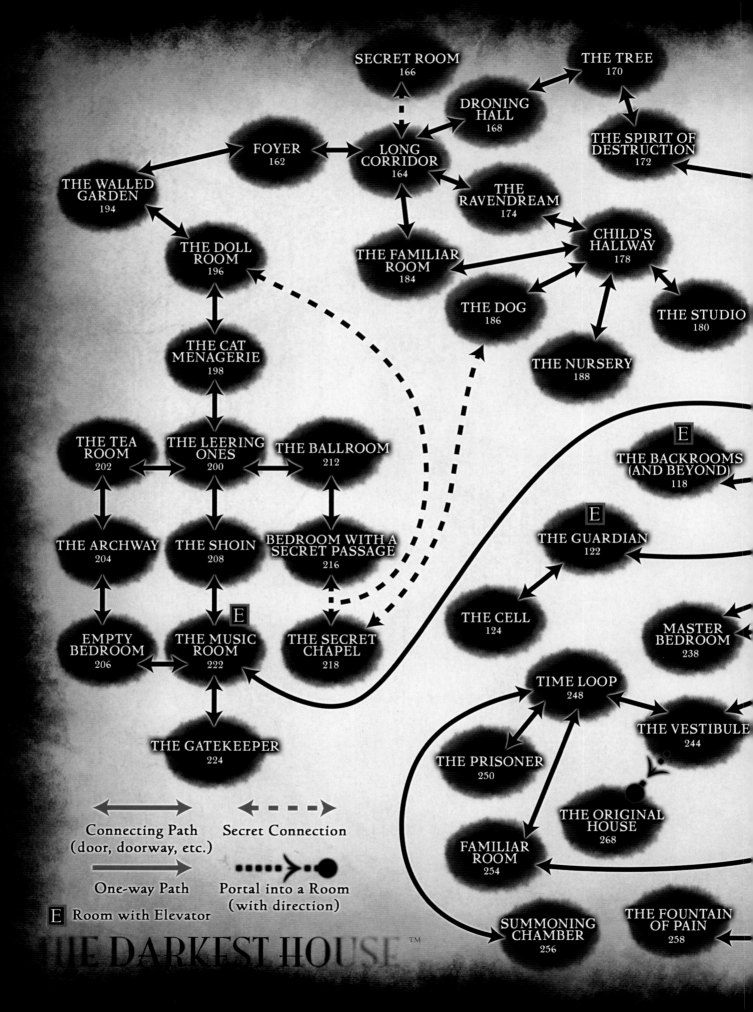

SECRET ROOM
166

THE TREE
170

DRONING
HALL
168

FOYER
162

LONG
CORRIDOR
164

THE SPIRIT OF
DESTRUCTION
172

THE WALLED
GARDEN
194

THE
RAVENDREAM
174

CHILD'S
HALLWAY
178

THE DOLL
ROOM
196

THE FAMILIAR
ROOM
184

THE DOG
186

THE STUDIO
180

THE CAT
MENAGERIE
198

THE NURSERY
188

THE BACKROOMS
(AND BEYOND)
118

E

THE TEA
ROOM
202

THE LEERING
ONES
200

THE BALLROOM
212

THE GUARDIAN
122

E

THE ARCHWAY
204

THE SHOIN
208

BEDROOM WITH A
SECRET PASSAGE
216

THE CELL
124

MASTER
BEDROOM
238

EMPTY
BEDROOM
206

THE MUSIC
ROOM
222

E

THE SECRET
CHAPEL
218

TIME LOOP
248

THE VESTIBULE
244

THE GATEKEEPER
224

THE PRISONER
250

THE ORIGINAL
HOUSE
268

FAMILIAR
ROOM
254

Connecting Path
(door, doorway, etc.)

Secret Connection

One-way Path

E Room with Elevator

Portal into a Room
(with direction)

SUMMONING
CHAMBER
256

THE FOUNTAIN
OF PAIN
258

THE DARKEST HOUSE ™

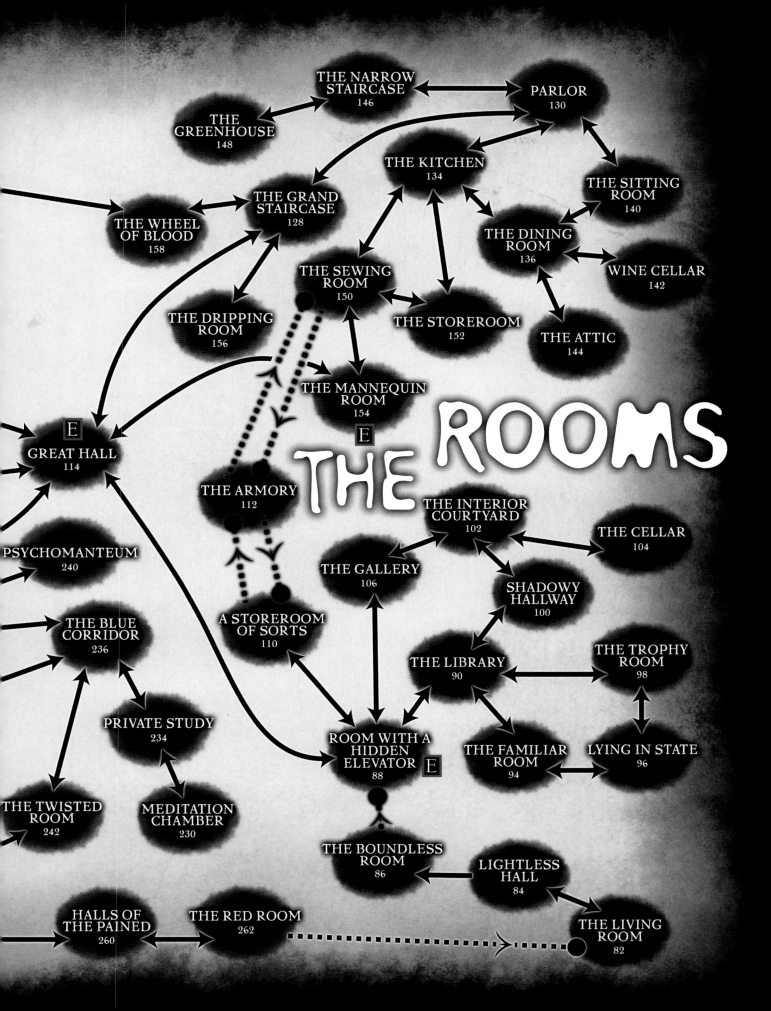

THE ROOMS

THE NARROW STAIRCASE 146

PARLOR 130

THE GREENHOUSE 148

THE KITCHEN 134

THE SITTING ROOM 140

THE WHEEL OF BLOOD 158

THE GRAND STAIRCASE 128

THE DINING ROOM 136

WINE CELLAR 142

THE SEWING ROOM 150

THE DRIPPING ROOM 156

THE STOREROOM 152

THE ATTIC 144

THE MANNEQUIN ROOM 154

E

GREAT HALL 114

THE ARMORY 112

THE INTERIOR COURTYARD 102

THE CELLAR 104

THE GALLERY 106

SHADOWY HALLWAY 100

PSYCHOMANTEUM 240

A STOREROOM OF SORTS 110

THE LIBRARY 90

THE TROPHY ROOM 98

THE BLUE CORRIDOR 236

PRIVATE STUDY 234

ROOM WITH A HIDDEN ELEVATOR 88 E

THE FAMILIAR ROOM 94

LYING IN STATE 96

THE TWISTED ROOM 242

MEDITATION CHAMBER 230

THE BOUNDLESS ROOM 86

LIGHTLESS HALL 84

THE LIVING ROOM 82

HALLS OF THE PAINED 260

THE RED ROOM 262

SECTIONS OF THE HOUSE

The first thing you might notice is that there is no map of the house. What? Well, that's because instead, there's a flowchart. It shows how the rooms connect to other rooms, which can sometimes be nonintuitive and is frequently nonlinear. In other words, the interior layout of the house makes no sense if applying Euclidean geometry. Piece together all the room maps and you'll just have a jumble. So, simply refer to the flowchart to keep track of where the characters are in the house, and where they can go from there. Use the maps of each room as a guide only while in that particular room.

The flowchart will also be your best guide to tell you what section of the house a room might be in. The sections are all different, and the differences are important, if for no other reason than they dictate which of the entities of the house (Father, Mother, Brother, Sister, or the Lover) holds sway there.

There are five different sections of the house, plus it's possible to find one's way into the Original House. The sections all represent, not to put too fine a point on it, love gone wrong. Yet each is a different kind of love, and each ultimately manifests in a different role that should be a loving part of a person's life. But this is the Darkest House, and the house hates you. So these manifestations are terrifying and awful. Feel free to make it clear that each section of the house has a different "feel" to the players. The characters might know, crossing from one section to another, that things have subtly changed.

The sections are Pater (page 80), Mater (page 126), Frater (page 160), Soror (page 192), and Amator (page 228).

PATER

The **Pater** section of the house is cruel, domineering, and distant. This section represents the fear of disappointing one's father, and the fear of punishment as a child.

+ The Eyes of the Child affect many of the rooms in this section. They allow a character to see and interact with things in this section that they couldn't otherwise.

+ The entity known as Father may take action (as determined by the House Die) against the PCs at some point. He appears impossibly tall, with a dark face and yellow eyes, and usually carries a massive leather belt as a weapon. He's always angry and violent.

MATER

The **Mater** section of the house is cloying, smothering, and emotional. This is the essence of motherly love, gone horribly wrong, with aspects of guilt, abandonment, and more. None of the entrances to the house take characters directly to the Mater section. It can only be reached by making one's way through another section of the house first and finding a path to this one.

+ The telephone complicates things in this section. The PCs will hear it ringing throughout the rooms here, but won't find it until they reach the Sitting Room, where they can decide to answer it or not.

+ The entity known as Mother may take action (as determined by the House Die) against the PCs at some point. She appears as a large woman with only a skull for a head. Skeletal upper torsos of children cling to her clothing desperately. She is always emotional and controlling.

SOROR

The **Soror** section of the house is sly, deceptive, and vindictive. It of course represents the sister role of the traditional Western nuclear family, but only in its worst aspects—dependence, lies, and sneakiness.

+ The music of the radio haunts this section. The PCs will hear it playing mysterious, creepy music throughout this section, and eventually may find the radio itself—and hear the mysterious voices that come from it.

+ The entity known as Sister may take action (as determined by the House Die) against the PCs at some point. She appears as a young woman with half of her face missing, broken as if she was a hollow porcelain doll. We can see into her head through the missing part of her face and it's full of moths. She is stealthy, deceptive, and creepy, but not physically imposing.

FRATER

The **Frater** section of the house is jealous, angry, and violent. This is the manifestation of a brother's relationship, but gone horribly wrong, representing resentment and jealousy.

+ The Lurker is an entity that can enter the house if the PCs let it in through the door in the Foyer, complicating things in this section and potentially elsewhere in the house.

+ The entity known as Brother may take action (as determined by the House Die) against the PCs at some point. Generally speaking, he is a lanky, male humanoid figure with hands balled into fists and one eye bulging unnervingly. His face shows a sneer, but he never takes actions. Instead, his axe-wielding shadow acts for him. He is always jealous and violent.

AMATOR

The **Amator** section of the house is mysterious, withholding, and untrustworthy. This is the essence of romantic love, but only the dark side of it: the obsession, the duplicity, and the loss of self.

There are only three ways to reach the Amator section and none of them involve finding the right door or passage. One is to use the right key on the lock in the Doorman's head. The second is to visit all four other sections and say the words *Mater, Pater, Frater,* and *Soror,* as presented in the Corridor of the Wheel of Blood. The third is when everyone in the group suffers from wounds with Ratings equal to their own and is transported to the Fountain of Pain.

+ The Storm complicates things in this section. Throughout this section, every window shows a storm raging outside the house. Worse, there's something alive out there, peering in the windows, trying to get in.

+ The entity known as the Lover may take action (as determined by the House Die) against the PCs at some point. The Lover has no physical appearance, and rarely takes direct physical action against the PCs, but rather undermines what they do behind their backs. Each room description provides the details.

THE ORIGINAL HOUSE

Lastly, the Original House (page 266) contains some of the answers to the questions raised elsewhere in the house and holds the keys to severing the house from the PCs' world, should they want to undertake such a monumental quest. It has no conceptual entity tied to it, nor any special object complicating things, other than the recursive dollhouse, but that is another matter entirely.

THE ROOMS

Obviously, the house is far bigger on the inside than the outside. The house might, in fact, be infinitely large. What's more, not all the rooms of the house follow a similar architectural style. Actually, many do not match at all, as if they came from completely different structures made of different materials by different cultures in different time periods. And that's because they did—the House That Hungers devours the rooms of other buildings and claims them for its own.

The house's layout should be confusing to the players. If they hear mysterious footsteps on the level above them, they should have no idea what room that might be coming from. This disorientation is created intentionally. It helps with the mood. This isn't an adventure locale the players should ever figure out or master in any way.

There are rooms where little or nothing happens. Sometimes, these will be little more than a corridor or an antechamber. Often, there is a sound, an odor, a sight, or a feeling coming from an upcoming room, where something (probably terrible) awaits. These are placed intentionally for the pacing and flow of the story. I call these the "building dread" rooms. Many of the rooms within the house conform to a stereotypical room type found in a home, such as a bedroom or a kitchen. That does not necessarily mean that such a room once had that purpose. On the contrary, the room types are more archetypes. That does not make them some kind of Platonic ideal of each room. On the contrary, if anything, they are dark and bitter perversions of such a thing.

Still, there's enough real about the rooms that if a character searches for something that would logically be there, like a spoon in the kitchen, or a pencil in a bedroom desk, it's there. Feel free to use that kind of logic to elaborate upon the rooms if necessary.

Lastly, remember that the rooms eventually reset. They return to normal even after the characters have passed through them, destroying things, changing things, or even slaying things. There is not a set time for this reset—let it flow naturally. There should be a feeling of dread that comes from the knowledge that the PCs cannot have any permanent impact on the house (even though that's technically not true), but it shouldn't become an irritant. A room that the PCs might have to pass through numerous times resetting too soon or too often will become tiresome.

ROOM DESCRIPTIONS

The room entries for the house have some or all of the following elements.

1. Name. In most cases the room's name is very descriptive to make them easier to remember.

2. Introductory Material. Each entry starts with a single summary sentence followed by a statement in italics with GM advice. Following this is the Overview, which is the descriptive text about the room. Anything in the Overview can be shared with the players—it's essentially the initial snapshot of the room and its contents.

3. QR code and URL. Scanning the QR code—or entering the URL in your browser—will take you to a webpage dedicated to this room. Here you will be presented with a list of all of the assets for this room that you might want as a separate element, such as the map, the art, or special handouts for the players called Remnants. Each asset will display its name and a small graphical representation of it—clicking on either of these items should take you to the asset itself. This means that you can get a map or a piece of art to either show as an electronic file while you play, or print it out to use as a separate visual aid if you desire. You can also share a copy of the file, or its URL, with your players if that would be useful in your game.

))) Sometimes there will be an additional QR code for special sound assets.

① THE INTERIOR COURTYARD

② The darkness above this very dangerous area has a good chance of grabbing a character and tossing them outside of the house, where they are changed, tinted with darkness.

This is a pretty dangerous area. Foolish actions or bad rolls might result in the loss of one or more characters.

OVERVIEW

Leaves and twigs fill this interior courtyard. A few bits of brown grass peek out from the stones, but they are dead. Everything in the courtyard is dead. It is cold and very still, but wind can be heard in the distance. Otherwise, there is the quiet of ancient despair hanging like a pallor over the entire expanse. In the middle is a statue of a weeping woman. At her feet lies a shattered stone tablet. The courtyard is open to the sky, but the sky is pitch black. There are three exits: two archways that lead to wide stone passages and a wooden cellar door in the ground near another wall.

ENTERING THE COURTYARD

Crossing the courtyard quickly is safe, although anyone watching the darkness above sees a gigantic human hand begin to emerge above a character passing underneath. All witnessing this event are subject to a Rating 3 mental attack from the shock.

Dawdling in the courtyard, or lingering anywhere in its confines risks an attack by the darkness itself. When this happens, a massive hand of pure darkness descends toward the victim, and its attack has a Rating of 8. Should this attack strike, the hand grasps the victim, who then only has a single chance to squirm free (Rating 6). Alternatively, they could attempt another action, but with a Bane from the crushing hand. If the victim remains in the hand's grasp after this one action, it pulls them up and out of the courtyard, into the darkness.

A saving grace is that the hand can attack only one victim at a time. Bright light will cause it to withdraw, but only long enough for one victim to get to safety. On the following turn, it attacks or otherwise extinguishes the light source.

VICTIM IN THE DARKNESS

The character can't be retrieved. They are gone, but not forever.

⑦ ...u are gone, but not dead. You are unconscious, ...outside the house. However, when the rest of the group exits the house and finds you, you are now tainted with darkness. Don't overdo it, but your personality now leans toward the darker, more negative side of things. You're not a homicidal maniac (at least not at first) but your ethical outlook is very likely skewed from where you are now, and it slowly—perhaps taking weeks—gets worse. You lean toward aggressive actions, and don't care too much about altruistic actions. You are quick to hate, but find difficulty in forgiveness or mercy.

When the others leave the Darkest House, they will find the missing character lying dead, unconscious. Soon, the PCs will begin to notice something strange about their friend. The character seems to have a darker personality and some very questionable ethics. This can be lifted like a curse if they have the means to do so; otherwise, they can try (years of) therapy. Returning to the Darkest House and completing a character arc will also restore the character to their original nature.

THE DARKNESS ABOVE

Anyone looking up into the "sky" sees that the darkness is not still. It roils with a life of its own.

THE STATUE

This marble statue is stained with age and moisture. At the statue's feet is a stone tablet that once bore the image of the sun, but is now shattered.

If the painting *An Old Woman and a Dog* is ren... from the Gallery and placed atop the tablet, peop... the courtyard are protected against the darkness. A... a giant hand looms from above in the courtyard, the old woman from the painting appears with her animal and motions the hand off with her cane. The hand then retracts into the darkness above.

SCRATCH MARKS

The stone wall bears scratch marks, with the words "Nothing more?" scratched into the stone. This isn't clear unless someone gets close.

EYES OF THE CHILD (GARGOYLE) ⑧

If someone has the Eyes of the Child, they see that there is a small ceramic gargoyle statuette behind the marble statue. Only someone with the eyes can see or touch the statuette. Even if they hold the statuette, to another observer, their hands are at their sides. There is no indication that the gargoyle exists to anyone without the eyes. If asked where a particular inhabitant or room lies, the gargoyle will point at the exit that will take the questioner to the destination or target the swiftest. However, the inhabitant or room must be named precisely as they are named in these notes. A general question, such as "Where is the door out?" or "Where's that big room with the brick pillars?" or "Where is the greatest treasure?" produces no result. This gargoyle is identical to the one that can be found in **the Library (page xx)**. If both gargoyles are held by the same person, they immediately animate and fight, destroying each other.

④

Map labels: To the Shadowy Hallway · Darkness Above · Statue · Gargoyle · The Cellar Door · To the Gallery · Scratch Marks · To the Gallery

⑨ ## THE CELLAR DOOR

The cellar door is unlocked, and there is a short flight of rough stone steps leading down to the darkness of the Cellar (page xx).

TO THE GALLERY

This staircase leads down to the Gallery (page xx).

TO THE SHADOWY HALLWAY

This passageway leads to the Library via the Shadowy Hallway (page xx).

FATHER

If the House Die indicates that Father arrives here, he descends out of the dark sky. The massive hand of pure darkness will not appear while he is present. Father is 9 feet tall, broad-shouldered, and wears simple clothing. His face is dark, and you can only see angry yellow eyes and a broad, roaring mouth. In one hand, he holds a long black belt.

Show the players the image of Father. ③

"I have to finish my Great Work," he bellows. "Only the Great Work is important. You mean nothing." Then, he attacks with the belt. He has a Rating of 6. He cannot be reasoned with, and will chase PCs that flee. He disappears if slain.

⑤ ⑥

---

4. Map. The map shows the general layout of the room and most of the important features (and where in the room they are located). These are GM maps, so they sometimes show secrets (like hidden objects or secret doors). If this is the case, there may also be a downloadable player version of the map in the web page with the other assets.

5. Art. Most rooms also have an illustration. These are all from the characters' point of view, intended to be shown to the players so you can say, "You see this." It should be obvious from the image and the Overview text as to whether you can show the illustration to the players as soon as they enter, or only after they trigger some turn of events. For example, a creature in the room may be hiding at first. There may also be other illustrations in certain rooms that you can show players later in the encounter, so that when they go into the Gallery, for example, you can show them images of most of the paintings.

6. Room Elements. Most of the content of a room's entry will describe the individual features of the room. This might include furniture, inhabitants, and so on. Many—but not all—of these elements will have corresponding labels on the map showing where in the room they can be found.

7. Private Message Text. Special information to send privately (by direct message, text, a passed note, or simply a whisper) to one or more specific players.

8. The Entity. Should the House Die indicate that one of the entities of the house comes to that room, the room will have an entry for the entity appropriate to the room (Father, Mother, Brother, Sister, or the Lover), and details of what they will do. Because we don't know where or when they will arrive, every room has such an entry. (See the House Acts, page 67 for more information.)

9. Exits. All egresses are labeled with room names and page numbers so you can move through to the next room...

SECRET ROOM

THE TREE
170

DRONING
HALL
168

THE SPIRIT OF
DESTRUCTION
172

FOYER
162

LONG
CORRIDOR
164

THE WALLED
GARDEN
194

CHILD'S
HALLWAY
178

THE DOLL
ROOM
196

ROOM
184

THE DO

THE STUDIO
180

THE NURSERY
188

THE CAT
MENAGERIE
198

THE TEA
ROOM
202

THE LEERING
ONES

LLROOM

E
THE BACKROOMS
(AND BEYOND)
118

E
THE GUARDIAN
122

THE ARCHWAY
204

THE CELL
124

MASTER
BEDROOM
238

EMPTY
BEDROOM

TIME LOOP
248

THE VESTIBULE
244

THE PRISONER
250

THE ORIGINAL
HOUSE
268

FAMILIAR
ROOM
254

SUMMONING
CHAMBER

THE FOUNTAIN

PATER

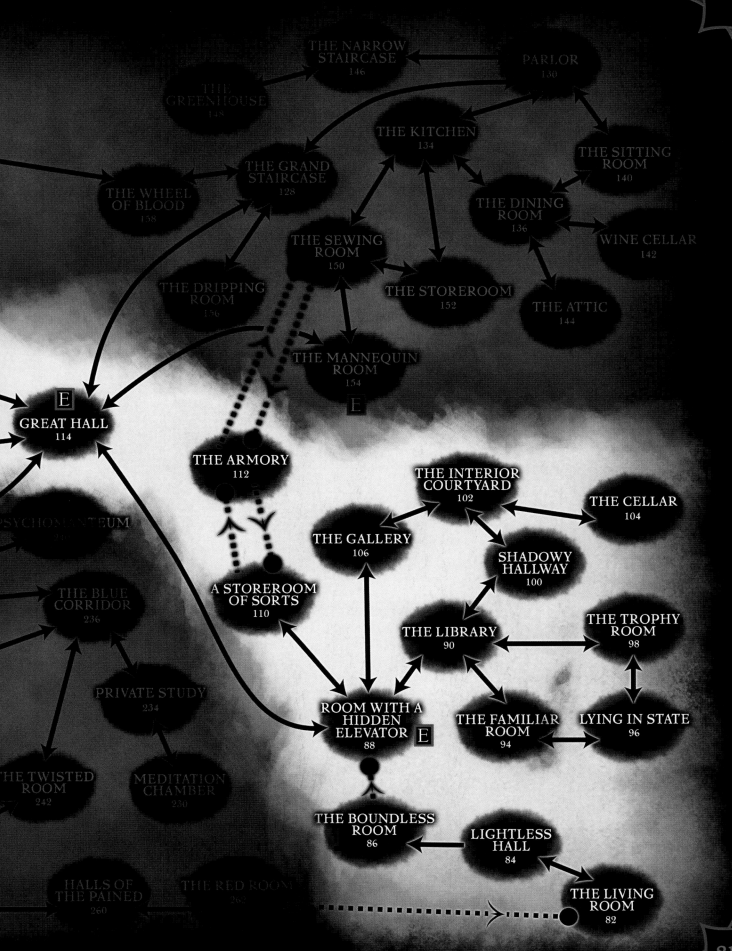

THE NARROW
STAIRCASE
146

PARLOR
130

THE GREENHOUSE
148

THE KITCHEN
134

THE SITTING
ROOM
140

THE WHEEL
OF BLOOD
158

THE GRAND
STAIRCASE
128

THE DINING
ROOM
136

THE SEWING
ROOM
150

WINE CELLAR
142

THE DRIPPING
ROOM
156

THE STOREROOM
152

THE ATTIC
144

THE MANNEQUIN
ROOM
154

E

E

GREAT HALL
114

THE ARMORY
112

THE INTERIOR
COURTYARD
102

THE CELLAR
104

PSYCHOMANTEUM
246

THE GALLERY
106

SHADOWY
HALLWAY
100

A STOREROOM
OF SORTS
110

THE LIBRARY
90

THE TROPHY
ROOM
98

THE BLUE
CORRIDOR
236

PRIVATE STUDY
234

ROOM WITH A
HIDDEN
ELEVATOR
88

THE FAMILIAR
ROOM
94

LYING IN STATE
96

E

THE TWISTED
ROOM
242

MEDITATION
CHAMBER
230

THE BOUNDLESS
ROOM
86

LIGHTLESS
HALL
84

HALLS OF
THE PAINED
260

THE RED ROOM
262

THE LIVING
ROOM
82

THE LIVING ROOM

The room beyond the Front Door, the living room holds one of the Child's Eyes.

Think of this as the kind of living room you'd see in a large American house as portrayed in an old black and white movie. There's nothing here to suggest what time period it's from—it could be anytime from the 1920s to the 1980s, although there is no television, radio, or anything like that.

OVERVIEW

This is just what it appears to be, a very mundane-looking living room in a house. It's dusty and touched with cobwebs. At least half the furnishings are covered in dusty sheets. The lighting is dim. The walls are plaster. There are windows (as you'd expect) and a closet. A single exit leads into a dark room or hallway (it's hard to tell from here). There's a piece of paper on the ground, near the door.

Once the PCs are inside, the door they came through slams shut behind them and then vanishes.

FRONT DOOR

The door slams shut and disappears after the PCs enter.

WINDOWS

Although the windows allow someone outside the house to look into this room, those inside the room look out onto just blackness. The windows are indestructible.

THE PIECE OF PAPER

This appears to be a page torn from a book—perhaps a personal journal. Show the players Remnant 1 (page 272).

CLOSET

The closet holds coats and jackets. There's a shelf above with a single glove and a broken umbrella. On the floor in the closet is a small cardboard box. In addition to a few dead flies, it holds three very old pieces of mail addressed to Philip Harlock:

+ An offer from an insurance agent (now long dead).
+ A postcard advertising a sale at a local hardware store (the business burned down years ago)
+ An invoice from a mail-order bookseller for two books: *Automatic Writing*, and *The Bell Signals Night*.

The box also has a small bit of torn canvas with a large green eye painted upon it, about life-size. This is one of the Eyes of the Child, and it was torn from a painting in **the Gallery** (page 106). If the characters find **the other eye** (page 91) and make a deal with the Curator, one of them can be granted special sight.

TO THE LIGHTLESS HALL

This doorway leads to **the Lightless Hall** (page 84).

FATHER

Father won't ever be encountered in this room.

LIGHTLESS HALL

This pitch-black room cannot be lit by any light.

This is one of the rooms described in the Secrets of the House *as a "building dread" room.*

OVERVIEW

Only 20 feet long, this hall leads from **the Living Room** (page 82) to **the Boundless Room** (page 86). This place is remarkable only in that it is always as dark as the inside of a skull.

DARKNESS

No light of any kind will ever light this hallway. It is always utterly dark.

TO THE LIVING ROOM

This doorway leads to **the Living Room** (page 82).

TO THE BOUNDLESS ROOM

This innocuous door leads to **the Boundless Room** (page 86). It is unlocked.

FATHER

Father won't ever be encountered in this room.

To the
Living Room

To the
Boundless
Room

No matter how fast light
travels, it finds the darkness
has always got there first,
and is waiting for it.

~Terry Pratchett,
Reaper Man

THE BOUNDLESS ROOM

A trap with infinite space in the darkness, but a buried clock holds the way out (which is to go deeper in).

> *The idea here is that the room is infinite and seems to repeat, but it doesn't actually. It follows its own strange rules.*

OVERVIEW

This is a huge room with wooden flooring and brick walls. Brick pillars rise to the ceiling in a single row. From the doorway, it's impossible to see the edge of the room on the left-hand side—it's too dark. On the right-hand side of the room, the brick wall has several large, high-placed windows that show only darkness, but what little light there is somehow comes from them. The far side of the room fades into darkness as well.

Near the second pillar's base, it looks like someone has pried up some of the floorboards.

FROM THE LIGHTLESS HALL

This door leads to **the Lightless Hall** (page 84). Once the characters move out of sight of it, however, they will not find it again.

WINDOWS

Like almost every window in the house, the windows look out into utter darkness, but these somehow also let in a bit of dim light. They're unbreakable and inoperable.

THE DARKNESS ON THE LEFT

Moving to the left reveals another row of brick pillars, another brick wall with windows, and another door back the way the PCs came from originally. And now the right side of the room is dark. This isn't just the other side of the room, however. It's an optical trick creating a mirror of the right side of the room. If the PCs check, there's an area where the floorboards have been pried up here too (it's the

same spot). If they go through the doorway, it leads back into **the Lightless Hall** (page 84), where there is but one entrance back into the Boundless Room, not two. In other words, the doorway on the left and the one on the right—that the PCs used to get here—are the same doorway.

THE DARKNESS STRAIGHT AHEAD

The room goes on forever into the darkness ahead. More pillars, more windows on the right. After about a hundred paces, the characters will see a place in the floor where someone has pried up floorboards. But this isn't a different spot from the first one—it's the same one. The room just keeps repeating over and over into infinity, like the background in a cartoon chase scene.

There are a few different actions the PCs can take to investigate this further:

✦ Go Back. If the PCs look back behind them, they can't see the door or the original damaged spot in the floor, but if they go back, they can find the original spot (you can't see more than one at a time). However, they no longer can see the door or the south wall. Just darkness. Now the room extends forever (always repeating the same layout) to the south as well. Going to the western half continues to reveal a mirror version of the eastern half, so there's no door there, either.

✦ Leave a Mark. If anyone tries to leave something behind, put a mark on the floor, or do anything else to mark the repeating pattern of the room and then move ahead or back to see if they find the mark, it doesn't work. The mark or object left behind is gone. Even if they alter the pried-up floorboards, this won't be true the next time they reach those floorboards.

✦ Spread Out. If the characters spread out, even with multiple lights of their own, they will begin to lose sight of each other in the darkness, even though it physically shouldn't work that way. Each character will feel like they're the one in the light.

✦ Split Up. If the characters split up in this room so that they can't see each other, they won't meet again in the repeating nature of the room. They won't ever meet up again until they try to simply find each other, probably by calling out. This takes a lot longer than they would expect—perhaps hours—reflecting the weird spatial issues in this room.

Should the PCs split up and take some time to find each other, one or more is taunted by the ghost in the room. When they all rejoin, the ghost whispers suggestions like "Those aren't your friends," or "That's not really him," or "That just looks like her," and so on.

Ahead

Windows

To the Left

Hole

From the Lightless Hall

THE PRIED-UP FLOORBOARDS

The hole left by the removed boards is about a foot across and reveals a lower, wooden subfloor. Anyone spending much time in the area hears a distant ticking sound, like a clock but much faster. If the subfloor is pried up, the hole continues down but curves to one side so that even though it's only a few feet deep, you can't see the bottom from above. Reaching down into it, however, reveals a large metallic object: an ornate pewter mantle-style clock, with two clock faces, each showing a different time.

The clock is magical, and it is activated by setting the time on the two different clock faces. What happens is based on what the PCs try:

Set the clocks so that the left clock's time is earlier than the right clock's (this is what is true when found).

✦ Nothing happens.

Set the clocks so that the right clock's time is earlier than the left clock's

✦ A small, black doorway appears in between the two clock faces. If anyone even thinks about going through the door, they disappear and reappear in **the Room With a Hidden Elevator** (page 88). *This is the only way out of this room.* There is no way to bring the clock along.

Set the clocks to the same time

✦ A dozen blood-red eyes appear and swarm around the clock. Each has a Rating of 1, but if they manage to touch a character, that character has a chilling vision of their own gruesome death and they suffer a mental injury with a Rating of 3.

Even if the PCs move farther into the room to more areas of pried-up floorboards, there are no other clocks to be found. Just the one.

THE GIGGLING GHOST

One person in the room will hear the giggling of a young child. Give the player this message:

> You hear the soft sound of a giggling young child somewhere in the darkness.

If they relate this, and everyone stops to listen, everyone hears it. If they don't, someone else sees a small, darting shadow near a pillar. Send that player this message:

> You see the shadow by one of the distant pillars move. Is someone there? If they are, they're small. A small glimpse of movement is all you get. There are no other shadows.

Investigation turns up nothing. There's a very minor spirit here (Rating 2, 8 for hiding) that seems like the ghost of a young girl. It's actually a demon interested mainly in taunting. It can move anywhere in the room in a heartbeat, and so it stays well away from the characters. It has no special abilities other than an immunity to attempts to control, banish, turn, or command it. Any such attempts, including just plain old talking, provoke more laughter.

Once they are in this room for quite a while, the characters spot the ghost from time to time, and if they do anything else in the room, it mocks them, but in the manner of a shy child. It quietly says things like "silly adults," and giggles as it vanishes into the dark.

FATHER

If the House Die indicates that Father arrives here, he emerges from the darkness. He is 9 feet tall, broad-shouldered, and wears simple clothing. His face is dark, with only angry yellow eyes and a broad, roaring mouth visible. In one hand, he holds a long, black belt. "Stupid!" he bellows. "You're too stupid to ever find your way out of here."

Show the players the image of Father.

Everyone who hears his voice is subject to his Rating 9 mental attack, after which he fades into the darkness, saying, "You are not worthy of my name."

ROOM WITH A HIDDEN ELEVATOR

Seemingly empty, the hidden elevator connects many areas of the house.

> *The elevator is key to fully exploring the Darkest House, but using it will quickly take unprepared, injured, or inexperienced characters into some truly dire situations.*

OVERVIEW

Arrival spot after escaping **the Boundless Room** (page 86), but without the Eyes of the Child, this room is empty.

Without the Eyes of the Child (obtained in **the Gallery** [page 106]), this just appears to be an empty room with a very stout door and two passages leading to the left and the right. An oval blue rug with gold embroidery lies upon the stone floor. It is worn and stained. Possibly bloodstains, but quite old, with signs that someone scrubbed them to try to get them clean.

APPEARING FROM
THE BOUNDLESS ROOM

Characters who escape **the Boundless Room** (page 86) arrive at this point.

UNDER THE RUG

There is a folded piece of paper beneath the rug. It appears to be a page torn from a book—perhaps a personal journal. Show the players **Remnant 9** (page 277).

EYES OF THE CHILD (ELEVATOR DOOR)

If anyone has the Eyes of the Child, they also see in the wall opposite the door what seems like a brass cage, with a scissor gate door in front of it, also made of brass, slightly tarnished. Only the person with the Eyes can open the door (those without it see and feel a blank wall). Once the door is opened, the interior of the elevator is revealed to all.

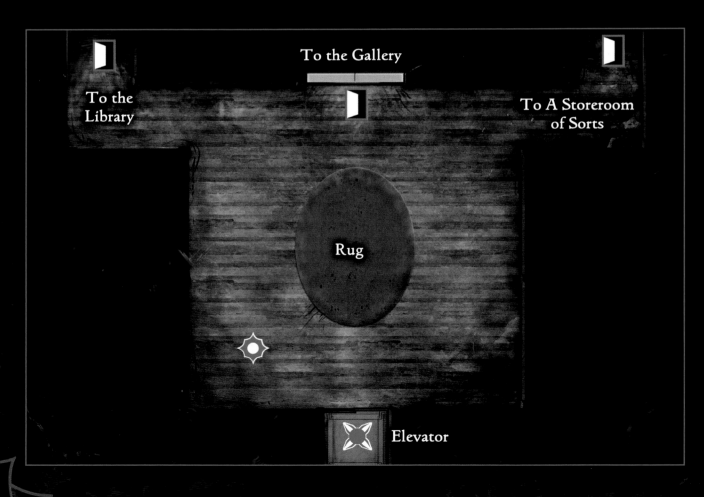

THE ELEVATOR

Anyone with the Eyes of the Child can see that the elevator is a large brass cage set into the back wall.

Show the player with the Eyes of the Child the elevator image.

On the floor is a heavy lever with six positions. It's currently in position 4. The elevator moves very slowly, taking almost a full minute to reach the next level up or down. There is a mechanical sound when it moves, and a clinking of chains. Through the cage, chains and gears can be seen moving. Damaging any of them renders the elevator inoperable for 24 hours before it resets.

✦ Position 1: Takes the elevator to **the Music Room** (page 222)

✦ Position 2: Takes the elevator to **the Great Hall** (page 114)

✦ Position 3: Takes the elevator to **the Mannequin Room** (page 154)

✦ Position 4: Where the lever is now (if the elevator goes to another level, 4 returns it to this room)

✦ Position 5: Takes the elevator to **the Backrooms** (page 118)

✦ Position 6: Takes the elevator to **the Guardian** (page 122)

TO THE GALLERY

The very stout door leading to **the Gallery** (page 106) is locked (Rating 9). The key can be found in **A Storeroom of Sorts** (page 110).

TO THE LIBRARY

This innocuous door leads to **the Library** (page 90). It is unlocked.

TO A STOREROOM OF SORTS

This innocuous door leads to **A Storeroom of Sorts** (page 110). It is unlocked.

FATHER

If the House Die indicates that Father arrives here, he storms in. He is 9 feet tall, broad-shouldered, and wears simple clothing. His face is dark, and you can only see angry yellow eyes and a broad, roaring mouth. In one hand, he holds a long, black belt.

Show the players the image of Father.

Should Father come to this room and the elevator has been revealed, he smashes it, rendering it inoperable for 24 hours. If the elevator has not been revealed, Father attacks the PCs physically using the belt as a weapon, bellowing that he will punish them for what they've done. He has a Rating of 6. He cannot be reasoned with, and will chase PCs that flee. He disappears if slain.

THE LIBRARY

A room full of books, with many secrets and treasures.

> *There's a lot to discover in this room. Don't rush through this encounter.*

OVERVIEW

This large rectangular chamber has bookcases along three walls, as well as a simple wooden desk and matching chair. The desk has a reading lamp upon it, a few pens, and a single notebook. Rather than the somewhat pleasant smell of old books, this room has an odor of stifling loneliness.

THE DESK

The desk has no drawers or cabinets, although affixed to the underside is a leather holster holding a small handgun. If the characters come from a setting where handguns are common, this will likely be of little significance. It is fully loaded, and has five shots. If the characters come from a setting where handguns are not common, treat it as a very easy to use and accurate ranged weapon that inflicts impressive but not overwhelming damage.

THE NOTEBOOK

The notebook is blank, but tucked within it is an older page, seemingly torn from a journal. Show the players **Remnant 4** (page 274).

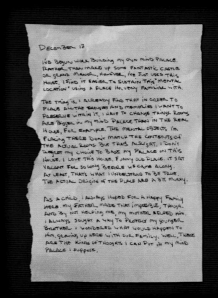

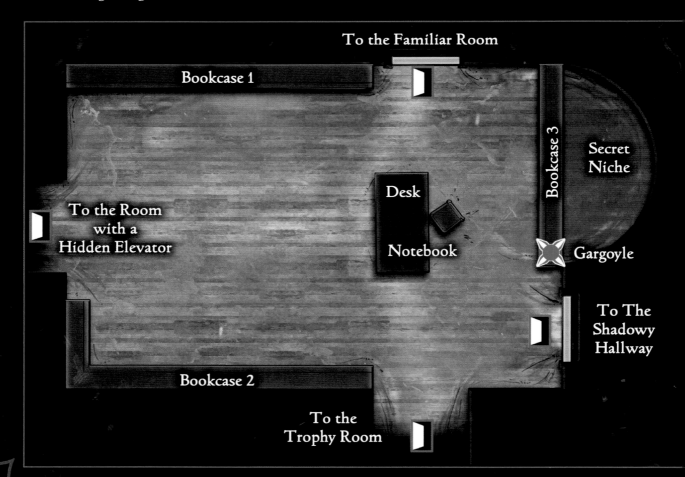

To the Familiar Room

Bookcase 1

Bookcase 3

Secret Niche

Desk

To the Room with a Hidden Elevator

Notebook

Gargoyle

To The Shadowy Hallway

Bookcase 2

To the Trophy Room

BOOKCASE 1

This is a fairly full bookcase, although not as full as the others. There are three books of particular note here:

1. *The Dream Eaters*. This seems like a mediocre novel set in the "land of dreams." However, if someone has the ability to sense the presence of magic, this book seems magical. If placed in the room where a single character sleeps, that character will have no dreams, good or bad. It only works if there is one sleeper in the room.

2. *Cornucopia*. This book also shows the presence of magic if looked for. It seems to be a rather dull philosophical treatise on joy and despair; however, if left alone overnight on a table or shelf (that is to say, not with other books), in the morning the book will be flipped open and next to it will be a different book. There is a 50/50 chance that *Cornucopia* will be open to a section about joy or despair. Should it be a section about joy, the new book that it has produced will be useful and pertain to the owner's current circumstances. For example, if a thief owns the book and is planning a robbery, they might find a book on lock-picking techniques or maybe even a book that happens to have a map showing the place they're going to rob. If *Cornucopia* opens toward despair, however, the book produced will not be useful and will cover a topic that the owner might very well find disheartening or sad. The thief might find a book detailing local laws and the severe punishments that await thieves, for example, or an autobiography of how someone ruined their life by stealing rather than earning a living within the law.

3. *Eyes of the Child*. Not at all magical, this is, in fact, a book of whimsical notions about seeing the world with fresh, innocent eyes. The important thing is that tucked in its pages is one of the Eyes of the Child. It is a small bit of torn canvas with a large green eye painted upon it, about life-size. It was torn from a painting in **the Gallery** (page 106). If the characters find the other eye and make a deal with the Curator, one of them can be granted special sight.

In addition to the books, there are three stoppered crystal vials with liquid inside. Each of these is a magical potion and only works once.

+ The first allows someone to read a single book with just a quick flip through its pages. It tastes like flat, bitter soda.

+ The second makes the drinker feel refreshed, as if they just ate a nutritious lunch and had a nap. If they are injured, their least serious wound heals.

+ The third allows someone to peer through one barrier (like a door or a wall, up to 6 inches thick) for about a minute.

BOOKCASE 2

This bookcase is a series of shelves, well-stocked with mostly nonfiction of a variety of ages and amount of use. There is a wooden box (hidden, Rating 3) disguised to look like a book with a spine that says, "History." Inside is a gold pocket watch (that doesn't work) worth about $30 and a large costume jewelry ring with a secret compartment. Inside the compartment is a dose of Rating 6 poison.

BOOKCASE 3

The bookcase is packed with books of different sizes, colors, and ages. Only about half of the books have titles on their spines. Should anyone approach the rear wall, the books shuffle and move as if someone invisible is rearranging them blindingly fast. When they go still a moment later, the word "STOP" can be seen spelled out faintly in the new arrangement of books, based on the colors and appearance of all the book spines. If this warning goes unheeded, the books rearrange again to present an upraised hand with the palm forward, as if to signal "stop."

If the characters persist in approaching the rear bookcase, books fly off the shelf to strike them, making attacks with a Rating of 4. After one attack per character, the bookcase gives up.

This is when the PCs might notice a special book simply titled *I'm Alive*. As the title suggests, this is a living, sentient book. When open, it can carry on a conversation by rearranging the letters on its pages. Getting it to do so (and be friendly) is a task with a Rating of 5. If persuaded to communicate, it is happy to "talk" about itself, but it knows very little about the Darkest House. It knows that it was once owned by a woman named Synovaria and eventually found itself here. (This detail is not relevant to the Darkest House adventure, and you may change it to fit the context of your campaign setting if you wish.) It knows that a man named Phillip Harlock once lived in the house, and that he's been gone for quite some time. It might mention that a being known as Father does sometimes wander through the library. The book suggests running or hiding should Father make an appearance. The book (which likes to joke that it's a "living document") is happy to be taken by someone that treats it well, and could even operate as a spy or something similar, as it's aware of its surroundings, but looks just like a normal book. "Treating it well" means keeping it stimulated with conversation, and writing it poetry. The book is fairly capricious, though, and will abandon the character that takes it if it gets a better offer.

Behind one book near the middle of the shelf is a hidden switch (Rating 6). If the switch is depressed, the entire bookcase pivots in the center just enough for one person to slip behind it.

BEHIND THE BOOKCASE

A small, empty niche carved out of solid rock, just large enough for a single person to stand within, lies behind bookcase 3. At about shoulder height, there is a square hole drilled into the stone, a few inches across—just large enough for an arm. Deep within the hole, just within reach, is a book. It takes some effort to pull it out. It's a small tome with the name of the character that found it on the cover and the spine. It details their entire life, as if it were an autobiography. However, every event is described in a negative light. Successes are downplayed, while failures are magnified—a biography written by someone that hates them.

Show players art of the **Library Map—After Discovery**.

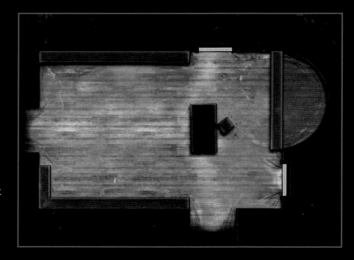

EYES OF THE CHILD (GARGOYLE)

If a character has the Eyes of the Child, they see a small ceramic gargoyle on the far right end of the highest shelf of the rear bookcase. Only someone with the eyes can see or touch the statuette. Even if they hold the statuette, to another observer, their hands are at their sides. There is no indication that the gargoyle exists to anyone without the eyes. If asked where a particular inhabitant or room lies, the gargoyle will point at the exit that will take the questioner to the destination or target the swiftest. However, the inhabitant or room must be named precisely as they are named in these notes. A general question, such as "Where is the door out?" or "Where's that big room with the brick pillars?" or "Where is the greatest treasure?" produces no result. This gargoyle is identical to the one that can be found in **the Interior Courtyard** (page 102). If both gargoyles are held by the same person, they immediately animate and fight, destroying each other.

BOOKS

Other than those already mentioned, some of the books in this library include:

- *Into the Dust*
- *Book of Lies*
- *Occult Majesty*
- *Outside the Circles of Time*
- *Longest Night*
- *The Key of It All*
- *Liber Null*
- *The Spirit Realm*
- *Eyes of the Centipede*
- *Automatic Writing*
- *The Tooth and the Claw*
- *H.P. Lovecraft's Tales of Horror*
- *The Book of the End*
- *Nestor's Nine Rules*
- *Eyes on the Skies*
- *Donjon Deep*
- *The Bell Signals Night*
- *House of Leaves*
- *The Anarchist's Cookbook*
- *Dune*
- *The Trial of Stamasos*
- *Moonchild*
- *Roget's Thesaurus*
- *Arul's Spirit Guide*
- *Non-Euclidian Geometry*
- *The Shape of Our Souls*
- *Seeking Realms Beyond*

TO THE SHADOWY HALLWAY

This innocuous door leads to **the Shadowy Hallway** (page 100). It is unlocked.

TO THE TROPHY ROOM

This doorway leads to **the Trophy Room** (page 98).

TO THE ROOM WITH A HIDDEN ELEVATOR

This doorway leads to **the Room With a Hidden Elevator** (page 88).

TO THE FAMILIAR ROOM

This innocuous door leads to **the Familiar Room** (page 94). It is unlocked.

FATHER

If the House Die indicates that Father arrives here, he storms in.

Show the players the image of Father.

He is 9 feet tall, broad-shouldered, and wears simple clothing. His face is dark, and you can only see angry yellow eyes and a broad, roaring mouth. He shouts, "You're disturbing my work. I must have peace and quiet to finish the Great Work!" And then he attacks by throwing handfuls of books at characters. He has a Rating of 6. He cannot be reasoned with, and will chase PCs that flee. He disappears if slain.

THE FAMILIAR ROOM (PATER)

his room is different from the others, as its details are dictated by the background of one or more of the PCs.

An NPC trapped in this room offers a fantastic way to bring in a new PC, should that need arise in the course of playing through the scenario.

OVERVIEW

This room is a location from the past of one or more of the characters. It might be their childhood bedroom, a prison cell where they were incarcerated, the taproom from a bar they frequented, a training dojo where they studied, or the library where they first saw an early crush. Or someplace else. The important thing is, it is not a replica—it's actually that room. The details might have changed somewhat, but that's only because time has passed. Or, it might be precisely as if they had just left it. It comes complete with furnishings, but any windows just look out into pitch blackness. There are no occupants.

FITTING THE ROOM IN

The room should conform to the needs of the map. In other words, where the diagram shows entrances and exits, the room needs to have them as well. It must have a door that connects to **the Library** (page 90) and one that connects to **Lying in State** (page 96). If the original room didn't have the same exits, it appears the way it did originally, but you must modify the room as needed with new, hidden doors, or original doors that no longer open. A secret panel might slide to reveal an exit where there wasn't one originally, or a now-extraneous door cannot be opened, or perhaps leads to a solid black wall through which passage is impossible.

COORDINATING WITH THE OTHER FAMILIAR ROOMS

There are two other similar rooms in the house (possibly more if the PCs explore **the Backrooms** [page 118]). They are always different rooms, and very likely, they are from the pasts of different characters. What happens when PCs visit them depends not on which room they discover, but the order in which they are discovered.

The first time the PCs come to a familiar room, it is just that—nothing more.

The second time the PCs come to a (different) familiar room, it is as the character acquainted with the room remembers it, but there is blood on the floor or perhaps on the furniture. Some recognizable memento of an NPC associated with this room can be found near or in the blood.

The third time the PCs come to a (different) familiar room, it is different because it is occupied. The PC acquainted with the room recognizes the NPC; they're someone the PC would normally expect to find in this room (in a world outside the house).

The NPC is just as surprised to see the PC, whom they likewise recognize. Their shock is quite genuine. "What are you doing here?"

From the NPC's point of view, they are still in the room where the room should be. They aren't in the Darkest House. When the NPC looks through the entrance the PCs came through, they don't see where the PCs have been, but rather where the original room's entrance would normally lead.

This changes should a PC attempt to persuade the NPC to come through one of the exits of the room (or forces them to do so). In this eventuality, the NPC *is* now in the Darkest House, trapped there alongside the PCs. It doesn't matter if they go back into the familiar room. They are now with the PCs, and likely in a lot of danger.

There is no way to reverse this process. A character within the Darkest House cannot escape through a familiar room, and all effects of being in the house still apply while within.

As long as the NPC remains in the familiar room, it's impossible to convince them that they aren't where they appear to be (because in a very technical sense, they are). The safest and kindest thing would, in fact, be to leave them where they are. Should the PCs leave and return, the NPC is gone.

FATHER

Nine feet tall, broad-shouldered, and wearing simple clothing, Father storms into this room if the House Die indicates it, shouting "I told you not to come in here while I'm working!"

Show the players the image of Father.

His face is dark, and you can only see angry yellow eyes and a broad, roaring mouth. In one hand, he holds a long black belt with which he attacks the PCs physically. He has a Rating of 6. He cannot be reasoned with, and will chase PCs that flee. He disappears if slain.

LYING IN STATE

Someone has died.

> *If you want to play "Bela Lugosi's Dead" by Bauhaus while the PCs are in this room, I won't stop you.*

OVERVIEW

A new casket of dark wood rests atop a bier in the middle of the room. A mirror hanging on the wall is draped in black cloth. Flowers fill vases around the room. There are a few pages of handwritten notes on the table by the door.

THE FLOWERS

Although they look alive, the flowers and their stems blacken, shrivel, and then turn to dust at the slightest touch.

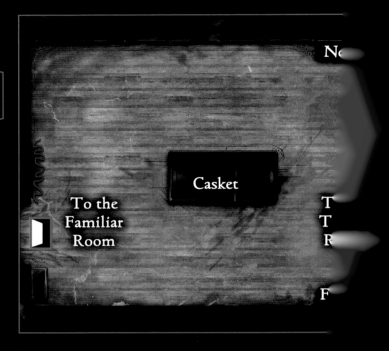

To the
Familiar
Room

Casket

T
T
R

F

THE MOURNERS

After a short time, an eerie, translucent processional of mourners slowly enters the room and passes by the casket, each pausing for a minute to gaze at the coffin as though they can see the figure within, despite it being closed. These mourners bring with them low, mournful music, but they're really just ghostly images replaying actions that happened long ago. Most of the mourners are older people, but a few are middle-aged or younger.

They do not react to, or interact with, the characters in any way. They are insubstantial and cannot be touched.

THE NOTES

These are Phillip Harlock's notes from v
died. The handwriting is the same as in
found throughout the house. Show the
(page 273).

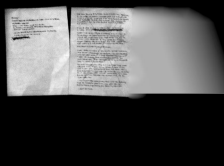

THE CASKET

The casket has a hinged, two-part lid. Opening the casket reveals the corpse inside. The corpse is of the oldest male PC. (If there is no male character, then it's the oldest, most domineering of the PCs instead.) Everyone *other* than the PC depicted in the casket gets a direct message:

> You hear a faint whisper. "It wears a human face."

There is nothing affecting the character who looks exactly like the corpse inside the coffin. Although they, too, have to admit the resemblance, they are certainly not dead. The house is trying to isolate them from the others, perhaps influenced by Philip's hatred of his father.

EYES OF THE CHILD (THE TINY DOOR)

There is a tiny blue door set in the wall. The door is about 18 inches high and 10 inches wide. It is locked (Rating 7), and the key is in **the Trophy Room** (page 98). Behind the door is a small niche 2 feet high and a foot wide. As soon as the door opens, a weird clockwork child scrambles into the room.

Show the players the image of **the Clockwork Child**.

It holds a terrible-looking knife with a bloodstained blade. It doesn't attack anyone, and instead runs about the room screaming with a terrible whine, half like an infant's cry and half like a mechanical screech. The clockwork child has a Rating of 3, unless someone attempts to catch it or strike it, in which case it has a Rating of 7. A single strike or grab is all it takes to render it inert, but not before it slashes with its knife one time.

Its weapon is called the **Eager Knife**. The Eager Knife is a magical knife that grants its wielder a Boon to attacks and damage. However, it also bears a curse in that, as its name might suggest, it is eager for violence and bloodletting. When a character has the knife in their possession, they must resist a Rating 4 effect or immediately attack anyone new they encounter. While using the knife to kill a living person or other mammal quells this

effect for about three days, not using it in this way for more than three days means that the character must start resisting the knife's effect to attack even their friends. Bringing the Eager Knife to **the Armory** (page 112) has special significance.

CLOCKWORK CHILD LOOSE IN THE HOUSE

If left completely alone, the child runs off into **the Trophy Room** and then throughout the house, screaming all the way. Occasionally, the PCs will hear it in the distance as they further explore the house. Thankfully, its screaming makes it easy to find if they ever need to.

TO THE FAMILIAR ROOM

This innocuous door leads to **the Familiar Room** (page 94). It is unlocked.

TO THE TROPHY ROOM

This innocuous door leads to **the Trophy Room** (page 98). It is unlocked.

FATHER

If the House Die indicates Father's appearance here, the corpse sits up in its casket, no longer looking like the PC, but instead like a broad-shouldered man, wearing a suit. His face is dark, and you can only see angry yellow eyes and a broad, roaring mouth. "If I die, I'm taking you all with me!" he shouts. Then the corpse lies back down and returns to how it was before. This all happens so suddenly that the shock is a Rating 6 mental attack.

THE TROPHY ROOM

illed with the trophies of years of hunting, this room has spirits that are very angry.

The focus in this room is anger and revenge upon living humans. The spirits here don't care if the PCs are hunters or not.

OVERVIEW

A room of death, to be certain. This room presents a taxidermist's pride, with animal heads mounted across all the walls, and smaller, stuffed beasts displayed on tables as well as the floor. A pair of hunting rifles hang above a fireplace, which is dark and cold.

Two bearskin rugs lie upon the otherwise bare stone floor.

The most striking specimen in the room is mounted on the wall directly opposite the fireplace. It is the head of an impressively large buck, with antlers rising up in an almost impossibly massive and intricately tangled crown.

EYES OF THE CHILD (ANTLERS)

If a character has the Eyes of the Child, they see that within the shockingly large antler rack of the main deer, the ghostly visages of at least a dozen severed human heads are impaled, or hang from sinewy threads. Each seems at least vaguely aware, slowly writhing, mouths working, bulging eyes moving.

THE DEER HEAD

The spirits of all the animals in this room, plus likely hundreds of other animals killed by hunters as trophies, reside within this buck's head. These are angry, violent spirits that seek vengeance against any and all living humans (or humanoids). If any should enter the room, the buck emits a ghastly roar as its neck elongates with a horrible wet crunching noise. Anyone witnessing this is subject to a Rating 3 mental attack from the shock. It attacks first and has a Rating of 5, although all of its attacks have a Boon due to its position. Fully extended, it can reach anywhere in the room and looks like a giant brown-furred snake with a deer's head. It fights until destroyed, or until there are no offensive creatures in the room.

TALKING TO THE DEER HEAD

If addressed, the buck will speak with a thousand savage voices at once—growls, shrieks, screeches, snarls, and howls. "Murder! You have murdered us. Not as prey but for reckless sport. You have reduced our existence to trophies to decorate your grisly home. Now you will pay."

Anyone managing to calm it (considering its disposition, the Rating is 8) can get it to stop attacking, but it still seethes with anger. It will allow the group to pass, however, and if asked will tell them that the Eager Knife is in the next room. It won't say or discuss anything else.

Deer Head

To the Library

To Lying In State

Fireplace

Rifles

ΙΕ OTHER ANIMALS

wolf head, a bear head, a tiger head, two antelope
ds, a jackalope head, and a few smaller deer heads
rn the walls. A stuffed falcon, wings spread, sits upon
de table. A stuffed boar and a stuffed puma stand on
floor in dramatic, life-like poses.

JNTING RIFLES

ese are functional but not loaded, and there is no
munition for them here. If the characters come from
tting where firearms are common, these will likely
of little significance. If the characters come from a
ing where firearms are not common, and somehow
ammunition for the rifles, treat them as accurate
ged weapons that inflict overwhelming damage but are
derately difficult to care for.

IE FIREPLACE

ere is a hidden shelf (Rating 5) inside the firebox,
ve the lintel. Upon it rests a key, coated in soot.
aned off, the key reveals itself to be made of blue glass.
pens the tiny door in **Lying in State** (page 96).

) LYING IN STATE

is innocuous door leads to **Lying in State** (page 96). It
nlocked.

) THE LIBRARY

is doorway leads to **the Library** (page 90).

FATHER

If the House Die indicates that
Father arrives here, he storms in
through the door.

Show the players the image
of **Father**.

He is 9 feet tall, broad-
shouldered, and wears tough,
outdoor clothing. His face is
dark, and you can only see angry
yellow eyes and a broad, roaring
mouth. He grabs one of the
rifles from above the fireplace or
from a character if they've taken
one. The rifle grows in size
to match Father's height, and
he swings it like a club, with
which he can strike two foes at
once if they are relatively near each
other. "I told you to stay out of this
room, you worthless little demons!"
He has a Rating of 6. He cannot be
reasoned with, and will chase PCs
that flee. He disappears if slain.

SHADOWY HALLWAY

This short hallway leads to the Interior Courtyard from the Library.

This is one of the rooms described in Secrets of the House as a "building dread" room.

OVERVIEW

An arched passage leads from the top of the stairs in **the Library** (page 90) to **the Interior Courtyard** (page 102). The passage is about 30 feet long and 12 feet wide, made of large fitted stones. There are scratch marks on the stones, making it look like something or someone was dragged toward the courtyard. The air smells of a cool night's breeze, of course coming from the courtyard.

SHADOWS

The shadows seem to dart and lurch strangely in this hallway, almost as if they're occasionally moving of their own accord. There is no overt effect here other than to unnerve the players.

TO THE LIBRARY

This innocuous door leads to **the Library** (page 90). It is unlocked.

TO THE INTERIOR COURTYARD

This doorway leads to **the Interior Courtyard** (page 102).

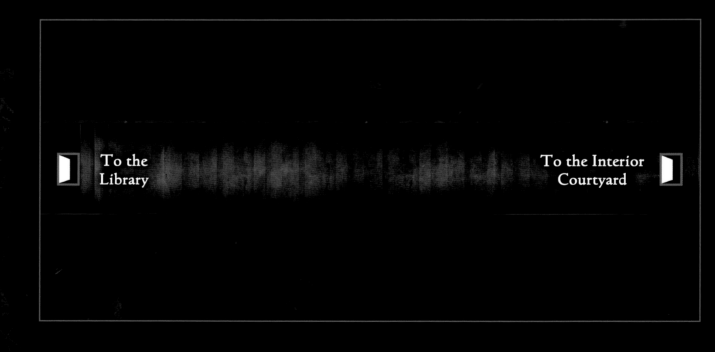

To the Library

To the Interior Courtyard

FATHER

If the House Die indicates that Father arrives here, he storms in. He is 9 feet tall, broad-shouldered, and wears simple clothing. His face is dark, and you can only see angry yellow eyes and a broad, roaring mouth. In one hand, he holds a long black belt.

Show the players the image of Father.

"You are all too stupid and too weak to be mine!" he shouts as he attacks with the belt as a weapon. He has a Rating of 6. He cannot be reasoned with, and will chase PCs that flee. He disappears if slain.

THE INTERIOR COURTYARD

The darkness above this very dangerous area has a good chance of grabbing a character and tossing them outside of the house, where they are changed, tinted with darkness.

This is a pretty dangerous area. Foolish actions or bad rolls might result in the loss of one or more characters.

OVERVIEW

Leaves and twigs fill this interior courtyard. A few bits of brown grass peek out from the stones, but they are dead. Everything in the courtyard is dead. It is cold and very still, but wind can be heard in the distance. Otherwise, there is the quiet of ancient despair hanging like a pallor over the entire expanse. In the middle is a statue of a weeping woman. At her feet lies a shattered stone tablet. The courtyard is open to the sky, but the sky is pitch black. There are three exits: two archways that lead to wide stone passages and a wooden cellar door in the ground near another wall.

ENTERING THE COURTYARD

Crossing the courtyard quickly is safe, although anyone watching the darkness above sees a gigantic human hand begin to emerge above a character passing underneath. All witnessing this event are subject to a Rating 3 mental attack from the shock.

Dawdling in the courtyard, or lingering anywhere in its confines risks an attack by the darkness itself. When this happens, a massive hand of pure darkness descends toward the victim, and its attack has a Rating of 8. Should this attack strike, the hand grasps the victim, who then only has a single chance to squirm free (Rating 6). Alternatively, they could attempt another action, but with a Bane from the crushing hand. If the victim remains in the hand's grasp after this one action, it pulls them up and out of the courtyard, into the darkness.

A saving grace is that the hand can attack only one victim at a time. Bright light will cause it to withdraw, but only long enough for one victim to get to safety. On the following turn, it attacks or otherwise extinguishes the light source.

VICTIM IN THE DARKNESS

The character can't be retrieved. They are gone, but not forever.

You are gone, but not dead. You are unconscious, but outside the house. However, when the rest of the group exits the house and finds you, you are now tainted with darkness. Don't overdo it, but your personality now leans toward the darker, more negative side of things. You're not a homicidal maniac (at least not at first) but your ethical outlook is very likely skewed from where you are now, and it slowly—perhaps taking weeks—gets worse. You lean toward aggressive actions, and don't care too much about altruistic actions. You are quick to hate, but find difficulty in forgiveness or mercy.

When the others leave the Darkest House, they will find the missing character lying outside, unconscious. Soon, the PCs will begin to notice something strange about their friend. The character seems to have a darker

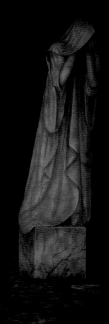

...rsonality and some very questionable ...nics. This can be lifted like a curse if ...ey have the means to do so; otherwise, ...ey can try (years of) therapy. Returning ... the Darkest House and completing ...character arc will also restore the ...aracter to their original nature.

...HE DARKNESS ABOVE

...nyone looking up into the "sky" sees ...at the darkness is not still. It roils with ...ife of its own.

...HE STATUE

...his marble statue is stained with age ...nd moisture. At the statue's feet is a ...one tablet that once bore the image of ...e sun, but is now shattered.

...If the painting *An Old Woman and a Dog* is removed ...om **the Gallery** and placed atop the tablet, people in ...he courtyard are protected against the darkness. Anytime ...giant hand looms from above in the courtyard, the ...d woman from the painting appears with her animal ...nd motions the hand off with her cane. The hand then ...tracts into the darkness above.

...CRATCH MARKS

...he stone wall bears scratch marks, with the words ..."Nothing more?" scratched into the stone. This isn't clear ...nless someone gets close.

...YES OF THE CHILD (GARGOYLE)

...f someone has the Eyes of the Child, they see that ...here is a small ceramic gargoyle statuette behind the ...arble statue. Only someone with the eyes can see or ...ouch the statuette. Even if they hold the statuette, to ...nother observer, their hands are at their sides. There is ...o indication that the gargoyle exists to anyone without ...he eyes. If asked where a particular inhabitant or room ...es, the gargoyle will point at the exit that will take ...he questioner to the destination or target the swiftest. ...owever, the inhabitant or room must be named precisely ...s they are named in these notes. A general question, ...uch as "Where is the door out?" or "Where's that big ...oom with the brick pillars?" or "Where is the greatest ...easure?" produces no result. This gargoyle is identical to ...he one that can be found in **the Library** (page 90). If both ...argoyles are held by the same person, they immediately ...nimate and fight, destroying each other.

THE CELLAR DOOR

The cellar door is unlocked, and there is a short flight of rough stone steps leading down to the darkness of **the Cellar** (page 104).

TO THE GALLERY

This staircase leads down to **the Gallery** (page 106).

TO THE SHADOWY HALLWAY

This passageway leads to the Library via **the Shadowy Hallway** (page 100).

FATHER

If the House Die indicates that Father arrives here, he descends out of the dark sky. The massive hand of pure darkness will not appear while he is present. Father is 9 feet tall, broad-shouldered, and wears simple clothing. His face is dark, and you can only see angry yellow eyes and a broad, roaring mouth. In one hand, he holds a long black belt.

Show the players the image of Father.

"I have to finish my Great Work," he bellows. "Only the Great Work is important. You mean nothing." Then, he attacks with the belt. He has a Rating of 6. He cannot be reasoned with, and will chase PCs that flee. He disappears if slain.

THE CELLAR

A dark, dank cellar offers a way out of the house, if it can be found.

> *The Doorman is eternally in a lot of pain. He is a pathetic, miserable figure. But if the PCs try to help him or rescue him from his situation (if that's even possible), how will they get out of the house?*

OVERVIEW

It is very dark and musty down here. Creaky wooden steps lead down to a bare, damp stone floor. In one corner, an old wooden bin holds long-rotted vegetables. A rusty bicycle hangs upside down from hooks in the ceiling, and a few old tools hang from pegs on the wall. An equally rusted metal barrel and a closed wooden crate stand next to the far wall. The damp, utterly still air carries a slight hint of gangrene.

VEGETABLES

Nothing more than what they appear.

BICYCLE

Unusable unless it is significantly repaired.

TOOLS

Hanging on the wall characters can find a hammer, pliers, shears, a mallet, a wrench, and a clamp. They're all rusted and worthless. Each of the pegs they hang from can be depressed, like a switch. If the pegs are depressed in the right order, a panel in the wall opens. The correct order is alphabetical, based on the tools: clamp, hammer, mallet, saw, shears, and wrench. The secret compartment behind the panel holds a saw, which is one of the eight **Mystic Tools**. Finding the secret panel just by searching is a Rating 8 action, and opening it without solving the puzzle requires a good prybar and a lot of strength—that's a Rating 7 action.

IF THE LURKER IS PRESENT

If the character possessed by the Lurker (from **the Foyer** [page 162]) is present when the saw is discovered, it forces the character to act.

> The spirit possessing you compels you to grab the saw and shout, "Mine!"

If this action causes any kind of questioning of the possessed character or their actions, the Lurker yet again compels its host.

> The spirit possessing you makes you say, "I'm fine. Don't worry about it. Now, where do you think the rest of these tools might be?"

Obviously, the Lurker wants the **Mystic Tools**. It will continue to compel its host to keep trying to find them. Should the entire set be found, the Lurker will attempt to kill all the other characters so that it can have the tools for itself.

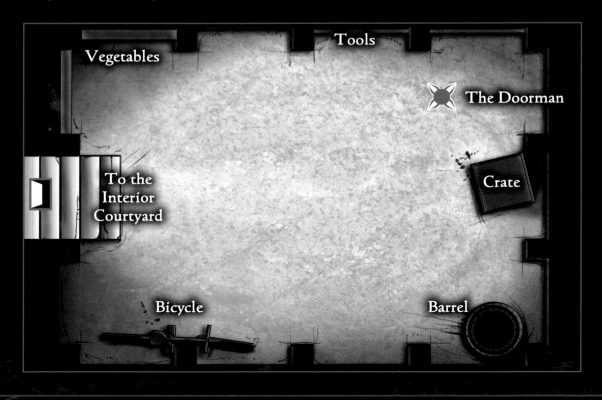

BARREL

About one-third filled with heating oil, which is neither flammable nor explosive (you have to heat it and turn it to vapor before it will burn).

CRATE

Filled with bits of rotten straw, packed around a random assortment of delicate, beautiful ornaments made of colored glass and crystal. They're clearly meant to be hung, as each has a small brass hook. There are ten ornaments, each worth about $20.

EYES OF THE CHILD (DOORMAN)

If a character has the Eyes of the Child, they will see the Doorman standing in the corner with his back to the characters.

THE DOORMAN

The Doorman can only be seen (and interacted with) by someone with the Eyes of the Child. He looks to be a human at first, and perhaps he once was. Now, however, his mostly bare skin is covered in a rough topography of scars while his eyes and mouth are stitched shut. Many padlocks have been sewn into his flesh, but prominently there is a large keyhole in his chest and another in his forehead.

Show the players the image of **the Doorman**.

The silver key found in **A Storeroom of Sorts** (page 110) or behind the bar in **the Ballroom** (page 212) opens the lock in his chest.

If the lock in his chest is opened, a door appears in the middle of the room. This is the **Front Door**, and PCs can use it to exit the house (even if that's not how they got in). Going back through the Front Door from the other side does not bring them back here, however; it takes them into **the Living Room** (page 82), as normal.

The plain key found in A Storeroom of Sorts opens the lock in his head. If the lock in his head is opened, a doorway of utter blackness opens next to him. This doorway leads to the secret room in **the Private Study** (page 230).

It's worth noting that this is the same Doorman that can be found with **the Gatekeeper** (page 224). When he's in that chamber, he can be seen by anyone. He moves around, but he can also be in two places at once. If slain in either place, he's dead in both. So if the PCs killed him in the other room, he won't be here. The PCs can only encounter him once in each place, so if they use him as an exit here, he will never be in the Cellar again (though they can still find him with the Gatekeeper, if they haven't already).

The Doorman has a Rating of 4, and will defend himself with his fists if he must.

TO THE INTERIOR COURTYARD

This innocuous door leads to **the Interior Courtyard** (page 102). It is unlocked.

FATHER

If the House Die indicates that he comes here, Father storms down the steps into the Cellar. He is 9 feet tall, broad-shouldered, and wears simple clothing. His face is dark, and you can only see angry yellow eyes and a broad, roaring mouth. In one hand, he holds a long black belt.

Show the players the image of Father.

"I've told you again and again, stay out of here!" he shouts as he attacks with the belt as a weapon. He has a Rating of 6. He cannot be reasoned with, and will chase PCs that flee. He disappears if slain.

A room filled with paintings, each with its own unique curse or haunting. The Curator here is a strange being that can grant the Eyes of the Child.

> *One of the most complex rooms in the house, the Gallery could end up being a significant portion of an RPG session all by itself.*

OVERVIEW

*The door from **the Room With the Hidden Elevator** (**page 88**) is locked (Rating 9). The key is in **A Storeroom of Sorts** (**page 110**).*

This is a long gallery with white walls bearing several framed paintings. Stone pillars run the length of the hall. A long red and gold carpet trails down the center of the room. The paintings are old, but some are older than others. Some of the frames appear . . . gnawed upon.

If a spirit within the Darkest House manages to exit the house and travel into a world outside, that is probably because it managed to create a painting keyed to itself in the Gallery. If the GM has used this as a way to get the PCs to come into the house—that they're chasing a spirit that has been disturbing the surrounding neighborhood—a painting keyed to that spirit should be placed here.

If the PCs have even one of the Eyes of the Child, the Curator appears in the middle of the room once they enter.

THE CURATOR

This person is a sinewy human (?) of indeterminate gender. Rather than a normal head, they have a large animal skull with wide, twisting antlers (in the end, they are so twisted and weird that they probably don't look like real antlers). The Curator wears strikingly strange but skin-tight clothing.

Show the players the image of the Curator.

"Are you a fan of art?" the Curator asks with a purring voice.

The Curator moves sensuously, as if each movement were part of a choreographed, albeit very slow, dance.

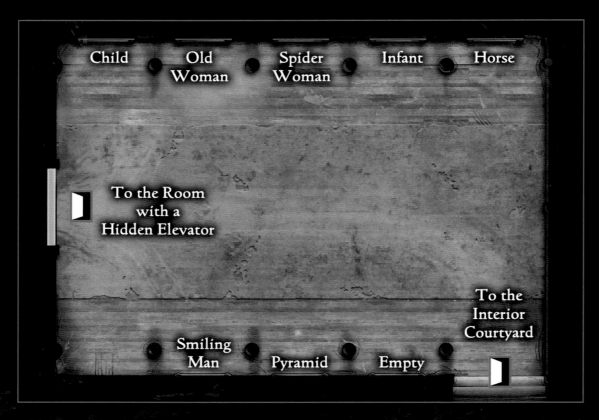

Child   Old Woman   Spider Woman   Infant   Horse

To the Room with a Hidden Elevator

To the Interior Courtyard

Smiling Man   Pyramid   Empty

If the PCs say yes, the Curator asks, "Which of these ches your eye?"

The Curator is happy to talk about each and every e of the paintings, and will tell them about the mposition, explain the use of color, or bring up random via about the unhappy life of the artist. The only one at provokes a different reaction is the damaged painting the child. If anyone mentions that painting, they say, hame about the eyes. I'm certain the child could see ch amazing things if only he had his eyes." If one of the Cs has one of the Eyes of the Child, the Curator will say at pointedly to that character.

If a character has one of the eyes, and mentions it in any ay, the Curator says, "If he had both eyes, that could be ite a gift." Then the Curator disappears.

If a character has both of the eyes, and mentions that the Curator in any way, the Curator says, "Would you e to see with the eyes of a child?"

If a character wants more information or clarification, e Curator will only purr, "Wouldn't you like to see ore than anyone else?"

If a character says yes, the Curator says, "A gift would be propriate in exchange for the one I offer, don't you agree?" A character can offer the Curator almost anything of lue. The more valuable or aesthetically pleasing, the tter. It simply needs to please them. If a character esents the Curator with a suitable gift, the Curator asks e character to hold out the eyes. The Curator takes the aracter by the hand and holds the child's eyes up to the aracter's eyes. In a painful flash, the character's eyes now ok like the painting's eyes—childlike and green. Then e Curator vanishes.

The character with the Eyes of the Child can now see d interact with things in the house that they otherwise uld not. For example, the elevator in **the Room With e Hidden Elevator** (page 88), the gargoyle in **the brary** (page 90), the Doorman in **the Cellar** (page 104), d more.

It is not possible for more than one character to gain e Eyes of the Child.

GHTING THE CURATOR

ghting the Curator is almost impossible, as they vanish soon as they are attacked, and very likely won't return. ne Curator has a Rating of 7. Their touch can drain meone's appearance of value and meaning. The victim comes utterly nondescript and unmemorable. The ctim can no longer influence or persuade people, they nnot intimidate people, and no one will ever remember em. While a blessing for a thief, perhaps, a curse for most anyone else.

THE DAMAGED PAINTING OF THE CHILD

This is a haunted portrait of a young boy, but the portion of the canvas on which his eyes were painted has been removed. If these pieces are found (one is in **the Living Room** and one is in **the Library**) and a deal is struck with the Curator, a character can be granted the Eyes of the Child and can see things in the house that they otherwise could not.

THE PAINTING OF AN OLD WOMAN AND A DOG

This haunted painting depicts an old woman walking a beast that's probably (?) a dog on a leash, with a walking cane in her other hand. Thick woods are all around, and much of it seems to have an orange tint.

Show the players the image of **The Painting of an Old Woman and a Dog**.

Hidden in the woods, it says, "Take me to the shattered sun."

The "shattered sun" is the broken tablet at the statue's feet in **the Interior Courtyard**. If the painting is removed and placed atop the tablet, people in the courtyard are protected against the darkness. Anytime a giant hand looms from above in the courtyard, the old woman from the painting appears with her animal and motions the hand off with her cane. The hand then retracts into the darkness above.

THE PAINTING OF A WOMAN WITH EIGHT SPIDER-LIKE ARMS

Show the players the image of the **Painting of a Woman With Eight Spider-Like Arms**.

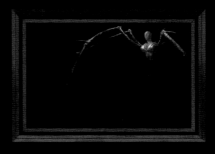

This is Ghorra, a spirit that can come and go from the Darkest House as she wishes, using this painting as a door. Only she can do so. Disturbing this painting is likely to draw Ghorra's attention. Depending on the situation, she might attack, or she might simply spy on the PCs. She definitely won't let anything bad happen to her painting, or allow it to be moved from the Gallery.

Ghorra has a Rating of 5, and can attack up to eight foes at once. Her spidery limbs are envenomed, so that anyone damaged by her has a Bane on all actions until their wound is healed. Their muscles feel weak and drained. Further, after the battle, anyone attempting to rest and recover from a wound she inflicted must succeed twice to heal the wound.

THE PAINTING OF A MAN AND AN INFANT

Show the players the image of the **Painting of a Man and an Infant**.

While staring at this painting, a random character sees the infant's head move slightly, as if to look at them more closely. No one else sees this phenomenon. That same character will see it again if they keep looking.

> As you look at the painting, you see the infant's head move, and its eyes focus on you, specifically.

THE PAINTING OF A MAN ON A HORSE

Ballamen the Rider is another spirit that can come and go from the Darkest House as he wishes, using his painting as a door. Only he can use this painting in this way. Disturbing this painting is likely to draw Ballamen's attention.

Show the players the image of the **Painting of a Man on a Horse**.

To defend his painting, he does not attack, but rather bestows curses. Anyone touching his painting must resist a Rating 6 magical attack. If they fail, they feel a bit of pain in some random portion of their body—not a wound, but just a pang. Things don't get horrible until the character next suffers a wound, which will be in the place Ballamen cursed. Rather than healing normally, the wound festers, and pus-filled tissue begins to slowly grow from the injury. That area of their body swells and turns purple-black, although the expanding tissue is a bloody red, oozing with pale yellow pus. The wound not only won't heal, but its Rating increases by +1 each day that passes. Magical or advanced healing retards the growth, but only magic that removes curses can end the affliction. If such magic is not available, the only thing that can truly help the afflicted character is to search the house to find Ballamen. If they appease him and approach him with respect, he bargains. In exchange for lifting his curse, the characters must—once they leave the house—perform some small task for him in the outside world. Perhaps it is the theft of a minor item, or perhaps it is leaving a message for someone he knew in life. And then they must return to the Darkest House to report the completion of the task. (This of course means the PCs need to find a way to leave the house and then have to return.) At no point will Ballamen reveal that he can leave and return to the house as he wishes.

Ballamen (Rating 4, Boon to all actions while on his steed) and perhaps his steed (Rating 3) might be anywhere in the house—the GM can decide.

THE PAINTING OF THE SMILING MAN

The Smiling Man (who can be encountered in **the Backrooms** [page 118] or **the Storeroom** [page 152]) is portrayed here. This painting is not magical or haunted, and carries no curse. It is merely foreshadowing.

Show the players the image of the **Painting of the Smiling Man**.

THE PAINTING OF A PYRAMID AND A SHRIKE

This is mostly gray tones, with a dark bird of prey swooping down at the viewer. In the background, we can see a pyramid structure of gray stones.

Show the players the image of the **Painting of a Pyramid and a Shrike**.

Even just touching this painting (or interacting with it, such as casting a magic spell upon it) irresistibly draws the character into the image. Those watching see the character disappear and then reappear in the scene in the painting, such that they are about half the size of the bird and painted in the same style and color palette as the rest of the image. From the character's point of view, they suddenly find themselves in a dark gray landscape with a gigantic bird swooping down to attack. The bird has a Rating of 5 and gains a Boon to attack and damage if swooping down from above. More characters can touch the painting and join in the first character's defense if they wish, but then there's the matter of getting out of the painting again.

The key to escaping the painting lies in the pyramid. Once inside the painting, a character can see that there is a door at the base of the structure. If they go to the door—which is a journey that takes them out of sight of anyone watching from outside the painting due to the distance—they find it very heavy to force open (Rating 7). Inside the pyramid are two objects.

One is an unlit candle that is a magical object called The Revelation. If a character lights the candle and meditates for at least 15 minutes upon a question that has a yes or no answer (or something similarly short), the GM provides the answer to the question. However, it should be noted that the answerer of the question is the Darkest House itself, and as such the character gains an immediate Doom.

The other object is a painting of the Gallery. It is fairly crude, but it shows not only the room but any characters that are still in the room. If anyone touches the painting of the Gallery, they appear back in that room.

THE EMPTY FRAME

There's no painting here. However, if someone puts a painting, even one that only roughly fits, into this frame, it resizes to fit perfectly. It must be a painting, not a photo or a drawing. (The paints in **the Studio** [page 180] might help.) There is no other effect unless the subject of the painting is one or more of the characters and the work is of at least Rating 3 quality. If it is, the character(s) can now magically travel to and from the Gallery to leave the Darkest House as they wish. However, there is a catch. Unless the character(s) are spirits, they cannot travel in this way unscathed. Each time they leave the house or return, they automatically suffer a mental wound with a Rating of 5.

TO THE ROOM WITH A HIDDEN ELEVATOR

This very stout door leads to **the Room With a Hidden Elevator** (page 88). The door is locked (Rating 9) and the key is found in **A Storeroom of Sorts** (page 110).

TO THE INTERIOR COURTYARD

This doorway leads up to **the Interior Courtyard** (page 102).

FATHER

If the House Die indicates that Father arrives here, he storms in. He is 9 feet tall, broad-shouldered, and wears simple clothing. His face is dark, and you can only see angry yellow eyes and a broad, roaring mouth. In one hand, he holds a long, black belt.

Show the players the image of Father.

"Don't touch my things! Don't poke your snotty little noses where they do not belong!" he shouts as he attacks with the belt as a weapon. He has a Rating of 6. He cannot be reasoned with, and will chase PCs that flee. He disappears if slain.

A STOREROOM OF SORTS

 grisly room filled with bones and important keys.

Not a significant challenge here, this room is mostly for mood and flavor, although it has a lot of important items in it.

OVERVIEW

This room smells of musty, dusty death and of misery long past. A person-sized brass birdcage hangs from the ceiling about 9 feet above the floor, holding the remains of some poor wretch that died within it. Bookcases and open cabinetry, empty other than for cobwebs, line the walls. Other human remains cover the floor in a carpet of what one can only assume must be murder. The room appears to be a dead end.

HUMAN REMAINS

Searching through the bones reveals two important things. The first is a key carved from a human femur (Rating 4). This key can be inserted into the air anywhere in this room or **the Sewing Room** (page 150) and a keyhole appears to accept it. If turned, every living thing in the room is transported to **the Armory** (page 112).

The second discovery is a page seemingly torn from a book—probably a journal. It is aged and stained, but not well hidden. Even a casual search will reveal it. Show the players **Remnant 2** (page 272).

THE CAGE

The desiccated skeleton in the cage clutches a large golden key in one hand and a silver key in the other. A careful eye can see that from below. What can't be seen from below is that there is also a key in the mouth of the skeleton's skull. The cage is sturdy (Rating 5) but the skeleton is extremely fragile.

+ Gold key: This opens the door to **the Gallery** (page 106).
+ Silver key: This opens the lock in the Doorman's chest. The characters must find him before using the key.
+ Plain nickel-brass key (from the mouth): This opens the lock in the Doorman's head. The characters must find him first.

The floor of the cage, on the inside, bears a scratched message, as if the dead person wrote it. It says, "Don't go to the armory without the eager knife."

The Doorman can be found in **the Cellar** (page 104) or with **the Gatekeeper** (page 224).

Cage

Human Remains

To the Room with a Hidden Elevator

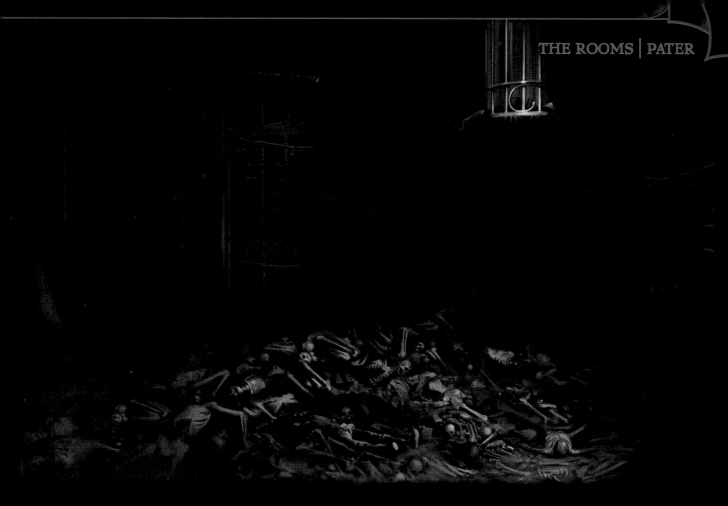

EYES OF THE CHILD

If someone has the Eyes of the Child, they see two ghastly spirits lurking invisibly in the corners of the room. Their naked flesh is pale yellow and their faces are nothing but a swarm of maggots. They cannot interact or be interacted with, even by someone with the Eyes of the Child. They only watch, and occasionally look wistfully at the bones in the room.

TO THE ROOM WITH A HIDDEN ELEVATOR

This innocuous door leads to **the Room With a Hidden Elevator** (page 88). It is unlocked.

FATHER

Nine feet tall, broad-shouldered, and wearing simple clothing, Father storms into this room if the House Die indicates it, shouting "Look what a mess you've made. You're worthless!" His face is dark, and you can only see angry yellow eyes and a broad, roaring mouth. In one hand, he holds a long black belt with which he attacks the PCs physically.

Show the players the image of Father.

He has a Rating of 6. He cannot be reasoned with, and will chase PCs that flee. He disappears if slain.

THE ARMORY

eachable only by magical transport via the bone key found in a Storeroom of Sorts (page 110), this weapon-filled chamber is home to a horrific entity of war and violence.

Play up the ominous mystery of this crouching figure that won't even turn toward the PCs when he speaks. There are clues throughout the house that the Eager Knife should be brought here. It's possible the PCs will get here, take a lot of damage from the spirit, flee, and then return when they understand the clues better.

OVERVIEW

The PCs appear in an oval-shaped room with no exits. It smells of steel and oil and the acrid tang of adrenaline. Empty, smashed weapon racks hang from the walls or lie about the floor. Broken weapons of all kinds—swords, spears, knives, axes, crossbows, pistols, rifles, and more—lay in ruin, strewn about the chamber. A figure clad head to toe in silver and black spiked armor, a cloak of fine chain wrapped around him, crouches on the floor, his back to the characters.

THE SPIRIT OF VIOLENCE

This fully physical entity is the embodiment of violence in its purest form. All it wants to do is inflict damage and pain.

It doesn't move when the PCs arrive, but it is absolutely aware of them.

"Who disturbs me?" Its quiet voice is like metal against metal—like a sword being drawn or a knife being sharpened.

The PCs can say whatever they want, but unless they immediately express that they have the Eager Knife (obtained in the room called **Lying in State** [page 96]), the spirit will stand and turn to face them, quietly saying "I am violence and bloodshed. To visit me is to court death." The being's face is a jagged mass of blades and its gaze is literally knives. Anywhere it looks is suddenly riddled with blades. There is no attack roll, only a damage die with a Rating of 6. It uses no tactics and takes no actions, it just gazes upon all its foes for its turn, disseminating raw violence.

It fights to the "death" because of course it does, but should it be slain it falls into a heap of jagged metal bits. It reforms in a few hours.

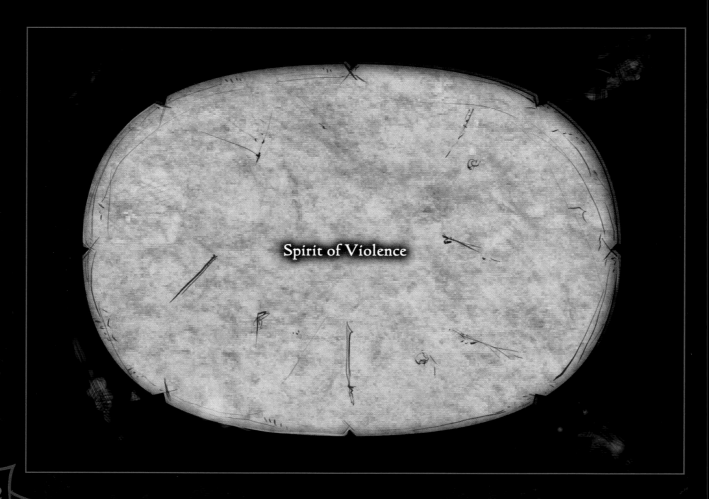

Spirit of Violence

PRESENTING THE SPIRIT WITH THE EAGER KNIFE

f the PCs say that they have the knife when they first rrive, the spirit holds out a mailed hand without urning toward the characters. If given the knife, it ays, "You have my dread blessing." The character who ave it the knife gains a permanent Boon on attack and lamage rolls. Moreover, that character has the ability to ommand Father to leave should they ever encounter him. ather recoils from the command, grits his teeth, and louches off.

EXITING THE ROOM

The same bone key that got them here gets them out. When the bone key is inserted into the air anywhere in this room, a keyhole appears to accept it. If the characters traveled from **A Storeroom of Sorts** (page 110), this action takes them to **the Sewing Room** (page 150). If the characters arrived here from the Sewing Room, the key takes them to A Storeroom of Sorts.

FATHER

Father will not appear in this room.

large open room with multiple levels where one can speak to the Host and maybe learn more about the house.

Play up the party aspect of the room. Being at a party you can't see is disorienting and strange.

OVERVIEW

This room is reached via the elevator or **the Grand Staircase** (page 128). It has three levels, each connected by wooden staircases. Even though the cage elevator passes through all three levels, it only stops at the bottom. This is also where the Grand Staircase begins as it connects to **the Parlor** (page 130). Note, however, that in both this room and the Parlor, the stairs seem to ascend—both rooms appear to be at the bottom of the staircase. The house obeys no rules of reality other than its own.

The bottom level is sparsely furnished with a few old but once-elegant pieces: a long table with a maroon runner, an L-shaped couch of fading gray, and a large, overstuffed chair, as well as some miscellaneous side tables. A massive fireplace burns at one end, and everything about the architecture and furnishings at the other end suggests that there should be a grand entrance, but no such door exists. Instead, the Host stands in front of the blank wall.

The level above the bottom is mostly just a balcony overlooking the lower level. The elevator passes through a brass cage here, but there is no door for it. A maroon carpet covers the wooden floor.

The elevator also passes through the upper level on its way up to **the Music Room** (page 222). This level has four doors, each of which leads to a side room. The maroon carpet is present here as well.

The entire room reeks of grandeur that has long since overstayed its welcome.

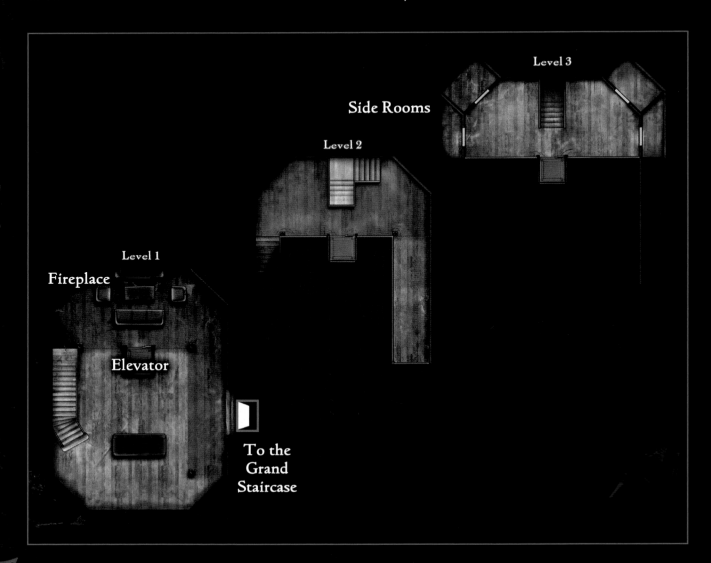

Level 3

Side Rooms

Level 2

Level 1

Fireplace

Elevator

To the
Grand
Staircase

THE HOST

A being of medium height and build, the Host wears a black turtleneck and a black tuxedo jacket over it. On his face, he wears what is presumably a mask of his own face (but who knows, it could be someone else) made of onyx. It covers his whole face and head and his neck as well—almost like a helmet more than a mask. Two other figures crouch behind him wearing animal masks and ragged clothing.

Show the players the image of **the Host**.

"Welcome," the Host says in a deep voice. "So glad you could make it." Please, make yourselves at home. There's all the food and drink you could want." He seems to motion around himself, as if there is a party going on, but there is not. There's no food or drink in sight. "Feel free to mingle. Many interesting folks here tonight."

Should the PCs ignore him, he will eventually just fade away, but not before sights and sounds of a loud, lavish party consume the area around where he stands. However, the Host presents an opportunity to get some questions answered. He is affable, if a little sinister or inappropriate. He talks to the characters as if he knows them and they know him.

+ He will only identify as the Host. He will not claim to own the house if asked. Instead, he'll just say something like, "Sometimes it feels like the house owns me, you know."

+ He says the characters are free to go wherever they wish, but warns them not to go down all the way to the bottom (and he'll motion toward the elevator). He won't elaborate.

+ If asked about other inhabitants of the house, he'll speak only generally, such as "It's a full house tonight." He will say that "the Curator in the Gallery might be interested in an exchange," but to "be careful of the Gatekeeper, for she'll ask a large price for her services and she doesn't bargain." He won't elaborate any further.

+ If asked about the Mystic Tools, the Host looks the characters up and down and says, "Perhaps I misjudged you. You know what you're talking about. Have you looked in the Cellar? The tools there are in a strange order, I think. Or perhaps below the checkerboard?" He won't say any more.

+ If any of the characters are injured, he will say, "You know, I think we have some ointment in the storeroom by the kitchen, uh . . . No. No, on second thought, do not go into the storeroom by the kitchen." He (of course) won't elaborate.

Beyond that, he won't reveal much that is useful.

FIGHTING THE HOST

If the Host is physically or verbally threatened, he commands the other two masked figures to "take care of this little problem." They attack as if animals, suddenly possessing claws and sharp teeth. Each has a Rating of 5. On the Host's turn, he'll direct what seems to be invisible hands to grab and hold one opponent. (The invisible hands are people from the party that it seems only he can see.) These grabbing hands have a Rating of 6, but inflict no damage. The held character can take no actions, however, except to try to break free. In addition, the Host can cause up to four victims of his choosing to suddenly see a room full of people as though there is a lavish party. Essentially, his victims can see the floor, walls, and furnishings, but

they can't see the other PCs (or any changes that the PCs make to the room). Instead, they see a mingling crowd of well-dressed partygoers, some in masks, all eating and drinking and laughing. This happens if they fail to resist this effect (Rating 6), and they remain affected for their next turn, after which point they can use their action each turn to roll to resist the effect again.

The Host has a Rating of 6, but he won't engage in physical combat unless he must.

THE FIREPLACE

The fire burns forever. Beyond that, it is unremarkable.

THE SIDE ROOMS

Each of the so-called side rooms off the top level are small bedrooms, and, like the outer room, appear to have once been elegant, but now the duvet on the bed is faded and tattered, the doilies draped over the dark wood dresser are moth-eaten and stained, and the wardrobes lean a bit to the side. Each of these rooms is relatively uninteresting, except that one has a piece of paper on the bed that appears to be a page torn from a journal. Show the players **Remnant 5** (page 274).

THE ELEVATOR

The elevator is essentially a large brass cage. On the floor is a heavy lever with six positions. It is currently in position 2. The elevator moves very slowly, taking almost a full minute to reach the next level up or down. There is a mechanical sound when it moves, and a clinking of chains. Through the cage, chains and gears can be seen moving. Damaging any of them renders the elevator inoperable for 24 hours before it resets.

+ Position 1: Takes the elevator to **the Music Room** (page 222)
+ Position 2: Where the lever is now (if the elevator goes to another level, 2 returns it to this room)
+ Position 3: Takes the elevator to **the Mannequin Room** (page 154)
+ Position 4: Takes the elevator to **the Room With the Hidden Elevator** (page 88)
+ Position 5: Takes the elevator to **the Backrooms** (page 118)
+ Position 6: Takes the elevator to **the Guardian** (page 122)

TO THE GRAND STAIRCASE

The Grand Staircase (page 128) leads up from here.

FATHER

If the House Die indicates that Father arrives here, he does so and the Host disappears.

Show the players the image of Father.

Father is 9 feet tall, broad-shouldered, and wears a fancy black suit as if he is attending a party, with a long-beaked mask on his face. He holds a glass tumbler filled with whiskey. You can only see angry yellow eyes through his mask. "I'll do today what I should have done years ago," he shouts as he grabs furniture or anything else nearby as weapons and violently attacks. He has a Rating of 6. He cannot be reasoned with, and will chase PCs that flee. He disappears if slain.

THE BACKROOMS (AND BEYOND)

An infinite(?) maze of repetitive rooms, which could hold both treasures and dangers—maybe even a way out—but exploring them might literally drive one insane.

These rooms are an homage to an internet story that's been around for a few years. Search for the Backrooms online and you'll get more ideas and even some images you can use.

OVERVIEW

The elevator brings the PCs to a lifeless room of stained carpet and peeling yellow wallpaper. So begins a sort of fractal structure of spatial expansion on the Darkest House's part. As the house spiraled into madness, it spread like a seeping fluid, or a mass of strangling vines, creating a vast network of rooms. There is no map for the Backrooms (there would be no point) and the GM can narrate time rather than detailing each specific room. In other words, after the first few rooms, you can simply say, "You travel through this seemingly endless progression of rooms for an hour. Do you want to keep going?"

TYPICAL ROOM

The backrooms are carpeted in beige, though the carpet is stained and frayed in places. Wallpaper covers the walls, probably originally yellow, but now more of a light brown in most places. The rooms smell a little damp, and the carpet feels that way as well.

The Backrooms are lit, although it's not clear how. There is a very low-level hum or buzz ever-present in every room. There are no doors. One rectangular room simply leads to another, or sometimes two others. Once in a while, there is a wide hallway or a stairwell (either up or down or both), and while most of these are short, some can get very, very long. Like I-hope-you-brought-provisions long.

Most rooms are about 500 square feet, but occasionally one is slightly less, and even more rarely one is more—a few of them are much more. Ceiling height varies, from quite low to quite high, being high only in the very large rooms (and not always then).

A typical room holds nothing. No furniture, no inhabitants.

DISCOVERIES IN THE BACKROOMS

For the most part, there's nothing in the Backrooms. There are exceptions, however. In the third room the PCs come to, they find a pile of crumpled pieces of paper. Three have multiple completed games of tic-tac-toe and Hangman drawn on them, and one is a handwritten letter or journal. The strange thing is, the handwriting perfectly matches that of one of the PCs. (Choose which of the PCs would be most likely to have written the letter or journal.) Show the players **Remnant 17** (page 281).

As for the rest of the exploration of the Backrooms, if the PCs press onward, you can sparingly populate the occasional room with items from the **rare discoveries list**, and very, very sparingly with items from the **very rare discoveries list**.

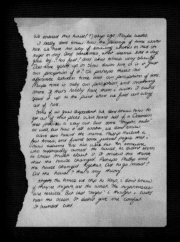

REPETITION AND GETTING LOST

The mind-numbing repetition and almost supernatural distastefulness of the Backrooms can affect one's mind and soul. Every day a character spends exploring the Backrooms, they must resist a Rating 1 attack that inflicts mental damage. Every consecutive day of exploring, the Rating of this attack increases by 1.

Eventually, characters taking no precautions get lost. Even those taking precautions, such as careful mapping, leaving a trail, and so on, might get lost. To avoid this, lost characters with no ability to travel via some kind of supernatural means or divine the right path must just wander. Each day of wandering, characters can attempt a task with a Rating of 9. Success means they get on the right path back out, but getting completely out will take as many days as they have already spent in the Backrooms. Eventually, lost characters will be found by the Smiling Man.

FAMILIAR ROOM

Similar to the rooms found in the main portion of the house (such as **this one** [page 94]), these are rooms stolen from elsewhere and incorporated into the house. The PCs might encounter one or more of these if they spend enough time exploring. Of course, some of these might not be "familiar" to the characters at all, and rather just an out-of-place room devoured by the house at some other time, like a bank manager's office, a gas station restroom, or a classroom.

THE VAST CHAMBER

At some point, dedicated explorers come upon a Backroom of truly epic dimensions. Perhaps a mile long and almost as wide, with a ceiling height that varies—most of it is about 50 feet, but it occasionally and abruptly drops down to 10 feet.

Multiple rooms, hallways, and stairwells branch off from the Vast Chamber, with some of the stairwells found within the room, not by the walls.

RARE DISCOVERIES

✦ Water dripping down the wall, staining the wallpaper. The source of the water can't be determined.
✦ A particularly foul odor, like urine.
✦ A deep, but distant rumbling sound. The source can't be found.
✦ A lone metal chair, lying on its side.
✦ An empty desk, pushed against one wall.
✦ An empty glass bottle.
✦ A Styrofoam coffee cup with a pencil poked into its side.
✦ Faint voices in the distance. The source can never be found.
✦ A scattering of human teeth
✦ A very large bloodstain on the carpet
✦ A pair of bloodstained pliers
✦ A vent blowing very cold air with a slight chemical smell. It's much too small to explore.
✦ Crawling insects. Beetles of some kind, although they seem unfamiliar. Should anyone pull up the carpet in that spot, they'll find a good deal more of the same bugs, and secretions that might be beds of eggs.

VERY RARE DISCOVERIES

+ A four-wheeled metal pushcart, the wheels of which squeak very loudly.
+ A power switch mounted on the wall that seems to control nothing.
+ An accurate map of the surrounding area drawn on the wall in black ink.
+ Three old rubber tires.
+ A human femur bone, well gnawed upon.
+ A crumpled, yellowed newspaper from somewhere no one in the group has ever heard of, relating information that makes little sense. Even the date seems like nonsense. (The 14th of Wyvober, 421 AA.)
+ A stone wishing well in the middle of the room. Fresh water lies at the bottom, and you can get some using the bucket that is there.
+ A working television and VCR with a single tape in the machine: *Poltergeist*.
+ A Familiar Room
+ The Vast Chamber
+ The Smiling Man

THE SMILING MAN

Should the characters wander in the Backrooms for days, they're likely to run afoul of the Smiling Man. They may have already encountered him in **the Storeroom** (page 152) after a fashion, or seen his image elsewhere. In the Backrooms, however, they can encounter him directly.

Show the players the image of **the Smiling Man in the Dark**.

Standing just under 5 feet tall, with an impossible grin and dead, staring eyes, the Smiling Man would unnerve just about anyone.

The Smiling Man loves to spread terror, so he is likely to toy with the characters for a while. He'll let just one of them see him and then run off. Then, hours later, perhaps, he'll do it again. Eventually, at the worst possible time, he'll launch a surprise attack. The teeth of the entity's horrific smile are actually each the head of a gigantic centipede, and at any time, he can send forth several of these (at least one per character) to attack with a large bite. The centipedes have a Rating of 2, but when it comes to inflicting damage, their Rating is 4.

The Smiling Man himself has a Rating of 9. When attacking with surprise, he gains a Boon on the attack. He can bite opponents, or somehow instantly produce cleaver-like weapons to hack and slash. Perhaps worst of all, his touch instills fear right into the most primal part of the brain, causing the victim to utterly freeze and lose their next turn. It might be best for most characters to run if they see him—he's very formidable. He will follow, but eventually the PCs should get away.

THE OCEAN

It would take weeks of exploring—and quite possibly covering *hundreds of miles* of Backrooms—but eventually the rooms begin to seem more and more cavern-like. Eventually, these damp caves lead to the shore of a mysterious, dark ocean. The sky is black and there is no moon, and it's never daytime. Scrawled on a large flat stone is an inscription. Show the players Remnant 12 (page 278).

If the PCs have found any of the journal entries in the house, they'll notice this has the same basic handwriting (it's Phillip Harlock's).

THE ELEVATOR

The elevator is essentially a large brass cage.

Show the players the image of the elevator.

On the floor is a heavy lever with six positions. It is currently in position 5. The elevator moves very slowly, taking almost a full minute to reach the next level up or down. There is a mechanical sound when it moves, and a clinking of chains. Through the cage, chains and gears can be seen moving. Damaging any of them renders the elevator inoperable for 24 hours before it resets.

+ Position 1: Takes the elevator to **the Music Room** (page 222)
+ Position 2: Takes the elevator to **the Great Hall** (page 114)
+ Position 3: Takes the elevator to **the Mannequin Room** (page 154)
+ Position 4: Takes the elevator to **the Room With the Hidden Elevator** (page 88)
+ Position 5: Where the lever is now (if the elevator goes to another level, 5 returns it to this room)
+ Position 6: Takes the elevator to **the Guardian** (page 122)

FATHER

Father will not come into the Backrooms. However, if the House Die indicates that he would, you can take that as an indication that the Smiling Man has taken notice of the explorers.

THE GUARDIAN

living statue guards a captive demigod-level being of darkness.

> *You cannot overstress the immensity of this chamber, and the ominous awe that hangs over it.*

OVERVIEW

The elevator stops at the lowest floor it can reach. Through the cage door, characters can see a chamber far larger than any they have encountered in the house. Reddish light comes from high up on the far wall. Across the vast expanse of the chamber, characters see a 100-foot-tall statue of a kneeling warrior bearing a sword in a vigilant pose. It's so cold here you can see your breath. If you didn't know better, you'd think you gazed into a vault miles below the surface.

THE STATUE

Just walking to the statue will take the PCs a few minutes. It is imposing and incredibly well done, with impressive details. Should any character attempt to make their way toward the stairs or the ledge above, the statue speaks with a booming but low-pitched voice that hurts a little to hear. "I guard here. I give but one warning. Do not ascend."

The statue will not engage in conversation. However, if the characters simply say, "We come here at the direction of Phillip Harlock" or something similar (they have to mention his name), the statue speaks again and says, "You may do as you wish, but the demon must remain imprisoned." She won't interact with them again.

If she is disobeyed and Harlock's name is not dropped, she will again speak, but this time only making a reverberating, low bass sound that rattles everyone and everything in the chamber. This is an attack with a Rating of 8.

If the characters do not back off and make to leave right then, she opens her mouth and spits out gobs of molten stone, once for each character. The stone transforms and hardens into a perfect duplicate of the statue, but human-sized, standing, and fully animate. Each statue has a Rating of 6, and resists damage as Rating 7.

The main statue will spit out more molten gobs to replace destroyed smaller statues, until she has created twice the number of characters. At that time, the statue herself stands (more than 100 feet tall, as she was kneeling originally) and engages foes directly. She has a Rating of 9, and resists damage as Rating 10.

If the guardian statue is destroyed, a low, evil chuckle comes from up the staircase.

GIANT STAIRCASE TO THE CELL

The staircase is smooth, carved stone and each step is 15 feet high. Ascending it by climbing will be like climbing a mountain for human-sized characters—they'll certainly need special gear and probably a fair bit of skill and stamina. This staircase leads to **the Cell** (page 124).

THE ELEVATOR

The elevator is essentially a large brass cage.

Show the players the image of the elevator.

On the floor is a heavy lever with six positions. It is currently in position 6. The elevator moves very slowly, taking almost a full minute to reach the next level up or down. There is a mechanical sound when it moves, and a clinking of chains. Through the cage, chains and gears can be seen moving. Damaging any of them renders the elevator inoperable for 24 hours before it resets.

- ✦ Position 1: Takes the elevator to **the Music Room** (page 222)
- ✦ Position 2: Takes the elevator to **the Great Hall** (page 114)
- ✦ Position 3: Takes the elevator to **the Mannequin Room** (page 154)
- ✦ Position 4: Takes the elevator to **the Room With the Hidden Elevator** (page 88)
- ✦ Position 5: Takes the elevator to **the Backrooms** (page 118)
- ✦ Position 6: Where the lever is now (if the elevator goes to another level, 6 returns it to this room)

FATHER

Father will not come to this room.

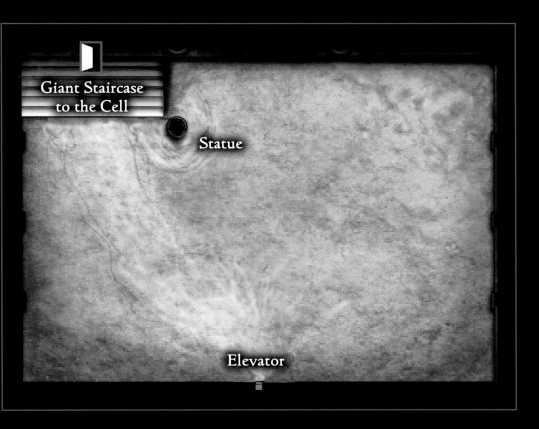

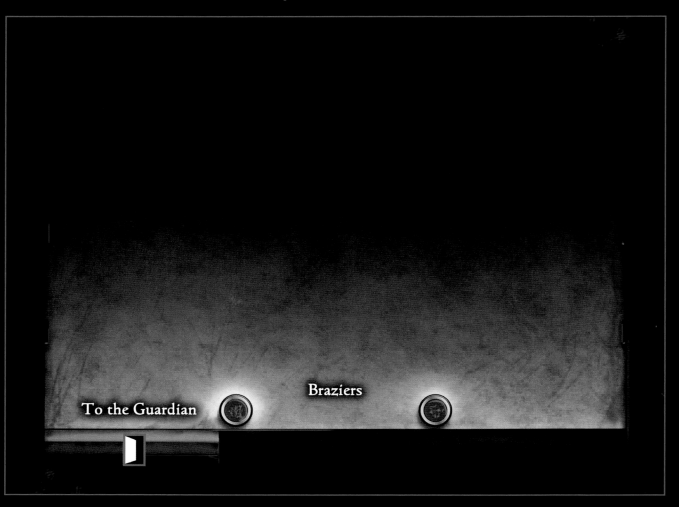

To the Guardian

Braziers

Master of the Darkest House? Prisoner? Both?

Want a little nihilism with your horror? How about talking to an evil, godlike being and having him describe how futile your existence is?

OVERVIEW

Two large, flickering braziers of brass, each 15 feet high, burn with a hellish light. Beyond them, an empty expanse of darkness no light will ever illuminate. The stench of hatred and the sensation of barely contained ferocity are palpable.

BRAZIERS

The braziers are extraordinarily powerful wards, effectively serving as shackles for an imprisoned being here known as **the Enemy of Light**. Only the most powerful effect that a mortal could obtain—whether spell, technology, etc.—could possibly affect the braziers or their flames in any way. It is relevant that even though they imprison a demon, the braziers are things of darkness and Hell themselves.

THE ENEMY OF LIGHT

This being is beyond the Rating system. It is as powerful as some kind of god in most game systems. It's not something you fight. Demon, god, something else? The truth is likely beyond mortal understanding.

If the PCs somehow got this far, they can speak to it. They won't see it, for it is only darkness within darkness. It has the deep voice of something almost incomprehensibly large. But its words are welcoming and kind.

REGARDING THE HOUSE

✦ It says that it knows nothing of the house. "I am older than this house. The house came to me, not the other way around."

REGARDING ITS SITUATION

✦ It says it does not leave this place, but that it is not a captive. It claims that freedom is of no value to it. "Liberty and independence only have importance in the light. They are fleeting. I am not." Similarly, it has no interest in speaking about the guardian, the braziers, or anything else. It won't speak of who placed them here, but the implication is certainly that it didn't do so itself.

REGARDING PHILLIP HARLOCK

✦ It says, "The little conjurer is gone now. He never really understood who he was or what he had done."

REGARDING ITS IDENTITY AND NATURE

✦ It says, "I am the Enemy of Light. I fight a war that is predestined. I will win, for light, like life, is finite. Darkness was, darkness is, and darkness will be. It is inevitable."

REGARDING ITS DESIRES OR NEEDS

✦ It says, "I wish for you to despair. Your existence is fleeting, and that is supremely unfair. I wish for you to hate. The world has no respect for you, and no place for you, so you should simply turn your resentment outward. Destroy. Extinguish the light. It is the only action with truly eternal consequences that you can even attempt."

THE STAIRCASE

This staircase leads to **the Guardian** (page 122).

FATHER

Father will not come to this room.

MATER

THE TREE
170

THE SPIRIT OF
DESTRUCTION
172

FOYER
162

RONING
HALL

THE
ENDREAM
174

CHILD'S
HALLWAY
178

THE WALLED
GARDEN
194

THE DOLL
ROOM
196

DOG

THE STUDIO
180

THE CAT
MENAGERIE

THE NURSERY
188

THE TEA
ROOM
202

THE LEERING
ONES
200

THE BACKROOMS
(AND BEYOND)
118

THE ARCHWAY
204

THE SHOIN
208

BEDR   WITH A
SECR   SAGE

THE GUARDIAN
122

MPTY
BEDROOM

THE MUSIC
ROOM
222

THE S
CHAPEL
218

THE CELL
124

MASTER
BEDROOM
238

TIME LOOP
248

THE GATEKEEPER
224

PRISONER
250

THE VESTIBULE
244

THE ORIGINAL
HOUSE
268

MILIAR
OOM

SUMMONING
CHAMBER

THE FOUNTAIN
OF PAIN

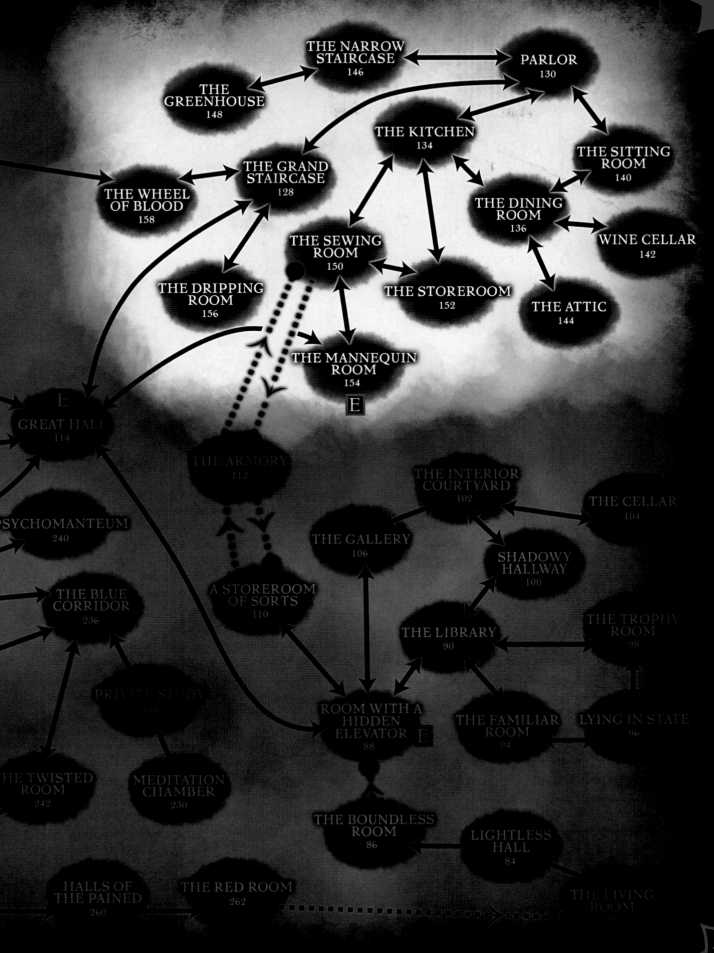

THE NARROW
STAIRCASE
146

PARLOR
130

THE
GREENHOUSE
148

THE KITCHEN
134

THE SITTING
ROOM
140

THE GRAND
STAIRCASE
128

THE WHEEL
OF BLOOD
158

THE DINING
ROOM
136

WINE CELLAR
142

THE SEWING
ROOM
150

THE DRIPPING
ROOM
156

THE STOREROOM
152

THE ATTIC
144

E

GREAT HALL
114

THE MANNEQUIN
ROOM
154

E

THE ARMORY
112

THE INTERIOR
COURTYARD
102

THE CELLAR
104

PSYCHOMANTEUM
240

THE GALLERY
106

SHADOWY
HALLWAY
100

THE BLUE
CORRIDOR
236

A STOREROOM
OF SORTS
110

THE LIBRARY
90

THE TROPHY
ROOM
98

PRIVATE STUDY
234

ROOM WITH A
HIDDEN
ELEVATOR
88

E

THE FAMILIAR
ROOM
94

LYING IN STATE
96

THE TWISTED
ROOM
242

MEDITATION
CHAMBER
230

THE BOUNDLESS
ROOM
86

LIGHTLESS
HALL
84

HALLS OF
THE PAINED
260

THE RED ROOM
262

THE LIVING
ROOM

THE GRAND STAIRCASE

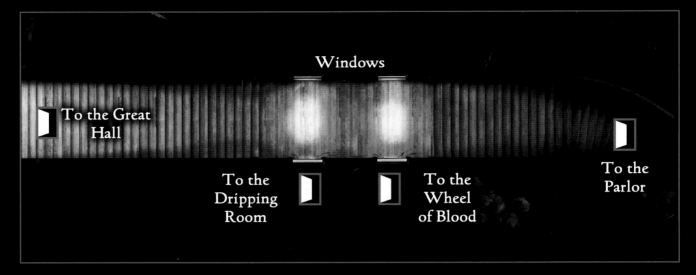

Windows

To the Great Hall

To the Dripping Room

To the Wheel of Blood

To the Parlor

---

he staircase is relatively safe, but the windows overlook a disturbing place.

This is one of the rooms described in Secrets of the House as a "building dread" room.

OVERVIEW

Sweeping up from **the Parlor** (page 130), this wide, polished wooden staircase is beautiful and impossibly large. It would appear to ascend hundreds of feet, as though the structure it was within were dozens of stories high. The landing at the center point is 30 feet wide with a pair of elegant wooden doors. The landing also has windows in the right-hand wall. The walls in the stairway have brown and white velvet wallpaper (same as the Parlor, but everything seems in much better shape here).

The top of the stairs is **the Great Hall** (page 114), but if one leaves from the Great Hall, the staircase also seems to ascend from there. Basically, the staircase seems to go up no matter which way you approach it.

THE RINGING

The ringing of the telephone from the nearby **Sitting Room** (page 140) can be heard here.

Play this audio clip for the players:

mymcg.info/tdh-mater-sound-ringingfromadistance

THE WINDOWS

The windows on the landing look out over a fantastically huge, well-manicured lawn at night, as if from a very high vantage. There are fountains, marble statues, and topiary. Only if one looks very carefully from the windows can it be seen that the statues and topiary bear hideous, monstrous countenances, and the water in the fountains is a deep red—perhaps it is blood. Dark, winged things flit almost unseen in the starless sky. Those seeing this hear a faint voice saying, "Here is night, brothers. Here the birds burn." Any characters who witness the whole scene with the winged things, fountains deep red, etc., are subject to a Rating 2 mental attack from the horror.

The windows are impermeable, but maybe that's actually for the best.

TO THE PARLOR

At the bottom of the stairs sits **the Parlor** (page 130).

TO THE GREAT HALL

The end of the stairs opens into **the Great Hall** (page 114).

TO THE DRIPPING ROOM

This innocuous door leads to **the Dripping Room** (page 156). It is locked (Rating 5). The key is in **the Greenhouse** (page 148).

TO THE WHEEL OF BLOOD

This innocuous door leads to **the Wheel of Blood** (page 158). It is unlocked.

MOTHER

If the House Die indicates that Mother arrives, a full-bodied woman in a thick dress climbs the stairs.

Show the players the image of Mother.

Over her dress, she wears a fancy (but slightly ragged) coat with large buttons. She has only a skull for a head, and the upper torso skeletons of children (just a skull, arms, a few ribs, and a spine) clinging to the coat and dress desperately. "Come to Mother, my lovelies," she shouts. Mother has a Rating of 7.

If the characters flee and reach **the Great Hall** (page 114) before she can catch them, Mother fades away into mist and shadow. If they flee to **the Wheel of Blood** (page 158) or **the Dripping Room** (page 156), Mother will follow them. The doors into those rooms will not open with Mother present, trapping the characters. If Mother catches up to them, she makes a physical attack against one of them that inflicts no damage but ensures that she has them in a firm grip. She then drags them down the stairs into **the Parlor** (page 130). The dragging is a Rating 4 physical attack. Once in the Parlor, she will squeeze her victim, inflicting a Rating 7 attack on them until they escape or are dead.

PARLOR

Though the Parlor looks innocuous, the entity here—the Arbiter—preys upon memories and fears.

Yes, there is a sitting room, a parlor, a living room, a shoin, a tea room (and don't forget the Great Hall and the lounge-type room where the Ravendream dwells) all in the same house. But the house devours the rooms of other buildings, remember? None of these rooms were ever originally part of the same house.

OVERVIEW

This room, with brown and white velvet wallpaper, a matching but slightly darker Victorian-style sofa, and an upholstered French chair, might very well be the point where the festering wound of the Darkest House first consumed the original house that it once was. Perhaps this is where the first house began missing the family it loved. Everything is old and tattered, even the wallpaper.

There's a large hole in the wall behind the sofa about the size of someone's head, and there's something dark and ominous about it.

A **broad staircase** (page 128) ascends out of this room, with smooth wooden steps and the same brown and white wallpaper.

THE RINGING

The ringing of the telephone from the nearby **Sitting Room** (page 140) can be heard here.

Play this audio clip for the players:

mymcg.info/tdh-mater-sound-ringingfromadistance

Door to the Sitting Room

Narrow Staircase to the Greenhouse

Grand Staircase

Sofa

Hole

Door to the Kitchen

THE HOLE

The hole is strangely deep. A character's arm will go in, but can't reach the other side. One might begin to suspect that there's a room behind the wall. While examining it, despite the ringing of the telephone, a searcher might hear a noise. Something that sounds like the grinding of teeth.

No light shines into the hole, no magic vision pierces the darkness.

Characters might try to widen the hole, or hack their own hole elsewhere in the wall, but doing so only reveals what one might expect—the interior of the wall.

Whether they examine the hole or not, one of the PCs will catch sight of a face in the shadows of the hole, barely visible, staring at them. It disappears if spotted, but returns soon enough. If addressed in any fashion, the face in the hole asks in a whispered voice, "What do you fear the most?"

The characters have three options.

1. They could say nothing. They could be ever so quiet and still for quite a while, perhaps even silently leaving the room. This is the wisest course of action. However, should they remain in the room or ever return to the room, the voice will ask the question again.
2. They could lie, or reply with something else (a question of their own, a clarification, and so on). This is the worst course of action. The voice asks them again, but this time it's not coming from the hole—it's coming from behind them. The Arbiter steps out of the shadows in the corner of the room.
3. They could answer and tell the truth. The voice whispers, "Describe it. Spare no detail." It seeks as much elaboration on the fear as the character can give. If they comply, when they're done, the voice whispers, "Delicious." The Arbiter steps out of the shadows in the corner of the room.

THE ARBITER

In his stately garb, the Arbiter appears formal, and yet the blood seeping from the bottom of his metallic mask twists his appearance in a macabre direction. He clutches a rolled piece of paper and wears a prominent, ornate ring.

Show the players **The Arbiter.**

His sudden appearance is a Rating 1 mental attack from the shock. The Arbiter only appears in reaction to someone's response to the whisper from the hole in the wall.

If the PCs didn't already tell the voice their greatest fear, the Arbiter is stern when he shows up. If the PCs continue to not give a proper, honest answer, he makes a fist with the hand wearing the ring. When he does, the speaking PC is subject to a Rating 6 attack as razors, hooks, and bladed chains appear from nowhere and slash their flesh. Then the Arbiter speaks aloud with a deep, resonating voice filled with absolute confidence. "Tell me your greatest fear." Sometimes, when he speaks, the metal plates of his mask shift of their own accord, and he bleeds more.

He keeps demanding that a PC tell him their fear, and attacking them if he doesn't get what he asks for. If a character finally relents, he says, "Describe it. Spare no detail." He seeks as much elaboration on the fear as the character can give. If the character does this, when they're done, he whispers, "Delicious."

Once a character has stated their fear, the Arbiter says, "Now, I can take that fear from you. I suspect you'd like to be free of it. Or, if you'd rather, I can take away any memory that you no longer want. Would you like that?"

Perhaps surprisingly, this is an honest question and an honest offer. If asked, he will say that there is a price to pay.

The price is negotiable, however. These are the things he greatly values:

+ Very powerful magic items (it has to really mean something to the character giving it, and it has to be the best item that the PCs possess)
+ *All* of a character's memories
+ The life of one character (taken in a slow, bloody sacrificial ceremony)

These are the things he values somewhat:

+ Powerful magic items (it has to be meaningful to the character giving it)
+ A significant pleasant childhood memory (your mother's face, your beloved family pet, etc.)
+ Blood. Every character willingly accepts a Rating 5 wound.
+ Trauma. Every character willingly accepts a Rating 5 mental wound.

These are the things he can provide that he greatly values:

+ Completely remove the character's deepest fear.
+ Remove an unwanted memory a character has, no matter how pervasive or vital.
+ Return a dead character back to life.
+ Instructions on how to leave the Darkest House (directions to the closest location of the Doorman and the closest location of the key that opens the door out)

These are the things he can provide that he values somewhat:

+ Remove any or all wounds he has inflicted.
+ Heal one wound (physical or mental).
+ One bit of knowledge in a specific skill or action (effectively giving a character a Boon on such actions while in the Darkest House).

If the PCs can't negotiate a deal that both they and the Arbiter are happy with, he disappears into the shadows, obviously perturbed. Should the PCs return to this room again, he will *demand* they make a deal with him, or he will just take what he wants.

FIGHTING THE ARBITER

The Arbiter has a Rating of 6, but physical attacks only seem to give him pleasure, not pain (or damage). So magical or mental attacks are the only way to inflict damage upon him. Meanwhile, his means of attack is to conjure razors, hooks, and bladed chains that appear and slash a victim. He can make this attack on up to three different targets on a single turn. He also has the ability to remove any wound he inflicts, and will offer to do so if his foes will surrender to him and give him what he wants, as detailed under the heading The Arbiter.

THE ARBITER'S CONTRACT

The rolled-up paper the Arbiter holds has a potent magical ability within it. The holder can determine if a statement said in their presence, or written where they can see it, is true or false. In the hands of a mortal (as opposed to some immortal, spiritual entity like the Arbiter), it can be used only one time, with one statement. Still, even used by a mortal, the magic has no limit. Even if the god of lies himself told a lie, the holder could determine it to be a falsehood.

THE ARBITER'S RING

This large ring is a powerful magical object. It allows the wearer to instantly undo any damage they inflict, whether physical, mental, magical, structural, and so on.

BENEATH THE SOFA

Should anyone look under the sofa, they will find a crumpled piece of paper amid some accumulation of dust and dirt. Show the players **Remnant 13** (page 279).

Even further beneath the sofa is a book, strangely translucent. If it weren't for the dust, it might not be visible at all. The book is difficult to grasp and hold, as if its tangibility fades in and out. The words on each page swim before the reader's eyes, impossible to make out. This is referred to henceforth as the Ghost Book. It can only be read in **the Private Study** (page 230).

GRAND STAIRCASE

This is **the Grand Staircase** (page 128).

NARROW STAIRCASE TO THE GREENHOUSE

A **Narrow Staircase** (page 146) leads down.

DOOR TO THE SITTING ROOM

This innocuous door leads to **the Sitting Room** (page 140). It is unlocked.

DOOR TO THE KITCHEN

This innocuous door leads to **the Kitchen** (page 134). It is unlocked.

MOTHER

If the House Die indicates that Mother arrives, a full-bodied woman in a thick dress storms into the room.

Show the players the image of **Mother**.

Over her dress, she wears a fancy (but slightly ragged) coat with large buttons. She has only a skull for a head, and the upper torso skeletons of children (just a skull, arms, a few ribs, and a spine) clinging to the coat and dress desperately. If any of the PCs has a wound, she rushes to them (or to the most wounded character, if more than one), whispering, "Oh, my poor, sweet baby. You're hurt! Oh, sweet child, let Mother take care of you." She then grabs them with great strength. This is an attack that inflicts physical damage, plus, a character struck is now a character stuck—she pulls them to her and holds them fast. The only action they can attempt is to try to break free. Meanwhile, on her subsequent turns, she attacks anyone nearby, saying, "Go away! Go away! Let them rest. There's no better balm than a mother's love." Mother has a Rating of 7. She won't follow characters that flee.

THE KITCHEN

here's some weird stuff here, but it's really mostly just a kitchen.

It almost feels like such a cliché that you might want to avoid having an encounter with Mother in the kitchen if you can help it.

OVERVIEW

It's strange to enter a room that was clearly once important and well-used and now stands empty. How long has it been empty? What happens to a beloved room when there's no life in it for a long, long time?

A tile countertop runs around much of the kitchen, with built-in cabinetry above. The room contains an icebox, a hooded gas stove, a large wall-mounted sink. A table with some drawers stands in the middle of the kitchen with a large wooden cutting board atop it. (The kitchen looks like something appropriate to a 1920's American kitchen.) There is a large window to the side of the sink, but characters can't see out of it until they get close.

THE RINGING

The ringing of the telephone from the nearby **Sitting Room** (page 140) can be heard here.

Play this audio clip for the players:

CABINETS

While most of the cabinets are empty, one contains a tin canister with a screw-on lid. It's filled with six paper packets that might be mistaken for tea, but each actually holds a powdered form of something akin to mold spores (Rating of 3). If sprinkled atop a living thing (plant or animal), the living thing is transformed, both physically and temperamentally, over the course of about thirty seconds into a hideous, vicious monster. The monster has the same Rating as the original creature, or a Rating of 4, whichever is higher. Flesh turns a mottled green and gray, eyes grow bulbous, hair sprouts in odd clumps, hands become claws, and so on. Every transformation is unique. The transformation wears off, but it takes a few hours.

DRAWERS

There is one drawer filled with knives, and one with a key (it opens the hatch in **the Dining Room** [page 136] that goes down to **the Wine Cellar** [page 142]), but the rest are empty.

mymcg.info/tdh-mater-sound-ringingfromadistance

The Window

Cabinets

Drawers

To the
Dining Room

To the
Sewing Room

To the
Storeroom

To the
Parlor

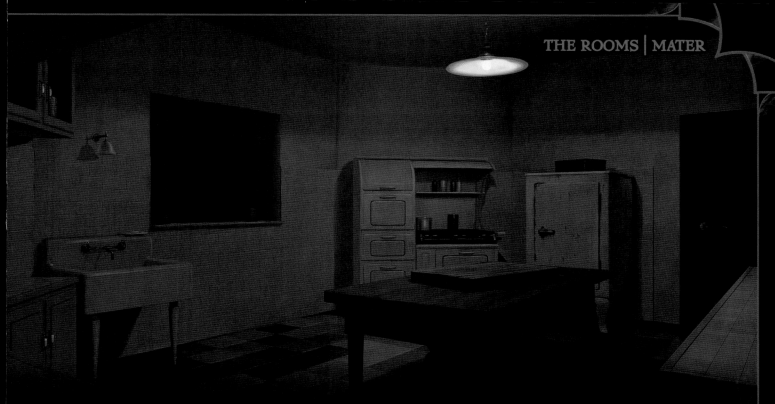

THE WINDOW

Unlike many of the windows in the house, this one does not look out into blackness. Instead, it looks out upon an overcast sky (a storm threatens) above a flat, dry landscape planted with some kind of grain. The window is utterly impermeable and offers no escape. If someone watches out it for a while, they'll see a few cows slowly enter the field of vision from the left, eating grass. A bit later, a man in what looks like farm clothes enters from the right, carrying an axe. At his feet is a dog. The man approaches the cattle very casually, and then, without warning, both man and dog begin brutally attacking the cattle. They kill two cows and hurt another before the rest manage to run away. The man does not give chase, but rather paints his flesh with the blood, using his hands. The dog begins to eat one of the cows. When the man is completely covered in blood, he sits on the ground, next to the feasting dog, and faces the window, staring blankly. Any characters watching this are subject to a Rating 2 mental attack from the shock and gore. If the characters leave the kitchen and return, the scene changes back to what it looked like when they first saw it.

TO THE DINING ROOM

This doorway leads to **the Dining Room** (page 136).

TO THE PARLOR

This doorway leads to **the Parlor** (page 130).

TO THE SEWING ROOM

This innocuous door leads to **the Sewing Room** (page 150). It is unlocked.

TO THE STOREROOM

This innocuous door leads to **the Storeroom** (page 152). It is unlocked.

MOTHER

If the House Die indicates that Mother arrives, a full-bodied woman in a thick dress climbs the stairs.

Show the players the image of **Mother.**

Over her dress, she wears a fancy (but slightly ragged) coat with large buttons. She has only a skull for a head, and the upper torso skeletons of children (just a skull, arms, a few ribs, and a spine) clinging to the coat and dress desperately. She says (to no one in particular), "Now, now, let me fix you something to eat." She moves over to the knife drawer, pulls out the biggest knife, and says to one PC, "You'll do nicely. The others will enjoy you." Then she attacks the character with the knife. If Mother is attacked, she howls and whines and says, "You never loved me!" and "You'll miss me when I'm gone!" Mother has a Rating of 7, but she won't chase opponents that run, instead just calling after them with words meant to instill guilt and despair.

THE DINING ROOM

A dangerous ghost haunts this room. But not the one you can see (or at least not that you can see easily).

Be generous if a character searches the wood storage area. Don't require a roll to find the secret door if someone actually goes in and looks around. Instead, talk about all the spiders and millipedes that swarm out of the old wood, some of them crawling over the character's skin.

OVERVIEW

You know that feeling of almost recognizing something or someone as the knowledge sits on the very tip of your mind? Everything in this room emotes that feeling. This is a large dining room, with dark green wallpaper and a long dining table of dark wood, with matching chairs. An unlit chandelier hangs above the table, and there is a bowl of fruit on the table beneath it. One wall bears a decorative mirror with a golden frame, and a prominent fireplace dominates the opposite wall, with a small wooden door next to it. A visible trapdoor in the wooden floor is near the mirror. It has an iron pull ring.

A feminine figure of chalk-white skin floats as if she is underwater, her lithe feet never touching the floor. No matter how hard you try, you cannot see her face-on. Her head is always turned away. And yet, she seems familiar somehow.

THE RINGING

The ringing of the telephone from the nearby **Sitting Room** (page 140) can be heard here.

Play this audio clip for the players:

mymcg.info/tdh-mater-sound-ringingfromadistance

THE FRUIT

The fruit is fresh, ripe, and delicious. If eaten in this room, it is fine. If taken out of this room, it quickly rots and is filled with worms and pupae. Beneath the fruit in the bowl are more torn pages from a journal. Show the players **Remnant 19** (page 282).

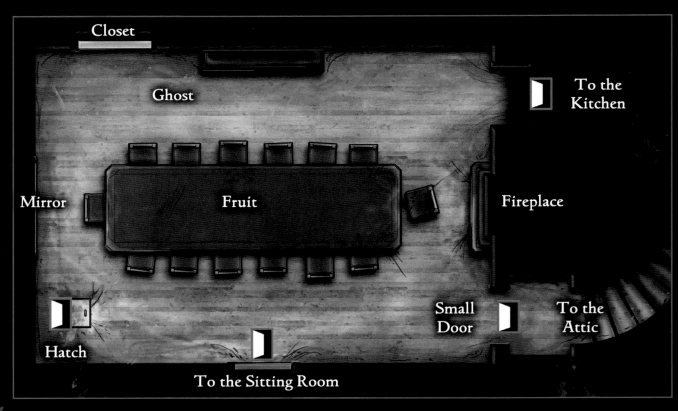

THE GHOST

The ghost has a Rating of 3 (Rating 5 for defense) and is not aggressive. She's not interested in the characters and wishes only to be left alone.

THE MIRROR

Characters will probably try to see the ghostly woman's face in the mirror. It won't work—the fact that she is always turned away is an inherent part of her essence. She doesn't want to interact with or even acknowledge intruders.

However, within the mirror, there is a second figure that does not physically appear in the room. It exists only in the reflection. At first, it hides well, but as the PCs move about, one of them may catch sight of a shadowy figure skulking in the background, in the mirror. It takes a while of careful study of the mirror to find it, but once someone really tries, they will see it—a skeletal apparition with a sheer shroud covering its head. This reflection spirit is Rating 5.

Show the players the image of the reflection spirit.

Eventually, as they stare and search for the figure, the PCs' reflections begin to change. Their faces grow more skeletal. The bones in their hands are visible. It is as though they quickly become dead—or rather undead. This only happens in the reflection, and it is the power of the apparition. However, the sight of it is shocking and horrific. This is a Rating 5 attack that inflicts mental damage. Should even just one character suffer this damage, that character can take no action and the apparition disappears from the mirror and reappears in the physical room. This switch only lasts long enough for the apparition (and everyone else) to take one action. It uses its skeletal hands to inflict physical damage. The character(s) who suffered the mental damage are subject to the same attack again. If they once again suffer it, they remain unable to act, and the apparition once again transfers to the physical world to attack.

The goal of the apparition is to kill one character. If this happens, the apparition fades away forever and the slain character is now a ghost trapped in the mirror. This means that the apparition, if it has multiple turns in which to act in the physical world, will probably attack the weakest character over and over again. (The weakest character might very well be the one who lost their action to the mirror because they can't defend or strike back.)

THE FIREPLACE

The fireplace has no wood.

THE SMALL DOOR

Behind the small door lies a closet-sized space for wood
storage. It's filled with a dozen or so logs. However,
if a character searches the back of this tiny area (this
would probably require entering the space), a hidden
door is revealed. Behind this second door is a very small
curving staircase that winds halfway around the fireplace
and chimney. The stairs lead to **the Attic** (page 144).
On the steps is a small book titled Donning Spiritual
Armor. It may sound like a religious text, but it is
actually a short treatise on fighting—and specifically on
defending against—ghosts, spirits, and similar beings.
If someone takes an hour to read it, they gain a Boon
on defending against attacks (mental and physical)
from spiritual entities of any kind. Once read, the book
mysteriously vanishes.

HATCH

The hatch is locked (Rating 4, the key can be found in
the Kitchen [page 134]). Once unlocked, it is difficult
and slow to pull the hatch up to reveal a very steep, very
narrow staircase—really almost a ladder—down to **the
Wine Cellar** (page 142).

CLOSET

This small closet holds an extra chair matching those
around the table and a small chest on a shelf containing
silverware. The silverware set is heavy, but worth $200.

TO THE KITCHEN

This innocuous door leads to **the Kitchen** (page 134).It
is unlocked.

TO THE SITTING ROOM

This innocuous door leads to **the Sitting Room**
(page 140). It is unlocked.

MOTHER

If the House Die indicates that Mother arrives, a full-bodied woman in a thick dress climbs the stairs.

Show the players the image of **Mother.**

Over her dress, she wears a fancy (but slightly ragged) coat with large buttons. She has only a skull for a head, and the upper torso skeletons of children (just a skull, arms, a few ribs, and a spine) clinging to the coat and dress desperately. She attempts to force characters to sit at the table with a physical attack that inflicts no damage. "Sit," she says. "Eat. Eat for your mother. I have slaved for so long to make you this meal." If she's successful, the affected character in the chair is immediately subject to a mental attack that does inflict mental damage and forces the character to remain in the chair, compelling them to see a meal she has laid out on the table. The character trapped in the chair cannot leave the table while Mother is in the room. She remains until everyone is seated or has fled the room, at which time she says, "I made your favorite dessert," and moves into **the Kitchen** (page 134), where she disappears.

If Mother is attacked, she howls and whines and says, "You never loved me!" and "You'll miss me when I'm gone!" Mother has a Rating of 7, but she won't chase opponents that run, instead just calling after them with words meant to instill guilt and despair.

THE SITTING ROOM

The Telephone and the Portrait.

> *There's an opportunity for some really deep roleplaying in this room if you have a group that finds that rewarding.*

OVERVIEW

A family gathering place without a family, this room has retreated into a realm of pure loneliness. There is a couch along one wall, and a small decorative table against another. A large, rather old-fashioned telephone rings. It is heavy and black, with a steel rotary dial rather than buttons. A small notebook sits on the table next to it. A framed family portrait hangs on the wall.

THE TABLE

In the single drawer of the table is a small address book. It contains about a dozen names, appropriate to the setting the PCs come from, with addresses and (if appropriate to the home setting) phone numbers. They're real but hold no actual significance. In addition, the book has all the PCs' names and addresses (and phone numbers if appropriate). If a PC has no permanent residence, the address just says "????"

THE RINGING TELEPHONE

If the PCs come from a setting where phones aren't common, you'll need to describe the device very differently. "A strange sculpture made of an unknown but heavy material, with a wheel on the front. Part of the device, shaped a little like an arm, can be removed from the sculpture, but it remains connected by some kind of cord. The device trills like a shrill bell rung over and over, and then there's a pause, and then the bell rings again just like before."

Play this audio clip for the players:

mymcg.info/tdh-sittingroom-sound-ringing

If a character picks up the receiver of the ringing phone, they hear a familiar voice say hello. The voice is that of someone from the character's past—someone who is no longer alive. Their voice seems very faint and far away, accompanied by an occasional crackling static sound. They tell the character who they are, and if need be, to prove their identity, say things that only they would know. A character listening to this is subject to a Rating 2

mental attack from the shock. Once this has been established, the voice begins speaking with the character, discussing topics that are important to them: life advice, family secrets, and so on. This is either an actual communication with the dead or a very clever deception. The PC might have questions:

> PC: What's it like in the afterlife?
> Dead voice: I don't want to talk about that.
> PC: How can you be talking to me?
> Dead voice: You are somewhere I can reach right now.
> PC: How did you know I was here?
> Dead voice: I can see you sometimes.

Eventually, the PC either hangs up or the line goes dead. Once the character puts the receiver down, however, a minute or two later, the phone begins to ring. If the same character picks it up, there is only a buzzing and clicking noise on the other end. If a different character answers the phone, they too get a chance to speak with a loved one that has passed.

That conversation too, eventually, comes to an end. And a few minutes later, the phone rings again. This time, regardless of who answers, a child's voice on the other end says, "Mother is very cross. You should probably hide." Then the line goes dead. At this point, the progression of the house's actions immediately moves to step 1, 5, or 9, whichever is the closest subsequent step. This means that Mother might very well arrive. If this happens, the characters hear her coming, but you'll want to give them at least a turn to act before she arrives—the phone call is a legitimate warning.

Play this audio clip for the players:

mymcg.info/tdh-sittingroom-sound-motherisverycross

The phone is going to keep ringing regardless of what the PCs do (short of destroying it, in which case it starts ringing again when the room resets). Subsequent voices just say cryptic things and then go silent. Examples include:

- ✦ "When you get where you're going, I'll already be there."
- ✦ "I know your name."
- ✦ "I see you."
- ✦ "Sic transit gloria mundi."
- ✦ "Mono no aware."

THE FAMILY PORTRAIT

A family sits together, wearing nice clothing.

Show the players the **Family Portrait**.

The portrait is contained by a pleasant wooden frame. Someone has scratched big Xs over the eyes of the man, the woman, and the girl in the image. Only the boy remains unscathed. The word "LOST" is scratched into the frame.

If someone looks closely, there's a very faint, shadowy figure in the image just over the boy's shoulder—maybe another boy his same age? Or just a shadow? (This presages the significance of Brother's shadow.)

TO THE DINING ROOM

This innocuous door leads to **the Dining Room** (page 136). It is unlocked.

TO THE PARLOR

This innocuous door leads to **the Parlor** (page 130). It is unlocked.

Family Portrait

Telephone

Table

To the Dining Room

To the Parlor

MOTHER

If the House Die indicates that Mother arrives, a full-bodied woman in a thick dress storms into the room.

Show the players the image of **Mother**.

Over her dress, she wears a fancy (but slightly ragged) coat with large buttons. She has only a skull for a head, and the upper torso skeletons of children (just a skull, arms, a few ribs, and a spine) clinging to the coat and dress desperately. She moans, "You're leaving me, aren't you? Leaving your mother and never looking back." She attempts to grab one or more of the PCs. This is a physical attack, but she inflicts no damage. Instead, a grabbed victim is held tight. Mother can hold two PCs at once. Once one or more held, she crushes the PCs to her, inflicting physical damage until they escape.

If attacked, Mother howls and whines and says, "You never loved me!" and "You'll miss me when I'm gone!" Mother has a Rating of 7, but she won't chase opponents that run, instead just calling after them with words meant to instill guilt and despair.

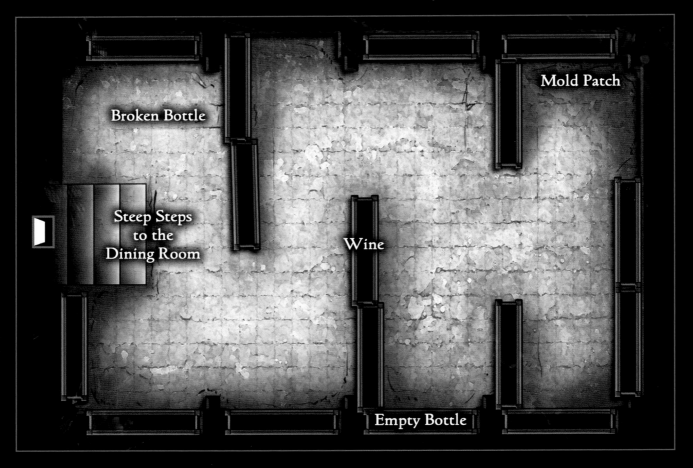

Broken Bottle

Mold Patch

Steep Steps
to the
Dining Room

Wine

Empty Bottle

Cellars and basements are filled with mold. Everyone knows that, right?

Despite the names, there is no connection between the Wine Cellar and the Cellar.

OVERVIEW

*The hatch in **Dining Room** (page 136) leading down to this cellar is locked (Rating 4, the key can be found in **Kitchen** [page 134]).*

Dark and dank, the wine cellar has an arched ceiling and is filled with many wine racks, both along the wall and free-standing. There are plenty of wine bottles in here, but one has shattered on the stone floor in the middle of the room, spreading glass and wine everywhere. The space is a bit dusty, and smells of mold.

THE BROKEN BOTTLE

The only remarkable thing about the shattered bottle is that the wine has not dried.

THE WINE

There are 158 wine bottles in the cellar, and while most are worth about $50, ten of them are worth $100, four of them are worth $200, two are worth $500, and one is worth $1,000. You'd have to know a fair bit about wine and look at every bottle to determine that.

THE EMPTY BOTTLE

A thorough search of the room will reveal that there is a single empty bottle stored with the rest of the wine bottles. Stranger still, the empty bottle is corked. This bottle is magical, and should it be uncorked, it will fill with whatever relatively common liquid the opener is thinking of. Thus, it can produce wine, but also clean water, fruit juice, coffee, syrup, weak acid, lamp oil, or even—depending on the context the character is from—gasoline. It can be corked and uncorked twenty times before it shatters.

THE MOLD PATCH

That same thorough search of the room that reveals the empty bottle also reveals a patch of black and green mold growing in one corner. The character making the discovery (and anyone with them) is subject to a Rating attack from the spores. This attack does no damage, but the victims are now sickened and suffer a Bane to all physical activities for the next hour.

STEEP STEPS TO THE DINING ROOM

A steep set of steps leads to the hatch to **the Dining Room** (page 136).

MOTHER

If the House Die indicates that Mother arrives, a full-bodied woman in a thick dress shows up in **the Dining Room** (page 136).

Show the players the image of **Mother**.

Over her dress, she wears a fancy (but slightly ragged) coat with large buttons. She has only a skull for a head, and the upper torso skeletons of children (just a skull, arms, a few ribs, and a spine) clinging to the coat and dress desperately. She says, "My sweet babies will be safe down there," and slams the trapdoor closed. It locks. The key, if it's in the cellar, can't be used from the underside. The lock is only accessible from the top. In such a case, the characters are trapped in the Wine Cellar, with the only likely escape being smashing through the hatch. The hatch has a Rating of 5. If the characters are trapped for an hour or more, they are subject to an attack every hour from inhaling the mold spores. This time, the spores inflict direct damage. Each hour, the attack Rating increases by +1. If the characters can't brute force the trapdoor open, they can use tools or weapons to slowly take it apart. This will take about five hours.

THE ATTIC

Sled

Window

Trunk

Puzzle Hole

Boxes and Stuff

To the Dining Room

The hidden attic is a focal point of many of the systems secretly operating in the house, including the only way to cut off a world from the house's reach.

This is a strange room, but as long as the PCs aren't reading from The Ghost Book *here, it's actually a safe place for them to rest and recuperate with no threat of Mother or other dangers.*

OVERVIEW

It is utterly quiet and still here, as though the sounds of the house are absorbed and consumed. This is a fairly normal-looking attic space, with a slight angle to the ceiling indicating that it is directly below the apex of a pointed roof. The narrow, winding stairs into the room curve around the chimney in **the Dining Room** (page 136). Old boxes and trunks sit on the floor, along with a pile of old coats and an old rocking chair. A sled hangs on the wall.

There's a single round window in one of the walls. It's dark outside.

Far more interesting than any of that is what appears to be a hole in the air in the shape of a massive puzzle piece. The hole is pure black and is about 6 inches across.

PUZZLE HOLE

While a character putting a hand into the hole will find it to be bone-chillingly cold, and the hand will throb for a few moments after being pulled back in, anything placed entirely within the hole is lost forever. The hole goes off into the void between worlds.

However, if the characters make it to **the Original House** (page 268), they'll see within the recursive dollhouse there that they can see the hole in that attic as well. The puzzle piece that fits can be found in the Original House, and if it is placed in the attic of the dollhouse, the dark house's connection to the characters' world is severed forever. From the characters' point of view, the hole here will only serve as a visual reminder of the significance of the scene in the recursive dollhouse when they find it, but it is, in fact, the very nexus of the house's ability to extend into all worlds. As such, it's much too potent for mere mortals to affect in any way.

THE BOXES AND OTHER STUFF

Everything in the attic is old, mundane, and mostly worthless. Trunks contain old clothing, most of which is likely from eras or settings very different from that of the characters. Photo albums of unrecognizable people,

pictures drawn by children, old school assignments, and miscellaneous keepsakes with no significance are piled unceremoniously in boxes.

However, even a cursory examination of the room's contents reveals two pieces of paper tossed haphazardly into a corner, covered in a bit of dust and cobwebs. Show the players **Remnant 21** (page 284).

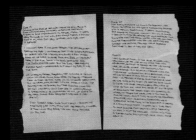

THE SLED

The word "Rosebud" is painted upon the sled.

THE LOCKED TRUNK

Only one of the containers here is locked. It's a very sturdy, built-in lock (Rating 6). The key is in **the Private Study** (page 230). Within the trunk are still more clothes, as well as a jewelry box. When opened, the box plays a twinkling, perhaps slightly eerie little tune (it's a simple, mechanical music box). Within is a collection of worthless costume jewelry, a pair of gold rings set with small emeralds (worth $800 each), a string of pearls (worth $4,000), and a Harlock family heirloom known as the Familial Diamond pin (worth a whopping $150,000).

THE ROUND WINDOW

The round window shows a dark night sky with an oncoming storm in the distance—another visual connection to the Amator section of the house as well as the Original House. Like all the windows, it is impervious to harm or manipulation by the PCs.

NAMES FROM THE GHOST BOOK

If the Ghost Book is found in **the Parlor** (page 130) and read in **the Private Study** (page 230), the reader will learn a variety of unholy names, representing the monarchs and princes of Hell and demonkind. If (as described in the book) these beings are called upon while gazing upon the void (through the puzzle piece-shaped hole) surrounded by candles, one of them may very well answer the call. Rather than immediately appearing, the diabolical king, queen, prince, or emperor observes the characters and intervenes in their lives much later on. This is almost certainly something that will take place after the PCs have left the Darkest House, and may involve a bargain, a possession, or something even grander. It will, however, be fraught with danger both physical and spiritual.

TO THE DINING ROOM

This staircase leads down to **the Dining Room** (page 136).

MOTHER

Mother will not come into the attic.

THE NARROW STAIRCASE

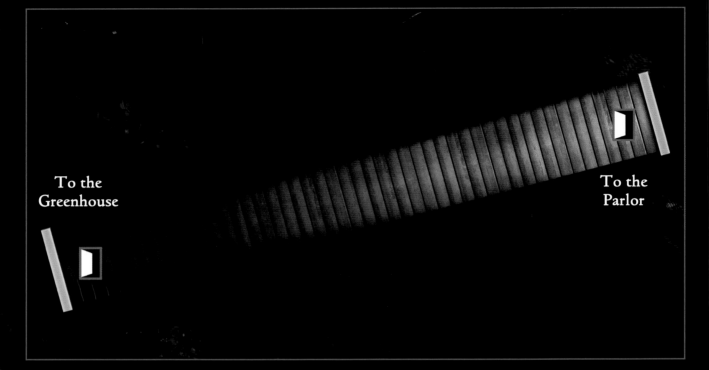

To the
Greenhouse

To the
Parlor

 n innocuous stairway down to the Greenhouse. No, really.

This is one of the rooms described in Secrets of the House as a "building dread" room.

OVERVIEW

Steep and narrow, these stairs impart a feeling of danger and vertigo. The hallway is only wide enough for one person to fit down, and only just barely that. The walls are painted off-white, and the stairs themselves are dark brown wood. Everything is a bit worn, and the stairs and walls are downright dirty at the bottom, where a thin metal door with a square window looks out into **the Greenhouse** (page 148). As the characters descend, the smell of earth and sweet-smelling plants is overpowering.

THE RINGING

The ringing of the telephone from the nearby **Sitting Room** (page 140) can be heard here.

Play this audio clip for the players:

mymcg.info/tdh-mater-sound-ringingfromadistance

TO THE GREENHOUSE

This innocuous door leads to **the Greenhouse** (page 148). It is unlocked.

TO THE PARLOR

This innocuous door leads to **the Parlor** (page 130). It is unlocked.

MOTHER

If the House Die indicates that Mother arrives,
a full-bodied woman in a thick dress stands at the top
of the staircase.

Show the players the image of **Mother**.

Over her dress, she wears a fancy (but slightly ragged)
coat with large buttons. She has only a skull for a head,
and the upper torso skeletons of children (just a skull,
arms, a few ribs, and a spine) clinging to the coat and
dress desperately. "Don't go out there!" she yells.
To reinforce her point, she squeezes to fit into the
stairs and descends like a terrifying charging beast.
She makes a physical attack against the closest
character that inflicts no damage but ensures
that she has them in a firm grip. She then
drags them up the stairs into **the
Parlor** (page 130). The dragging
is a Rating 4 physical attack.
Once in the Parlor, she will
squeeze her victim, inflicting a
Rating 7 attack on them until
they escape or are dead.

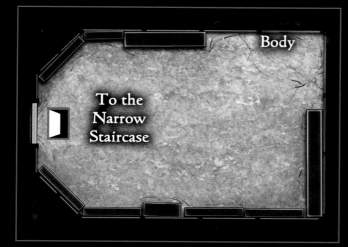

To the Narrow Staircase

Body

P lants growing here threaten the very physical integrity of characters that poke about.

This room presents the potential for some ghastly body horror. Be aware of players truly bothered by that.

OVERVIEW

In this simple glass enclosure, the plants have utterly taken over. The air is humid, and is thick with heavy floral and herbal fragrances. The greenhouse is filled with tables, and each table is overflowing with plants in pots, planters, and various raised beds. The glass itself is covered in ages of that green slime that accumulates in a greenhouse (it's algae) and offers no view outside. In one corner, growing vines have threaded their way through a human skull and ribcage, but even these bones are barely visible with all the growth.

PLANTS

None of the plants in the greenhouse are recognizable by any of the characters. Not even—or perhaps especially—those with knowledge of botany or nature.

BODY

If the body is examined, it's clear that not only are the vines entwined through the bones, but the body is horrifically altered. Bony protrusions from the sternum look as though the bones from a hand are pushing through it. Some ribs curve the wrong way. The skull bears a hole that doesn't look like a puncture; it looks almost natural.

At this point, if the characters leave, they're safe.

If they remain to look at things more closely, one or more of them *will* brush up against a leaf or vine and that is all it takes to trigger an awful fate (foreshadowed by the long-dead body here). The viny plant in this corner of the greenhouse burrows into flesh to gain nutrients. However,

to make this easier, its touch turns skin, muscle, and bone impossibly malleable and porous—almost insubstantial—but only for a very short time. This results in two terrors:

1. The plant has a Rating of 3. It can move its vines like limbs, but it cannot uproot itself. It stretches and grows in order to weave into the victim's body. This is a physical attack, but the plant has a Boon, as it has the element of surprise. Because the victim's flesh has the consistency of gelatin, this attack causes no damage. At first. On the plant's next turn, however, the character's flesh has already begun to turn to normal, and the plant—already deep within their muscles and still wrapping around bone and organs—immediately and automatically deals a physical wound with a Rating of 4. On subsequent turns, the character suffers additional wounds with a Rating of 2. Physically pulling the plant out is an action with a Rating of 3, and while success means the vine is pulled out, the character suffers another automatic wound with a Rating of 4.

2. On the character's first turn after touching the plant, they can very easily damage their own malleable body simply by trying to move. The character must either stand perfectly still (and remember, the character doesn't know what's happened to their body, so they don't know to stand still) or immediately make a roll. If the character fails an action with a Rating of 4, they inadvertently push some part of their body into the nearby table, into another plant or planter, into their own clothing or equipment, or—perhaps most horrifying of all—accidentally thrust their own hand or equipment into another part of their body. Before they realize what's happening, their weapon might be stuck in their rapidly solidifying arm, or their hand is stuck in their own head. And if two characters are close together and *both* fail their rolls, they likely fuse parts of their bodies together in some ghastly way. By the time the victim next has a turn, they automatically suffer a physical wound with a Rating of 4. Removing an inanimate object is as difficult and damaging as pulling out an invasive plant: Rating 3 action to remove, an automatic wound with a Rating of 4. Tearing apart two different body parts requires two rolls to succeed, and inflicts an automatic wound with a Rating of 6.

Lastly, any character inflicting an inadvertent injury upon themselves in this way is also subject to a Rating 5 mental attack from the shock and horror.

To add insult to injury, characters that escape this encounter alive might very well have permanent damage to their physical forms, with a bone now bent at a strange angle or something similar (or worse). This could very well cause complications later on.

The good news is, if the one extensive vine plant is destroyed, the rest of the room is relatively safe.

HIDDEN AMONG THE PLANTS

There are two valuable items in this room, obscured by the growing plant life. One is a key, which opens the door into **the Dripping Room** (page 156). The other is a canister filled with a coarse grey powder. The canister is labeled HERBICIDE. This is actually magical powder, and sprinkled onto virtually any plant—even some kind of intelligent plant monster—it will instantly cause the plant to turn pale, wither, and die. The canister holds enough powder for two uses.

LOOKING OUTSIDE

If someone manages to clean some of the glass on the sides of the greenhouse, they will see a large yard, overgrown with unidentifiable plants. It is night, but there are lights on in the surrounding buildings. The greenhouse appears to be within a compound of various grey stone buildings of different sizes. Dog-like creatures with six legs, raptor-like beaks, and four eyes prowl the open areas of the compound. The walls of the greenhouse are impervious to any attempts to break through them.

TO THE NARROW STAIRCASE

This innocuous door leads to **the Narrow Staircase** (page 146). It is unlocked.

MOTHER

If the House Die indicates that Mother arrives, a full-bodied woman in a thick dress enters the greenhouse.

Show the players the image of **Mother.**

Over her dress, she wears a fancy (but slightly ragged) coat with large buttons. She has only a skull for a head, and the upper torso skeletons of children (just a skull, arms, a few ribs, and a spine) clinging to the coat and dress desperately. "You don't look like you've been eating enough," she says. She then pulls a handful of leaves or vines from a planter and tries to shove it down one character's throat. This is a physical attack, and if she's successful not only does it inflict damage, but the character loses their next turn. If attacked, Mother howls and whines and says, "You never loved me!" and "You'll miss me when I'm gone!" Mother has a Rating of 7, but she won't chase opponents that run, instead just calling after them with words meant to instill guilt and despair.

A haunted dress may learn to wear a character here.

Gilravage is really like a Doom. For the most part, the downside of being controlled by her comes after the PCs leave the house.

Dress

To the Kitchen

To the Mannequin Room

To the Storeroom

OVERVIEW

The smell of mold and sweat fills the air. A few dead moths lie on the wooden floor. This rather simple workroom has an old-fashioned hand-crank sewing machine on a table. Bundles of cloth are piled on another table. There's a rocking chair in the corner, and a pair of dress forms, one empty and one with a tattered, ratty dress on it.

A dirty window is in one wall, but it reveals nothing by faint light, like moonlight.

THE DRESS

The dress is haunted by a spirit named Gilravage. She wants to be worn. She'll pick a character—regardless of gender—and make a Rating 5 attack. This attack inflicts no damage, but if the character is affected, they suddenly feel attracted to the dress, as if it is actually (despite its tattered appearance) quite beautiful.

> Wow, on second thought, suddenly that dress on the dress form looks amazing. You would look amazing in that dress. You feel like you should put it on, immediately.

The character believes they will look fantastic wearing the dress and desires to put it on immediately, even over their current clothing.

Once a character is wearing the dress, Gilravage can now control their actions. The only thing she does (at least at first) is to ensure that the wearer does not take the dress off.

> You hear a feminine voice purr in your ear. "Everything's going to be all right, hon. Just don't take off this dress and everything will be fantastic and wonderful. Oh, and don't tell anyone about me. Just make like you love the dress, and want to wear it and it will all be grand. Like candy and cake, you get me?" You are compelled not to take off the dress nor to say that the dress is controlling you or influencing your actions. Otherwise, you can act as normal.

Should anyone strongly object to the character wearing the dress, Gilravage makes a Rating 5 attack against the objecting character's mind as well. If she's successful, the affected character also feels that the wearer looks great in the new garment.

Send the newly affected character this message.

> Oh, wait. Actually, that dress makes them look truly fantastic. No wonder they want to wear it. You feel like you should just smile, nod, and admire such a smart look.

On the off chance that something is already possessing the wearer (such as the Lurker from **the Foyer** [page 162]), Gilravage makes the character take the dress off immediately and try to force it upon someone else.

> "Ugh. Too crowded in here. Yeesh, you'll just let anyone in, won't you? Have a little discretion next time, huh? Now, take me—the dress—off immediately and put me over someone else's head, will you? There's a good little one." The dress compels you to take it off and try to force it on one of the other PCs.

Right now, all Gilravage wants to do is get out of the Darkest House. So much so that she will help the wearer when that is also the wearer's goal by granting them a Boon to *all actions*. While in the Darkest House, if the character sets off with any intention other than getting out, they have a Bane in all actions. Once out of the house, Gilravage compels the character to leave the party, go off on their own, and become a serial killer, murdering people carefully and cautiously.

Gilravage has a Rating of 5, but any physical wound applied directly to the dress destroys it.

SING THE BONE KEY

he bone key found in **A Storeroom of Sorts**
age 110) can be inserted into the air anywhere in this
om and a keyhole appears to accept it. If turned, every
ving thing in the room is transported to **the Armory**
age 112).

O THE MANNEQUIN ROOM

his innocuous door leads to **the Mannequin Room**
age 154). It is unlocked.

O THE KITCHEN

his doorway leads to **the Kitchen**
age 134).

O THE STOREROOM

his innocuous door leads to **the**
oreroom (page 152). It is
nlocked.

MOTHER

the House Die indicates that
other arrives, a full-bodied
oman in a thick dress
orms into the room.
Show the players the
nage of **Mother.**

Over her dress, she wears a fancy (but slightly ragged)
coat with large buttons. She has only a skull for a head,
and the upper torso skeletons of children (just a skull,
arms, a few ribs, and a spine) clinging to the coat and
dress desperately. If one of the characters is wearing
the dress, she screams for them to "take off that rag."
Gilravage (the dress) can't compel Mother, so instead,
she compels the character to attack her (or, if this is
obviously foolhardy, to flee). Mother will attempt to tear
the dress from the character and then try to force another
dress on them that she produces from somewhere on her
person. "Here, wear this. I made it just for you!"

If no one is wearing the tattered dress, Mother will
immediately produce a garment and try
to force a character to wear it. "Here,
wear this. I made it just for you!"
If the character resists, she attacks
physically. "Listen to your mother,
you ungrateful wretch!" Mother
has a Rating of 7. She won't follow
characters that flee.

THE STOREROOM

he Smiling Man captures one of the characters in this room and fills their head with horrors.

When you use this room, think carefully about the player whose character will be primarily affected by it. This is the kind of encounter that will change a character forever. The direct message text for you to copy and send is fairly prescriptive compared to most in the Darkest House, meaning to some degree it tells the player what their character does and thinks. It does this because that's the horror here. The character is broken down and in some ways, corrupted. Obviously, you need to get consent from the player for this. In a perfect world, the player is the kind of person who likes this sort of challenge. It's the kind of thing that they can fall back on and draw from as their character progresses through this and future stories.

If, in the end, forcing someone to be trapped for a year with the Smiling Man is something you don't want to do, instead have a character see him glaring in the darkness just once. It's creepy and unnerving, but that's all.

OVERVIEW

Almost immediately upon looking into this room, at least one person will feel that something is not right. Something is watching.

This is a large storeroom, with multiple shelves. While it seems most of the stores here are canned foods and bagged or boxed dry goods, there is a section of non-food household items such as cleaning supplies and tools, medicines, and holiday decorations. All the goods of one type are stored together, and are organized alphabetically. There's a book on its side on a shelf by the door.

THE GOODS

Most everything here is spoiled or stale, but not so old as to be rotten. The medicines and medical supplies here would allow any injured character an immediate additional attempt to recover from their wounds. Someone intent on finding a particular household tool will find one (within reason).

THE BOOK

The book appears to be a journal. On the cover is the name Phillip Harlock. However, all of the pages have been torn out of it.

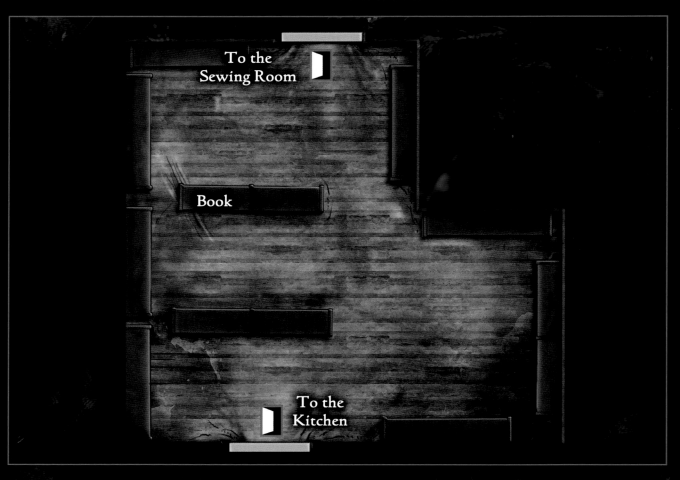

THE SMILING MAN

The Smiling Man is an inhuman entity that could *almost* pass for human. He looks like a man, but his almost impossibly wide grin is just *too* big, with just *too* many teeth, to ever truly pass as human.

Show the players **Smiling Man in the Dark**.

Very shortly after the PCs enter the room, choose a character and send them this lengthy message:

> Suddenly, the door is gone. Your friends are gone. You're trapped here. Alone. Hours pass. It doesn't seem to matter what you do—scream, pound, try to break out or escape—nothing seems to work. Nothing gets you out of here. After you've been here for, what? Ten hours? Twelve? Perhaps more . . . there is a voice from the darkness. It whispers, but you can't quite make out what it says. You catch a glimpse of a man. A smiling man. But then he's gone. Days pass. You've no food or water. You're weak. Perhaps delirious. The smiling man returns. He brings you food and water. And he whispers things to you from the darkness. Terrible things. You don't want to listen, but the smiling man is the only thing keeping you alive. Weeks go by. It's impossible to keep an accurate count of days, but it seems that he comes at night. You've begun to think of it as night, anyway. You turn him away, tell him to go, but eventually, you realize his mad, wretched whispers offer you the only escape you have from this prison. You curl up on the floor and listen. Months go by. Perhaps a whole year. Who can tell? Does it matter? Do such prosaic things have purpose or meaning? If they ever did, you've forgotten them. But then the smiling man tells you something new. It's time, he whispers. Time to return, and use what you've learned. You're leaving. He's sending you back. But you have questions to ask him . . . questions that go unasked, because without any further warning, you're standing in the light. Unsteady on your feet, you can't help but grip the wall. The room has not changed, except that the door is right there, where it once was. Right where it was so long ago. There's the exit out. And, your companions—can you even remember all their names? You never thought you'd see them again. They are back as well. And they look somehow unchanged. They stare at you strangely. Have they heard the smiling man's whispered words as well?

No time has passed since the character disappeared. Literally no time—the other PCs did not see them disappear or reappear, although the character is clearly haggard and worn. Clearly affected by their time with the Smiling Man.

If the player asks what the Smiling Man was whispering to them in the darkness, you can send them this message.

> He spoke of things too awful to contemplate. He explained ideas and related facts no one wants to know.

If they ask for more details, send them this message:

> You tell me. What's something your character would be horrified to have someone whisper about in the dark, night after night?

You may want to discuss this experience with them after the session is over.

One thing is certain: if the affected character sees the painting of the Smiling Man in the **Gallery** (page 106) or the doll made to look like him in **the Nursery** (page 188), or if they encounter the Smiling Man in **the Backrooms** (page 118), they are likely to experience an immediate mental attack with a Rating of 5.

No amount of searching of the Storeroom turns up any sign of the Smiling Man. Not now, and not ever.

TO THE SEWING ROOM

This innocuous door leads to **the Sewing Room** (page 150). It is unlocked.

TO THE KITCHEN

This innocuous door leads to **the Kitchen** (page 134). It is unlocked.

MOTHER

Mother will not enter this room.

THE MANNEQUIN ROOM

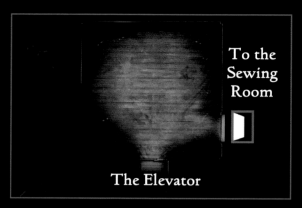

To the Sewing Room

The Elevator

The mannequins here want you to be a mannequin too.

There might be a temptation to play Mother for laughs here or elsewhere. Resist that temptation. She is the twisted essence of motherly love. Everything she does should be horrific.

OVERVIEW

This dark storeroom stinks of jealousy and hate. The occupants of this room are a bunch of mannequins who are jealous of the life and mobility of real people. A few near the elevator have clothing on, and are set a bit apart from each other and the rest. A much larger number are pushed to the back of the room, some leaning on the others. None of these have clothing, and a few are missing a hand or an arm.

MANNEQUINS

When someone comes into this room, the mannequins—who are controlled by a single spirit cursed to inhabit them all, so that it has physicality but no singular identity—single out a target. Once a character is in reach of the closest set of mannequins, those mannequins move as one and grab the character as if they were stiff-moving but living people. This is a Rating 6 attack that inflicts no damage. Instead, the grasped character is immediately

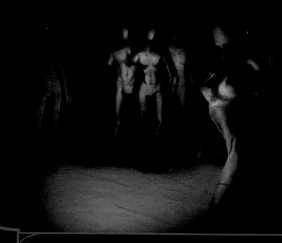

hurled into the mass of mannequins in the back. These figures envelop the victim so that they cannot be seen in a tide of limbs and body parts.

The mannequins in front then serve as a line of defense, attacking anyone that attempts to rescue the victim. These act as three individuals with a Rating of 3 each, so they can confront multiple foes at once.

Meanwhile, the victim thrown into the mass of mannequins faces another Rating 6 attack. If the attack succeeds, the mannequins encase a portion of the character's body with interlocking metal plates. Once encased, that body part is immobilized. Every time the mannequins take a turn, they make this attack, and every success means more of the character is enclosed within the insidious devices.

The mannequins start with an arm, then a leg, then the head, then the remaining arm, and finally the remaining leg. If they finish this process, they will attempt to do it to another character. A character trapped by the mannequins can take no action except to try to get free, and that action has a Rating of 6.

If the three mannequins at the forefront are all destroyed, the victim's allies can try to get them free, but this is still a Rating 6 action (simply attacking the remaining mannequins doesn't accomplish much). Should the victim get free, the mannequins all immediately disassemble and the parts become inert. Searching through the remains reveals several miscellaneous metallic plates with various hooks and protrusions to attach them together, and a wrench.

METAL ENCASEMENT

The devices closed around a character's body parts are quite debilitating. The effect of this depends on the body part:

+ Arm: The arm is utterly stiff, useless except perhaps as a club. It cannot move at any joints and the hand is completely within the metal containment.
+ Leg: The leg is completely stiff. The character can only move with a very slow, lumbering limp that makes a lot of noise. If both legs are encased, the character cannot walk or run (or, if they fall over, stand back up).
+ Head: The character cannot see or smell, and their voice and hearing are both extremely muffled.

A completely encased character can essentially take no physical actions.

To get free of the enclosure, one must have a special tool, called the encasement key. It can be obtained in **the Dripping Room** (page 156). Simply trying to pull or

...ry the encasement away without the key causes the ...etal plates to shift in devious ways, cutting the trapped ...haracter, who automatically suffers a Rating 1 wound. ...All subsequent attempts also cause a wound, and each ...me the Rating is +1 more, to a maximum of Rating 6.) ...emoving the insidious device is an action with a Rating ...7, and if successful, the trapped character still suffers ...e aforementioned wound. Much better to use the key ...which causes no harm to the victim).

...Every day a character spends with part of their body ...apped in one or more of these devices incurs an ...utomatic Rating 3 mental wound from the horror.

...If the articulated plates of these devices seem ...miniscent of the mask worn by the Arbiter in **the Parlor** ...page 130), that is intentional. These devices were created ...y the same devious demon in whatever Hell the house ...habitants hail from. The difference is, the Arbiter ...njoys the wounds.

THE WRENCH

...he wrench is one of the eight **Mystic Tools**.

F THE LURKER IS PRESENT

...the character possessed by the Lurker (from **the Foyer** ...age 162]) is present when the wrench is discovered, ...forces the character to act.

> The spirit possessing you compels you to grab the wrench and shout, "Mine!"

...If this action causes any kind of questioning of the ...ossessed character or their actions, the Lurker yet again ...ompels its host.

> The spirit possessing you makes you say, "I'm fine. Don't worry about it. Now, where do you think the rest of these tools might be?"

...Obviously, the Lurker wants the **Mystic Tools**. It will ...ontinue to compel its host to keep trying to find them. ...hould the entire set be found, the Lurker will attempt ...o kill all the other characters so that it can have the tools ...or itself.

THE ELEVATOR

The elevator is essentially a large brass cage.

Show the players the **Elevator** image.

On the floor is a heavy lever with six positions. It is currently in position 3. The elevator moves very slowly, taking almost a full minute to reach the next level up or down. There is a mechanical sound when it moves, and a clinking of chains. Through the cage, chains and gears can be seen moving. Damaging any of them renders the elevator inoperable for 24 hours before it resets.

- ✦ Position 1: Takes the elevator to the **Music Room** (page 222)
- ✦ Position 2: Takes the elevator to the **Great Hall** (page 114)
- ✦ Position 3: Where the lever is now (if the elevator goes to another level, 3 returns it to this room)
- ✦ Position 4: Takes the elevator to **the Room With a Hidden Elevator** (page 88)
- ✦ Position 5: Takes the elevator to **the Backrooms** (page 118)
- ✦ Position 6: Takes the elevator to **the Guardian** (page 122)

TO THE SEWING ROOM

This innocuous door leads to **the Sewing Room** (page 150). It is unlocked.

MOTHER

If the House Die indicates that Mother arrives, a full-bodied woman in a thick dress storms into the room.

Show the players the image of **Mother**.

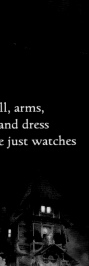

Over her dress, she wears a fancy (but slightly ragged) coat with large buttons. She has only a skull for a head, and the upper torso skeletons of children (just a skull, arms, a few ribs, and a spine) clinging to the coat and dress desperately. If the mannequins are active, she just watches the proceedings, saying, "This is what you deserve for your disobedience." If they are not active, or the characters defeat them, she tries to grab a character with a physical attack (that inflicts no damage) and, while holding them with one hand, apply the metal device to their leg with the other (the skeletons hanging onto her help). Mother has a Rating of 7 and will not follow the characters if they flee.

THE DRIPPING ROOM

A room consumed by wax, but what the wax covers might be even worse.

The wax woman's holes might freak out someone with trypophobia.

OVERVIEW

A brown substance, thick but still somewhat viscous, drips from the ceiling and runs down the walls. It collects on the smooth polished stone floor in ever-flattening mounds and upon the furnishings in blobs. The furnishings appear to be a glass-topped table, a pair of glass chairs, and a marble pedestal near the back of the room topped with an object that can't quite be made out. There are some objects on the table as well, but they also are not easily identified, as they are covered in the syrupy substance.

Near the pedestal stands a life-sized statue of a woman, perhaps made of the brownish waxy material prevalent in the room. Except much of the wax has dripped off her in places, revealing that underneath the layer of wax, the statue is made of a porous stone filled with mysterious, irregular holes.

The door to this room is locked (Rating 5). The key is **in the Greenhouse** (page 148).

THE SUBSTANCE

The yellow-brown dripping goo is more or less warm wax. It's too warm to solidify, but not quite warm enough to run quickly. It's harmless to touch, tacky but not overly sticky. There are small holes in the ceiling where it starts, and a few larger ones along the bottom of the walls to keep the wax from filling the room.

THE WAX WOMAN

The "statue" is, in fact, an animate object haunted by a dark spirit. The statue moves to guard what's on the pedestal. If the characters ignore the object and the woman, they are in no danger. That's probably unlikely, however. She has a Rating of 4 and resists damage with a Rating of 5, and should anyone get close to her, a yellow substance—not the wax of the room—oozes out of the holes in her stone body, filled with wriggling worms. Anyone witnessing this is subject to a Rating 3 mental attack, although the ooze and worms are mostly harmless (touching it might result in a rash). Worse, the creatures deep inside her that just vomited that substance peek out on her next action, insect-like mouths still dripping with the yellow spew. Far too many legs of oddly different lengths on their long, multisegmented yet somehow hairy bodies pull them out. Collectively, they make an additional Rating 4 physical biting attack in addition to the woman physically slamming and grabbing at foes with her hands.

Table

Wax Effigy

The Wax Woman

To the Grand Staircase

THE WAX EFFIGY

The object on the pedestal is just a formless blob of wax. Pick the character who is most object-focused. This character, upon entering the room, actually determines what the object *appears* to be. It is literally the most desirable object that character can conceive of. If a character loves treasure or money, it is a bejeweled crown (or orb, or miniature carousel, or anything else) made of gold. If the character loves guns, it is the finest-crafted weapon of that type they could ever desire, hand-tooled with an ivory grip. If they seek a specific object as a part of their overall character goals, such as a specific magical artifact or the holy grail itself, it's on the pedestal. The only requirement is that the object is something that could fit in that space—probably something that a typical person could lift without too much problem.

If any character doubts that it is what it appears to be, ask someone knowledgeable or smart to make a roll to determine its veracity. Ignore the die result—they believe it to be the real object. Basically, while in this room, the wax blob is the object (although it has no magical powers). When removed from the room, the object melts into a mass of warm wax after about an hour.

THE TABLE'S CONTENTS

Although there are a few minor, unimportant items amid the wax, like a vase and a crystal bowl (worth $50 and $180, respectively), there is also another torn journal page, a strangely shaped steel key, and a woodworking plane. All are partially covered by wax.

The piece of paper is still mostly legible, and if carefully done, the wax covering the page can be removed, leaving just an oily stain.

Show players **Remnant 20** (page 283).

The plane is one of the eight **Mystic Tools**.

The key is the encasement key that will allow someone to easily and painlessly remove the metal enclosures that might be placed upon a person in the **Mannequin Room** (page 154).

IF THE LURKER IS PRESENT

If the character possessed by the Lurker (from **the Foyer** [page 162]) is present when the plane is discovered, it forces the character to act.

> The spirit possessing you compels you to grab the plane and shout, "Mine!"

If this action causes any kind of questioning of the possessed character or their actions, the Lurker yet again compels its host.

> The spirit possessing you makes you say, I'm fine. Don't worry about it. Now, where do you think the rest of these tools might be?"

Obviously, the Lurker wants the **Mystic Tools**. It will continue to compel its host to keep trying to find them. Should the entire set be found, the Lurker will attempt to kill all the other characters so that it can have the tools for itself.

TO THE GRAND STAIRCASE

This innocuous door leads to **the Grand Staircase** (page 128). This door is locked (Rating 5), but easily locked or unlocked from within the room.

MOTHER

If the House Die indicates that Mother arrives, a full-bodied woman in a thick dress climbs the stairs.

Show the players the image of **Mother**.

Over her dress, she wears a fancy (but slightly ragged) coat with large buttons. She has only a skull for a head, and the upper torso skeletons of children (just a skull, arms, a few ribs, and a spine) clinging to the coat and dress desperately. "You like mother's candle-making crafts? Let me show you how to do it." She then pulls a handful of warm wax from the wall and tries to shove it down one character's throat. This is a physical attack, and if she's successful, not only does it inflict damage, but the character loses their next turn. If attacked, Mother howls and whines and says, "You never loved me!" and "You'll miss me when I'm gone!" Mother has a Rating of 7, but she won't chase opponents that run, instead just calling after them with words meant to instill guilt and despair.

THE WHEEL OF BLOOD

Door to the
Grand Staircase

Paintings

Door to the
Spirit of
Destruction

The four disturbing paintings here make this more than just a hall connecting the Grand Staircase and the Spirit of Destruction.

The paintings appear to have been painted by the same artist that worked in the Studio.

OVERVIEW

You can almost hear music in this room. Processional, ritual music. This is a long corridor with walls painted red, black carpet on the floor, and a door at each end. It's about 100 feet long, and every 20 feet, a very large painting hangs upon the right wall (as one comes into the hall from **the Grand Staircase**).

THE PAINTINGS

The paintings have no frames, but a single word or name is carefully painted below each canvas. Starting with the painting closest to the door to **the Grand Staircase**, the four paintings are as follows:

1. Hungry wolves wait in a forest of blood-red trees. A being with a head like a bird wearing a crown and holding a candelabra watches over them. Below the painting, it says, "Mater."

Show the players **Painting of Hungry Wolves**.

2. The wolf pack, having spotted a stag, chases it through the woods. A savage, two-headed wolf-being holding a spear and with daggers for breath howls in encouragement. Below the painting, it says, "Pater."

Show the players **Painting of Wolf Pack Chase**.

3. The wolves bring down the stag in a bloody display. A rat-headed being holding a gnarled staff watches the grisly scene without emotion. Below the painting, it says, "Frater."

Show the players **Painting of Wolf Attack**.

4. Wolves long gone, a deathly, skull-headed figure holding a candelabra stands vigil high above the skeletal remains of the long-dead stag. The animal's spilled blood seems to have caused the sprouting of a new blood-red tree. Below the painting, it says, "Soror."

Show the players **Painting of Wolves Long Gone**.

While the four painted words equate to four of the five sections of the house, their connection to each painting is somewhat tenuous.

What matters, however, is the order: *Mater*, *Pater*, *Frater*, and *Soror*. If these four Latin words re spoken aloud by a character who has visited at least ne room in each of the four sections, that character s instantly transported to **the Vestibule** (page 244). ne does not need to say the words in this corridor—hey can be spoken anywhere and achieve this effect. *Even utside the house.*

OOR TO THE GRAND STAIRCASE

This innocuous door leads to **the Grand Staircase** page 128). It is unlocked.

OOR TO THE SPIRIT OF DESTRUCTION

This innocuous door leads to **the Spirit of Destruction** page 172). It is unlocked. Sounds of great destruction and mashing can be heard from the other side.

MOTHER

If the House Die indicates that Mother arrives, a full-bodied woman in a thick dress storms in.

Show the players the image of **Mother**.

Over her dress, she wears a fancy (but slightly ragged) coat with large buttons. She has only a skull for a head, and the upper torso skeletons of children (just a skull, arms, a few ribs, and a spine) clinging to the coat and dress desperately. "You never seem to learn," she whispers. She then begins pulling the clutching skeletons from her bosom and hurling them as a physical attack. If she's successful, not only does she inflict damage, but the character loses their next turn as the skeletal child grasps, tears, and bites at them (there is no additional damage, however). If attacked, Mother howls and whines and says, "You never loved me!" and "You'll miss me when I'm gone!" Mother has a Rating of 7, but she won't chase opponents that run, instead just calling after them with words meant to instill guilt and despair.

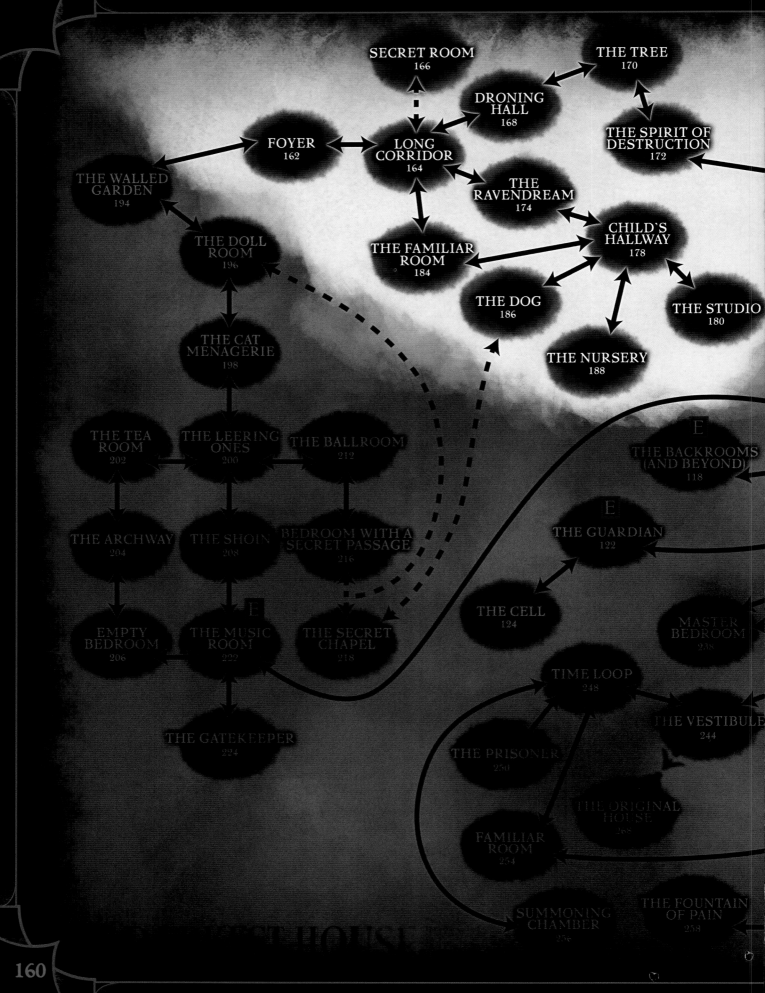

SECRET ROOM
166

THE TREE
170

DRONING
HALL
168

THE SPIRIT OF
DESTRUCTION
172

FOYER
162

LONG
CORRIDOR
164

THE WALLED
GARDEN
194

THE
RAVENDREAM
174

THE DOLL
ROOM
196

THE FAMILIAR
ROOM
184

CHILD'S
HALLWAY
178

THE CAT
MENAGERIE
198

THE DOG
186

THE STUDIO
180

THE TEA
ROOM
202

THE LEERING
ONES
200

THE BALLROOM
212

THE NURSERY
188

E
THE BACKROOMS
(AND BEYOND)
118

THE ARCHWAY
204

THE SHOIN
208

BEDROOM WITH A
SECRET PASSAGE
216

E
THE GUARDIAN
122

MASTER
BEDROOM
238

EMPTY
BEDROOM
206

E
THE MUSIC
ROOM
222

THE SECRET
CHAPEL
218

THE CELL
124

THE GATEKEEPER
224

TIME LOOP
248

THE VESTIBULE
244

THE PRISONER
250

THE ORIGINAL
HOUSE
268

FAMILIAR
ROOM
254

SUMMONING
CHAMBER
256

THE FOUNTAIN
OF PAIN
258

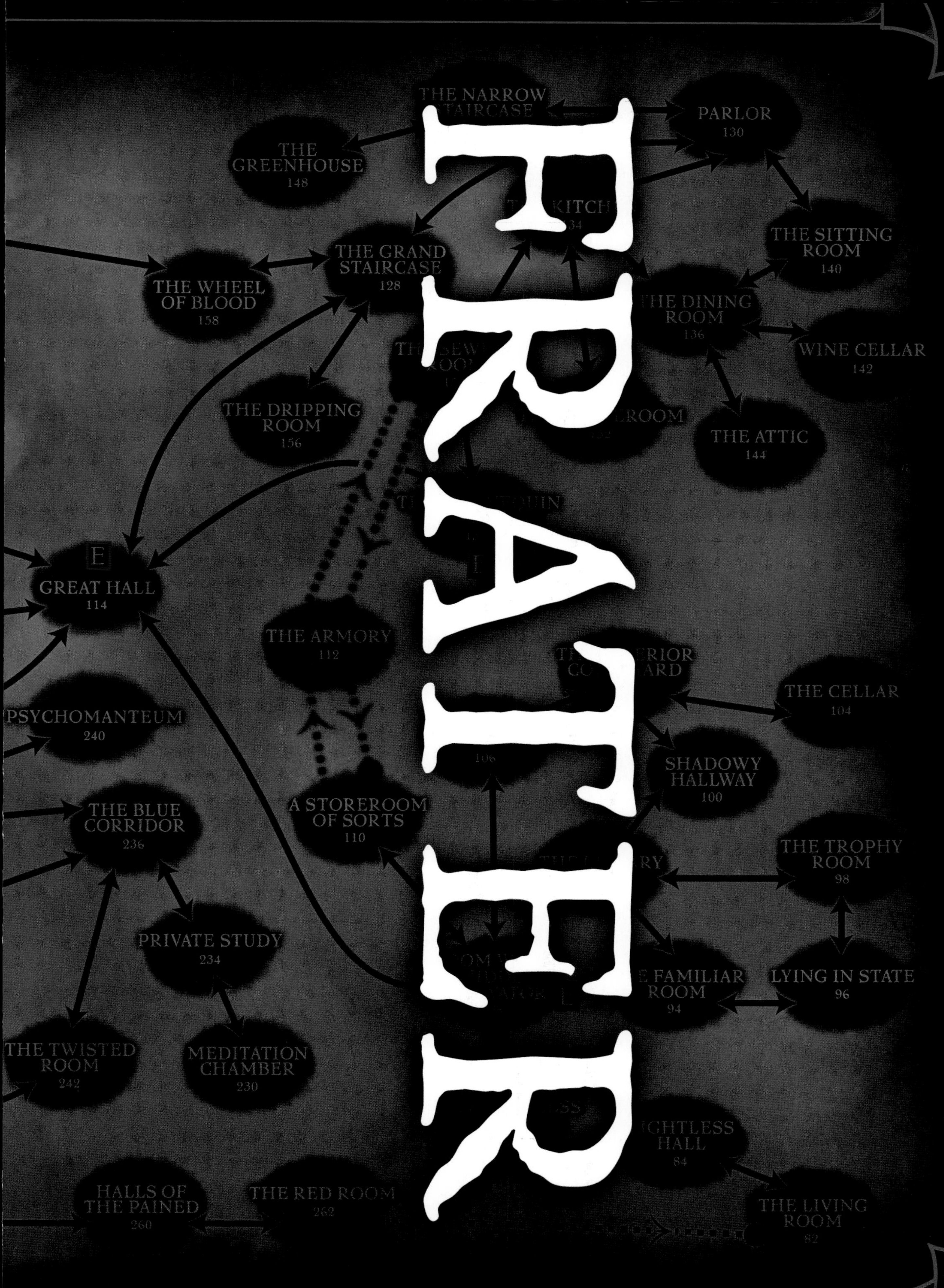

THE NARROW
STAIRCASE

PARLOR
130

THE
GREENHOUSE
148

KITCH
34

THE SITTING
ROOM
140

THE GRAND
STAIRCASE
128

THE WHEEL
OF BLOOD
158

THE DINING
ROOM
136

WINE CELLAR
142

THE SEW
ROOM

ROOM

THE DRIPPING
ROOM
156

THE ATTIC
144

E

GREAT HALL
114

THE ARMORY
112

RIOR
CO   RD

THE CELLAR
104

PSYCHOMANTEUM
240

106

SHADOWY
HALLWAY
100

THE BLUE
CORRIDOR
236

A STOREROOM
OF SORTS
110

THE TROPHY
ROOM
98

PRIVATE STUDY
234

FAMILIAR
ROOM
94

LYING IN STATE
96

THE TWISTED
ROOM
242

MEDITATION
CHAMBER
230

GHTLESS
HALL
84

HALLS OF
THE PAINED
260

THE RED ROOM
262

THE LIVING
ROOM
82

FRATER

The first room visitors using the Back Door will find, but the Lurker wants to come in too.

> *A character possessed by the Lurker can act normally for much of the exploration of the house, with the Lurker mostly "hiding" within the character. Rooms where the Lurker takes action will be clearly spelled out.*

OVERVIEW

This room seems very quiet and still, although surprisingly lived in. A polished wood floor appears spotless, and the walls bear dark green wallpaper with brown wooden wainscoting. The large, wooden double doors are closed, with dark windows on either side. A small table is pushed up against the wall; the only things on it are a small ring of keys and a notepad with one note written upon it: *They steal what we see.*

Pinned to the door is a note: *Don't answer the door.*

As the characters first begin to look around the room, they hear something knocking at the door.

ENTERING THE HOUSE HERE

Of course, it's very possible that the characters just entered the house through this very door. The door closes of its own volition as soon as they are in—nothing else about the room changes. They still hear knocking once they're inside. It's worth noting that the door looks quite different from the outside (out there, it's a single, not a double, door) and there are no windows on either side of it.

If the characters entered the house through the back door, but in their context there was no walled garden, if they open this door again, they will see (and can enter) **the Walled Garden** (page 194) regardless of what was on the other side of the back door before. As described in the Walled Garden, there is no exiting the house from there.

ANSWERING THE DOOR

If someone opens the door, there is no one there. If they close the door, the knocking returns a few moments later.

Should someone open the door a second time, they still see nothing, but they hear a whispered voice.

> You hear a whispered voice, just behind your ear, that says, "May I come in?"

If the character says anything other than yes, an invisible force (Rating 7) strikes them.

If the character suffers damage, they are knocked down and the door closes.

If the character says yes, send them this direct message.

> A whisper asks, "Is it safe here?"

Again, if the character says anything other than yes, the voice (no longer whispering, so now everyone can hear it) says, "You're right. It's not." A spirit called the Lurker—the source of the voice—then attempts to possess the character who answered.

Send the affected player this message:

> Something is attempting to possess your body. Don't say anything to anyone, but roll to resist its intrusion. It has a Rating of 7, so your target number is 14. Reply only to me to tell me if you fail or succeed.

The Lurker has a Rating of 7, but at this time, can only attempt to possess a living being. It cannot affect physical matter, nor can it be affected physically. If the character resists the Lurker's possession attempt, they are in total control of themselves, and immediately

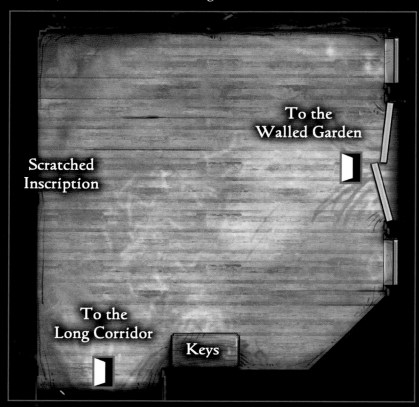

Scratched Inscription

To the Walled Garden

To the Long Corridor

Keys

ave the sensation of something passing by them, as if
hey've let something into the house. The characters
annot see it, or interact with it at this time. They
ear neither any more whispers nor knocking. But the
urker is now in the house. This can affect rooms in
ifferent ways.

However, if the character again says yes, the whisper
ays, "Are you certain? Have you checked behind the crib
n the nursery?" The character then has a sensation of
omething passing by them, as if they've let something
nto the house. They cannot see it, or interact with it
 this time. They hear neither any more whispers nor
nocking and there is no possession attempt. But the
urker is now in the house. This can affect rooms in
ifferent ways, but in particular **the Nursery** (page 188).

NOT ANSWERING THE DOOR

 no one answers the door, eventually the knocking stops,
ut only after a very long time. The knocking begins
gain if the characters return to the room.

F THE LURKER POSSESSES THE CHARACTER

he Lurker takes no immediate action. However, in other
ooms, you may see "If the Lurker is Present."

Read the information there, because if the Lurker is
ossessing a character, it is indeed present.

Give the possessed player this message:

> Don't say anything to anyone, but you are
> possessed. You are in control of your actions, but you
> can't say anything about the entity lurking within
> you. You'll likely get more updates later.

SCRATCHED INSCRIPTION

he green wallpaper has been cut and the wood beneath
 scratched, as if with a knife or a claw. The scratches
ear a message.

Show the players **Remnant 29** (page 290).

THE KEYS

There are six keys on a ring on the table. One goes to the
(currently unlocked) door in this room that leads out of
the house. One opens the door to **the Ravendream's room**
(page 174), one opens the door to **the Studio** (page 180),
and one opens the door to **the Familiar Room** (page 184).
The other two have no apparent use, at least not in the
current Darkest House.

TO THE WALLED GARDEN

This door leads to **the Walled Garden** (page 194). It is
not locked. Pinned to the door is a note: *Don't answer
the door*.

TO THE LONG CORRIDOR

This opening leads directly into **the Long Corridor**
(page 164).

BROTHER

Should the House Die indicate that Brother arrives, the
PCs see a lanky, male humanoid figure with hands balled
into fists and one eye bulging unnervingly in the doorway.
His face shows a sneer, and his shadow doesn't reflect
his pose at all, and in fact, seems to hold an axe. Brother
wears dark pants and a dark red shirt.

Show the players the image of **Brother**.

Brother doesn't do much besides lurk in the doorway
and smirk, but his shadow comes into the room and
attacks with the axe. Brother has a Rating of 6; however,
his shadow cannot be harmed except by magic. Brother's
physical form can be hurt, but if he is attacked, he will try
to use the doorway or furniture for cover and may even
run off, although he's likely going to hide and ambush
anyone who tries to follow him. He can be bribed to leave
the PCs alone (this time) with an extremely valuable
object, magical device, or very high-tech device, as long as
it comes from outside the house. He disappears if slain.

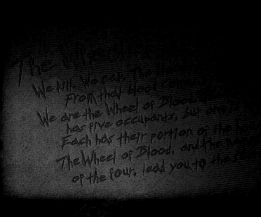

LONG CORRIDOR

Connecting many rooms, this hallway hides a secret of its own.

It's possible that the players will never think to look for the hidden hatch in the floor. Them's the breaks. Don't give them hints. The key in the drawer is enough of a clue.

OVERVIEW

This corridor has a door to the left and the right, an opening into **the Foyer** at one end, and a bend to the left at the other end, forming **the Droning Hall**. The floor is made of black and white tiles, like a checkerboard, and heavy red draperies hang upon the walls, even to the point of concealing the side doors, although it takes little to find them. There is a side table with a single drawer. On top are an envelope and a mostly burned-down candle in a hideous silver holder.

TABLE

In the drawer is the three-stemmed key. This object looks like three different keys, whose bows (the roundish part you hold while turning) have all been fused so that the stems (the long protruding parts that go into the lock, also called the blade) each extend in a different direction. The whole thing makes a triangle shape. If this key—using any of its three parts—is used in the locked doors to **the Ravendream** (page 174), **the Studio** (page 180), or **the Familiar Room** (page 184), it unlocks them.

However, the character unlocking the door must immediately face ghostly hands that tear through the veil of our world and grab for them with a cold, numbing clutch. The hands have a Rating of 5. Should they strike, they grasp the character by the throat and begin to strangle them, automatically inflicting a Rating 5 wound each turn the character does not get free of them. If the character does get free, the hands disappear. This happens each time the wrong key is used in one of these three locks. Worse, each time, the Rating of the ghostly hands increases by 1. The appearance of these hands might be

a Rating 2 shock (attack inflicting mental damage) for everyone present.

Unlocking these doors using any other manner, whether it be picking the locks or using the proper keys on the key ring found in **the Foyer** (page 162), does not produce the grasping hands. Likewise, using this key to open the secret hatch in this room does not result in the attacking hands either.

ENVELOPE

This has the name "Phillip" written on the outside. It's been opened, but the letter is still folded inside. If the PCs take a look at the letter, show them **Remnant 16** (page 280).

CANDLE

The ugly candle holder is solid silver, so it's probably worth $500.

HATCH TO THE SECRET ROOM

There's a secret hatch in the floor. If it's found, it's probably because there is a keyhole. If the three-stemmed key in the table drawer is inserted into the small keyhole between two tiles, it can open this hatch (otherwise, it is Rating 7 to open). Beneath the hatch is a dark shaft with wooden sides. On one side, planks have been hammered to create a sort of ladder. It depends for 30 feet down into **the Secret Room** (page 166).

TO THE FOYER

This end of the corridor opens into **the Foyer** (page 162).

TO THE RAVENDREAM

Concealed behind red draperies, a locked side door leads to **the Ravendream** (page 174). (The lock on this door is Rating 6. The key can be found in **the Foyer** (page 162), though the three-stemmed key in the side table also works.)

To the Familiar Room

To the Droning Hall

To the Foyer

Table

Envelope

Candle

Secret Hatch

To the Ravendream

TO THE FAMILIAR ROOM

Concealed behind red draperies, a locked side door leads to **the Familiar Room** (page 184). (The lock on the door is Rating 6. The key can be found in **the Foyer** (page 162), though the three-stemmed key in the side table also works.)

TO THE DRONING HALL

A bend at the end of the Long Corridor opens directly into **the Droning Hall** (page 168).

BROTHER

Should the House Die indicate that Brother arrives, the PCs see a lanky, male humanoid figure with hands balled into fists and one eye bulging unnervingly in the doorway. His face shows a sneer, and his shadow doesn't reflect his pose at all, and in fact, seems to hold an axe. Brother wears dark pants and a dark red shirt.

Show the players the image of **Brother**.

Brother doesn't do much besides lurk in the doorway and smirk, while his shadow comes into the hall and attacks with the axe. Brother has a Rating of 6; however, his shadow cannot be harmed except by magic. Brother's physical form can be hurt, but if he is attacked, he will likely run off, although he's likely going to hide and ambush anyone who tries to follow him. He can be bribed to leave the PCs alone (this time) with some extremely valuable object, magical device, or very high-tech device, as long as it comes from outside the house. He disappears if slain.

SECRET ROOM

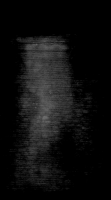

L ying beneath the floor, this hidden room contains treasures, and also danger.

> *If the Lurker acts here, eventually you'll have to start writing appropriate direct messages to the possessed character on your own, as it tries to (awkwardly) shake suspicion from itself all while forcing its host not to reveal anything about it.*

OVERVIEW

At the bottom of the 30-foot-deep shaft lies a room with a low ceiling. Compounding its compromised height is the fact that the floor is flooded up to about knee level (2 feet or so). Hidden in the cold, dank water are three metallic boxes. One is unlocked and contains nothing but water. The other two are locked and sealed. Each is rusted and corroded, but watertight. They're not obvious, though, as the water is dark. What is obvious is the stench of decaying, water-soaked flesh all but dissolved into the murk. The only sound is an occasional dripping, but try as you might, you can't find the source.

THE WATER

There are three corpses in the water. Wrinkled, greenish-black skin peels away from their swollen tissues due to the cold water. However, the spirits of the Darkest House stir them to life (or a semblance of it) if anyone comes down the ladder. The animate corpses each have a Rating of 3 and attack the intruders with claw-like hands of bare bone. Each attacks with surprise, gaining a Boon on the first attack. The initial appearance is a Rating 2 mental attack from the shock.

Show the players this version of the room image.

FIRST LOCKED BOX

The key to this box can be found in the room with **the Tree** (page 170). If the PCs don't have the key, the box's lock has a Rating of 4. The box is mostly waterproof. Within the box lie the following objects:

✦ **A simple ring carved from jade.** It is magical, and allows the wearer and up to six others to teleport directly to **the Living Room** (page 82). The ring only works in the house, and it only works once for each character. The characters could pass it around, however. No amount of study (or magical analysis) reveals the destination of the journey ahead of time. Only that the ring teleports to somewhere else in the house.

✦ **A glass flask with a magical potion.** This potion heals all wounds, mental and physical, that the imbiber currently suffers from. Further, it lifts any current curses they might be under.

✦ **A pair of eyeglasses.**

✦ **A variety of pencils and pens.** Depending on the context of the setting from which the characters come, these might be impressive or they might be garbage.

✦ **Crumpled up amid the other objects is a page torn from a book—perhaps a personal journal.** Show the players **Remnant 6** (page 275).

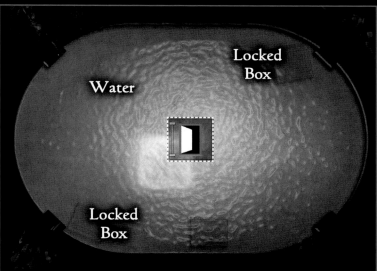

SECOND LOCKED BOX

The key to this box can be found in the room with **the Tree**. If the PCs don't have the key, the box's lock has a Rating of 4. The box is mostly waterproof. The box contains a pair of pliers that are part of the set of eight **Mystic Tools**. A piece of paper, stained and torn but with writing on it, lines the bottom of the box. Show the players **Remnant 15** (page 280).

IF THE LURKER IS PRESENT

If the character possessed by the Lurker (from **the Foyer**) is present when the second locked box is opened (whether here or elsewhere), it forces the character to act.

> The spirit possessing you compels you to grab the pliers and shout, "Mine!"

And after the note is read, the Lurker forces its host to act again.

> The spirit possessing you forces you to say, "We must seek out and find all of these tools! They will make us extremely powerful."

If these things cause any kind of questioning of the possessed character or their actions, the Lurker yet again compels its host.

> The spirit possessing you makes you say, "I'm fine. Don't worry about it. Now, where do you think the rest of these tools might be?"

Obviously, the Lurker wants the **Mystic Tools**. It will continue to compel its host to keep trying to find them. Should the entire set be found, the Lurker will attempt to kill all the other characters so that it can have the tools for itself.

SHAFT UP TO THE LONG CORRIDOR

A ladder runs up the 30-foot shaft to a hatch in the ceiling that opens into **the Long Corridor** (page 164).

BROTHER

Should the House Die indicate that Brother arrives, the PCs see a lanky, male humanoid figure with hands balled into fists and one eye bulging unnervingly looking down from above, on the ladder. His face shows a sneer, and his shadow doesn't reflect his pose at all, and in fact, seems to hold an axe. Brother wears dark pants and a dark red shirt. His face shows a sneer.

Show the players the image of **Brother**.

His axe-wielding shadow comes into the shadow-filled room and attacks with surprise, granting it a Boon. Brother has a Rating of 6; however, his shadow cannot be harmed except by magic. Brother's physical form can be hurt, but if he is attacked, he will climb up, although he's likely going to hide and ambush anyone who tries to follow him. He can be bribed to leave the PCs alone (this time) with an extremely valuable object, magical device, or very high-tech device, as long as it comes from outside the house. He disappears if slain.

DRONING HALL

s characters get closer to the Tree, they hear an ominous droning sound.

This is one of the rooms described in Secrets of the House as a "building dread" room.

OVERVIEW

This hallway's floor is covered by a ragged green carpet.

DRONING SOUND

This hallway is nothing but bare stone walls and floor, with an arched ceiling. As the characters move down this hall away from the Long Corridor, they begin to hear a droning sound. It might be a machine of some kind or it might be a large number of insects (it is, of course, the latter). It smells of rotting wood.

TO THE TREE

This innocuous door leads to **the Tree** (page 170). It is unlocked.

TO THE LONG CORRIDOR

The corridor bends and connects to **the Long Corridor** (page 164).

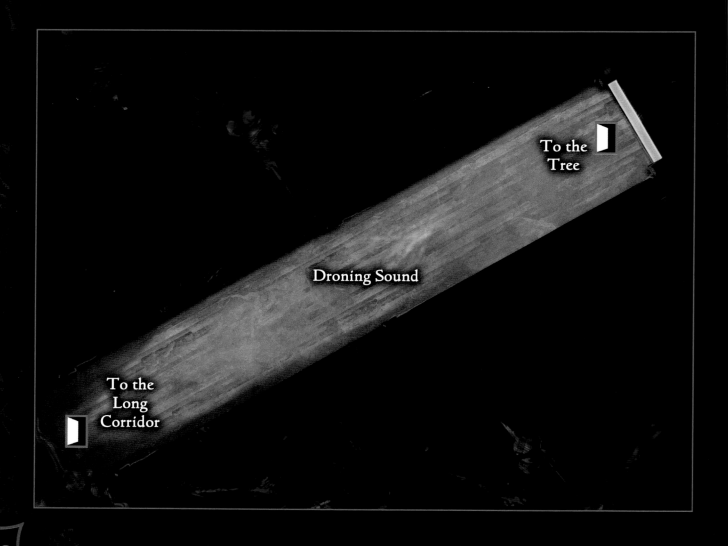

To the Tree

Droning Sound

To the Long Corridor

BROTHER

Should the House Die indicate that Brother arrives, the PCs see a lanky, male humanoid figure with hands balled into fists and one eye bulging unnervingly in the doorway. His face shows a sneer, and his shadow doesn't reflect his pose at all, and in fact, seems to hold an axe. Brother wears dark pants and a dark red shirt.

Show the players the image of **Brother**.

Brother doesn't do much besides lurk in the doorway and smirk, while his shadow comes into the room and attacks with the axe. He has a Rating of 6; however, his shadow cannot be harmed except by magic. Brother's physical form can be hurt, but if he is attacked, he will run off, although he's likely going to hide and ambush anyone who attempts to follow him. He can be bribed to leave the PCs alone (this time) with an extremely valuable object, magical device, or very high-tech device, as long as it comes from outside the house. He disappears if slain.

THE TREE

An undead tree attacks anything alive, sustained by its dead companion who feeds it insects and spiders.

> *The tree hates all that live. It doesn't feed to sustain itself so much as to destroy life.*

OVERVIEW

This room stinks not unlike rotten eggs—like a decaying marsh. A gnarled, black, and leafless tree rises out of the middle of a shallow, brackish pool. The walls are stone and the ceiling is vaulted, but there's no sunlight here. It's no wonder the tree is dead. Insects fly about the room or crawl across the various surfaces.

In the back of the room, a man stands next to a heavy wooden door. He is reaching into a barrel on the ground and pulling out a massive handful of insects and spiders. They swarm over his hand and arm but he seems almost oblivious. The buzzing and flittering of insects in the room is quite loud.

TREE

A thing of pure death and darkness (rather than life and health), the tree is much more akin to the *opposite* of a tree. Its branches reach out to gain sustenance to feed its dark, soggy roots which spread throughout the dank pool. If any living creature larger than an insect comes into the room, the tree moves and stretches its branches toward them. The tree is rooted to its spot, but the branches can move like an octopus's arms. The tree has a Rating of 5, although its resistance to damage has a Rating of 7. If it strikes a character, it immediately grabs them and lifts them in the air, where it attempts to hold them and drain the life from them. On the tree's turn, it can attempt to grab another character (to a maximum of four) and drain all those it is holding. The drain doesn't inflict wounds, but rather lowers the character's Rating by 1. If the character reaches Rating 0, they wither and die. If they escape before this happens, they return to their normal Rating after a few minutes' rest. While drained, however, all of their actions are modified accordingly. They use their new, drained Rating for everything.

THE MAN AND THE INSECTS

The man moves almost like an automaton, seemingly oblivious to what happens around him, always with a blank, glassy stare. It's his role to feed the insects and spiders in the barrel to the tree. He moves jerkily and does not speak (or even respond to speech), but if he or the tree is threatened or damaged, he reacts with immediate violence. When he opens his mouth, his teeth are

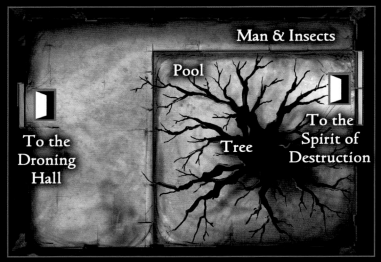

revealed to be keys, and it seems as though there might be something squirming in his throat. He has a Rating of 3, but his primary form of attack is to launch the barrel of stinging, biting insects at a foe. This one-time attack has a Rating of 4 and, if struck, the victim is covered in bugs. Until they are removed (such as with a large amount of water), the character has a Bane, and automatically suffers a Rating 1 wound each time it is their turn.

If the man suffers physical damage, the wound reveals that he is actually a mostly hollow husk of flesh, filled with still more insects. The wound splits open and insects crawl or fly out. This means that anyone inflicting damage upon him automatically suffers a Rating 1 wound. If he is slain, his body just collapses entirely, insects and spiders spilling out everywhere. (Yes, this means that the insects inside him, animating him, are feeding the *other* insects to the tree. It's a cruel ol' world.)

Amid his remains, characters can find the keys that made up his teeth. Most are bent, rusted, worn, or otherwise useless, but two are intact; explorers will find that these keys open the two locked boxes in **the Secret Room** (page 166).

THE POOL

Within the brackish water, the tree's shallow roots are surrounded by a few bones and a very large canid skull, all covered in black slime. Careful study might reveal that it all seems to have sprouted from a single body—probably the midsection of a large dog or wolf. A stubby bone, perhaps a digit, still bears a ring covered in slime.

Once cleaned, the ring gleams gold and is in the shape of the top half of the legendary Medusa's head, so you see her eyes and some of her snaky hair. Her eyes are each a small diamond. The ring is magical. When the wearer touches a living being and wills it to be so, the being turns to stone forever. The ring works once.

THE PAINTING

If the characters bring *Sacred Tree of the Wolf That Bleeds Darkness* from **the Studio** (page 180) and the tree hasn't been destroyed, it will grab the painting in its branches and affix it to the wall in this room. The tree will then gently touch each character on the forehead. They now know that should each of those characters ever—working in concert—call upon the Wolf That Bleeds Darkness, a terrible lupine entity will appear and tear out the throat of a single target indicated by the group. The victim must be corporeal (but not necessarily alive or mortal) and must be Rating 9 or less. The victim dies immediately. Characters that call upon the Wolf That Bleeds Darkness feel a dark uncleanliness well up within them, and will have feral, monstrous dreams for many nights to come.

TO THE DRONING HALL

This innocuous door leads to **the Droning Hall** (page 168). It is unlocked.

TO THE SPIRIT OF DESTRUCTION

The door leading to **the Spirit of Destruction room** (page 172) is locked (Rating 4). The key is lost. When standing by it, one can hear smashing and crashing in the distance, on the other side.

BROTHER

Should the House Die indicate that Brother arrives here, the PCs see a lanky, male humanoid figure with hands balled into fists and one eye bulging unnervingly in the doorway. His face shows a sneer, and his shadow doesn't reflect his pose at all, and in fact, seems to hold an axe. Brother wears dark pants and a dark red shirt.

Show the players the image of **Brother**.

Brother doesn't do much besides lurk in the doorway and smirk, while his shadow comes into the room and attacks with the axe. He has a Rating of 6; however, his shadow cannot be harmed except by magic. Brother's physical form can be hurt, but if he is attacked, he will try to use the doorway or even the tree for cover. The tree will not attack him. He can be bribed to leave the PCs alone (this time) with an extremely valuable object, magical device, or very high-tech device, as long as it comes from outside the house. He disappears if slain.

THE SPIRIT OF DESTRUCTION

A powerful demon has destroyed a whole area of the house, and it wants to destroy more.

The demon's not smart or observant. Careful PCs can slip through this room many times, although there should be some tense moments as they make their way through the wreckage and across the hole without drawing its attention.

OVERVIEW

The door leading to **the Tree room** *(page 170) is locked (Rating 4). The key is lost.*

This is a huge room. It's difficult to make out what its intended use ever was, as it's now haunted by a powerful animating spirit that psychokinetically creates a body for itself from whatever is at hand and then attempts to smash and destroy everything it comes upon, so the chamber now contains little more than rubble and wreckage. Broken masonry, smashed furniture, bent and twisted metal, splinters of wood, broken tools or implements, torn bits of curtain or rug, and so on fill the room. In fact, this was once a number of adjoining rooms, but the dividing walls have been mostly obliterated. The piles of rubble and wreckage create many places for hiding. Some areas appear impassable.

THE SPIRIT

The demon is Rating 6, although it is Rating 7 when it comes to damage and only Rating 5 when it comes to perception. It starts out made primarily of splintered wood and bricks. It is in the middle of the room and won't immediately notice characters at either doorway. The demonic spirit wants to destroy everything. *Everything.* Even the material making up its own form. This means that if someone damages it, it revels in the destruction rather than seeming to be hurt. Track the wounds, but destroying the physical form it gives itself does not truly affect it. It will just make another (which takes only one turn on its part). The new form will be fully healed of wounds, so the demon might make a new body even if its existing form isn't completely destroyed.

The only way to truly harm the demon is with mental or spiritual attacks. However, any of the **Mystic Tools**—even, strangely, the blueprints—can be used as a damaging weapon against this demon, even offering a Boon to attacks and damage. They are forces of creation, and it is a force of destruction, the tools' diametrically opposed opposite. Damage from any of these kinds of attacks cannot be restored by the demon.

THE WRECKAGE

As mentioned, there is enough cover in this room that if the characters just want to try to cross the room and slip past the demon, their stealth actions gain a Boon.

Amid the vast amount of wreckage lies the hammer of the **Mystic Tool** set. This would take at least 10 people hours to find, and that's assuming there's not a terrible demon in the room trying to smash them. If the characters have the blueprints, found in **the Private Study** (page 230), that guide them toward the tools, they will go right to the hammer.

IF THE LURKER IS PRESENT

If the character possessed by the Lurker (from **the Foyer**) is present when the hammer is discovered, it forces the character to act.

The spirit possessing you compels you to grab the hammer and shout, "Mine!"

If this action causes any kind of questioning of the possessed character or their actions, the Lurker yet again compels its host.

The spirit possessing you makes you say, "I'm fine. Don't worry about it. Now, where do you think the rest of these tools might be?"

Obviously, the Lurker wants the **Mystic Tools**. It will continue to compel its host to keep trying to find them. Should the entire set be found, the Lurker will attempt to kill all the other characters so that it can have the tools for itself.

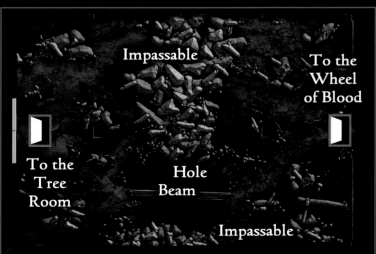

IMPASSABLE AREAS

The areas marked as impassable have a Rating of 8 to try to climb over or dig through.

HOLE

The hole is almost 30 feet deep and is filled with jagged rubble. Falling into it inflicts Rating 7 damage.

THE SINGLE BEAM

Crossing the room is probably going to require making their way across the hole, where there is but a single ceiling beam offering a sort of precarious bridge. The beam is steady, and crossing the beam slowly and carefully without anything stressing the character (like a demon trying to smash them) is only a Rating 2 task. In circumstances where the character is in a hurry or has other concerns, a Rating 5 is probably more apt.

TO THE TREE ROOM

This innocuous door leads to **the Tree** (page 170). It is locked (Rating 4). The key is lost.

TO THE WHEEL OF BLOOD

This innocuous door leads to **the Wheel of Blood** (page 158). It is unlocked.

BROTHER

Should the House Die indicate that Brother arrives, the PCs see a lanky, male humanoid figure with hands balled into fists and one eye bulging unnervingly in the doorway. His face shows a sneer, and his shadow doesn't reflect his pose at all, and in fact, seems to hold an axe. Brother wears dark pants and a dark red shirt.

Show the players the image of **Brother**.

Brother doesn't do much besides lurk in the doorway and smirk, while his shadow comes into the room and attacks with the axe. He may, however, try to alert the demon to the characters' presence or current location any way he can, without actually putting his physical body at risk. Brother has a Rating of 6, and the shadow cannot be harmed except by magic. Brother's physical form can be hurt, but if he is attacked, he will probably run off, although he's likely going to hide and ambush anyone who tries to follow him. He can be bribed to leave the PCs alone (this time) with an extremely valuable object, magical device, or very high-tech device, as long as it comes from outside the house. He disappears if slain. The demon cannot hurt Brother's shadow, but the shadow could hurt the demon—however, why would it want to?

THE RAVENDREAM

lthough it seems like an innocuous room, something horrible lurks quietly in the shadows.

> *It's very unlikely that a character will freely offer the Ravendream their dream. It just sounds too scary.*

OVERVIEW

*The door into this room from the **Long Corridor** (page 164) is locked (Rating 6). The key can be found in **the Foyer** (page 162).*

This chamber looks like a rather large sitting room with quite a lot of seating, although the style and furnishings seem distinct from anything else in the house. In fact, it looks more like a public lounge area than something you'd find in a home. A pair of dark, patterned couches and a low coffee table sit atop a wide, orange, oval rug. A scattering of a dozen or so chairs and a few side tables remain. There is a crumpled piece of paper on one of the couches.

A figure, at first unseen, lurks in the shadows of a bookcase filled with curios. There's a feeling of drowsiness here—not the pleasant feeling of welcome rest, but the heady, dizzying sensation of intoxication.

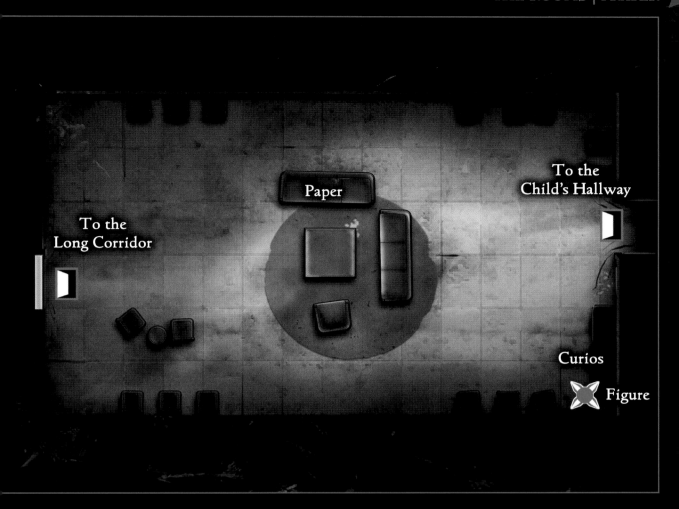

THE FIGURE

Just noticing the man requires that a character state that they're looking around the room and succeed at a Rating 5 task. The character then notices the shadow in the form of a man lurking at the opposite side of the room.

There's something unsettling about the shadowy form (beyond the obvious). While he keeps a humanlike shape, he moves unnaturally, as if he has no bone structure and his body parts aren't fully connected.

Show the players **the Ravendream**.

If anyone approaches him, the man's shadowy form transforms into a conspiracy of ravens. Far more ravens than seems possible. The ravens swarm about the room, buffeting characters and objects with their wings, and scratching with beaks and claws before coming back together on the opposite side of the room, in the form of a man. Then he tries talking to the characters.

If anyone speaks to him, or if he initiates the conversation, he speaks with a multitude of voices at once.

"I – We – Seek – Want – Only – Your – The – Dreams." The voices are shrill and grating, and then whispering. If a character offers their dreams, the Ravendream responds, "Yes – Thank You – Take – What – You – See." Then ask the player what one of their most vivid dreams was. When they describe it (whatever they describe), tell them that the ravens from the being's essence swarm around them for a moment, and then explain that their dream is gone now. They have no memory of it, although they can sense its loss. In return, the character gains the ability to drive Brother away whenever he is encountered. The image of the Ravendream will loom over and behind the character, and Brother will run away, terrified.

It's far more likely that the characters will refuse, or will want more information. Regardless, if no one freely offers their dreams, the Ravendream says, "I – We – Steal – Take – What – You – See – In – By – Your – The – Dream." He then attacks.

FIGHTING THE RAVENDREAM

When he attacks, the Ravendream, who has a Rating of 7, sends forth some of the ravens that comprise his form. This is a magical attack, and if successful, it inflicts mental damage. It also brings one of the victim's nightmares to life.

Ask the character what something from their nightmares would look like, or perhaps who or what it might be. Or, if you don't want to ask such a leading question, just ask, "What was the most recent nightmare your character had?" Consider sending the player a direct message to ask them this so that no one else can hear the answer.

> What was the most recent nightmare your character had?

Have something from the nightmare—a creature or person—appear in the room and describe it to the players. This nightmare entity has a Rating of 5 and lasts only long enough to take a single turn. Regardless of its appearance, it makes a physical attack.

If the Ravendream sustains a wound of Rating 4 or higher, he attempts to flee . . . into the characters' dreams. The ravens swarm about the room, and then are suddenly gone. Everyone must roll to resist a magical attack with a Rating of 7. Those that fail will see the Ravendream again . . . the next time they sleep. He haunts their dreams steadily for weeks, giving them terrible nightmares, but eventually pulls back so that he only makes an appearance once a week or so. Once a week becomes once a month and eventually, his nightmare appearances become very occasional. But they never truly go away.

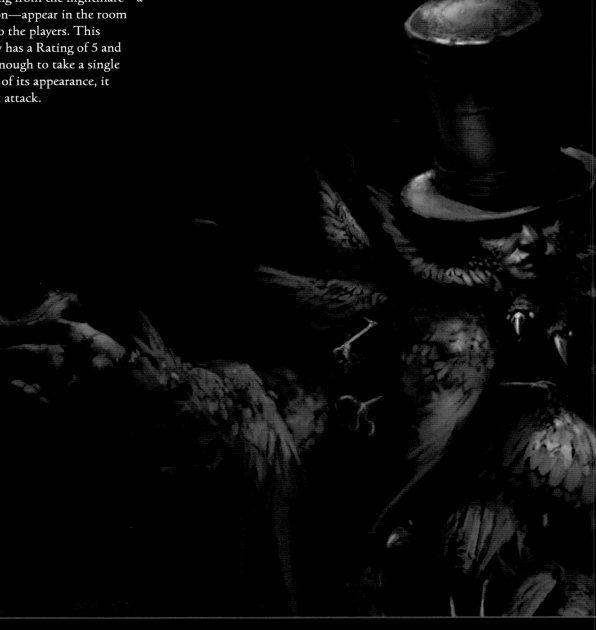

THE CURIOS

On the shelves sit miscellaneous and perhaps even tacky little ceramic figurines of animals with too-big eyes, children with large round heads, and mythical beasts like unicorns and dragons. Amid them is a small box of carved marble, just big enough to store a small brooch. The brooch is made of silver, with an inset ivory face. When wearing the brooch during a financial transaction, the character can ask one thing of the person they're bargaining with, and get what they ask for, even if it's an expensive item for free. (The GM of course is free to put any limitations on this they want.) The brooch is probably worth $150 otherwise.

THE PIECE OF PAPER

This appears to be a page torn from a book, perhaps a personal journal. Show the players **Remnant 7** (page 275).

TO THE LONG CORRIDOR

This innocuous door leads to **the Long Corridor** (page 164). It is unlocked.

TO THE CHILD'S HALLWAY

This opening leads directly into **the Child's Hallway** (page 178).

BROTHER

Brother will not enter this room. If the House Die indicates that he should arrive, he comes to the doorway, looks at the Ravendream, and flees, saying, "No, stay away! Not again!" The implication is clear that Brother and the Ravendream have come into conflict before, or that the Ravendream has somehow hurt or tormented Brother in the past. The Ravendream might simply be something that escaped Brother's nightmares long ago.

THE CHILD'S HALLWAY

To the
Dog Room

To the
Familiar Room

To the
Ravendream

Child's Laughter

To the
Nursery

THE STUDIO

To the Child's Hallway

Paintings

Paint

Blank
Canvas

Within an art studio, a being of pure artistic creativity waits, hungry for existence, seeking to duplicate and take over a character.

> *Characters who gain the ability to call upon the Wolf That Bleeds Darkness basically have a "get out of jail free" card, allowing them to essentially win one encounter, assuming they face a single foe of the right Rating. Let this be okay. They've earned it.*

OVERVIEW

*The door to this room is locked (Rating 6). The key can be found in **the Foyer** (page 162), though the three-stemmed key in **the Long Corridor** (page 164) side table also works.*

An easel, a cart covered with small pots of paint, and several canvases—some blank, others painted upon— mark this room to be an art studio. It seems to have been used fairly recently. No dust, and while the paint on the canvases is dry, some appear to be recently created. The wooden floor is spattered with paint of all colors and there's a smell of turpentine in the air.

THE PAINT

The paint is still fresh in the sealed pots. It has an odd smell, and if such a thing can be determined, one discovers that each is mixed with human blood.

THE PAINTINGS

There are a pair of unfinished paintings that seem recent, but it's not possible to determine their subjects. Two of the paintings are finished.

One is labeled *Tomorrow's Girls* on the back. It's a rather simplistic painting of little girls playing in a park. It's nothing special. This is a palimpsest, however. If the paint is carefully removed, the painting beneath is a scene of grisly horror, with a beheaded priest presiding over a religious ritual for skeletal figures. This painting, if brought to **the Secret Chapel** (page 218), grants a dark blessing over all characters present. Each is fully healed, and gains a Boon to all actions until they next sleep. However, they can feel a dark, unsettling energy coursing through their bodies. Those who are religious or spiritual in any way will need to eventually spend some time and energy ridding themselves of this taint, but that is likely a part of a story well outside the bounds of the Darkest House.

Show the players the following image.

The other is labeled *Sacred Tree of the Wolf That Bleeds Darkness*. It seems to be religious in nature, but dark and bloody. A tree springs from the back of a wolf with stained glass windows behind (each showing either a horrendous, almost draconic wolf, or castles or houses inhabited by monstrous entities). There are grave markers and robed figures as well. If the characters take the painting to **the Tree** (page 170) and the tree still (or once again) lives, it will grab the painting in its branches and affix it to the wall in that room. The tree will then gently touch each character present on the forehead. They know that now, should each of those characters ever—working in concert—call upon the Wolf That Bleeds Darkness, a terrible lupine entity will appear and tear out the throat of a single target indicated by the group. The victim must be corporeal (but not necessarily alive or mortal) and must be Rating 9 or less. The victim dies immediately. Characters that call upon the Wolf That Bleeds Darkness feel a dark uncleanliness well up within them, and will have feral, monstrous dreams for many nights to come.

Show the players the following image.

THE DUPLICATE

If a character stares overlong at a blank canvas (for example, if they were considering painting something to go in the empty frame in **the Gallery** [page 106]), a mystical entity without form or substance confronts them. There is nothing to see or hear, so to speak. Instead, the character simply senses that there is something without form or identity that wants to duplicate them. This is a spirit of creativity, a creation not yet created. It is something that is not yet anything, waiting for and craving existence so much that it is going to create itself, and it would like the character's help. It wants to duplicate them.

The duplicate wants to *be* the character, but it has no context other than what it perceives right at that moment. Appearance is relatively easy. Voice is also relatively simple. Thoughts and motivations are hard. The character can feel deep within their essence a question.

> Do not yet share this with the other players. You sense something. It hangs in this studio like a spark of creativity that has not yet been seized upon. This is something that wants to exist, and it wants your help. You can feel it asking you to give yourself to it. It wants to become you. All it wants is your memories, your thoughts, and your feelings. Do you give them?

If the character refuses, or asks for clarification, the duplicate attempts to take what it wants by force. It has a Rating of 5.

> Resist a mental attack. It has a Rating of 5, so your target number is 12. Reply only to me to tell me if you fail or succeed.

If the character cannot resist, it drains them of their emotions and their past.

> Quickly and horrifically, you are drained of all your emotions and your past. You're nothing but a burnt-out husk who can't even remember how to stand. However, the spirit creates a duplicate of you, for itself, with everything you are and all the mundane equipment you normally have. The duplicate is going to emerge from the canvas and paint in this room, and you need to play as the duplicate now. You need to insist that the drooling body on the ground is meaningless, and the duplicate is the real you. And for all intents and purposes, it is. This doesn't change anything about your character mechanically or narratively, other than inside you know you're a duplicate and you don't want anyone else to know that.

If the character succeeds in resisting, the spirit fills their mind with horrific pain and images of terrible suffering. The character feels as though this will continue until the duplicate gets what it wants.

> You have managed to hang on to the core of your own essence, but at a terrible cost. Your body is wracked with pain and your mind is filled with horrific images of suffering. You get the sense that this entity or spirit wants you to submit or it will continue.

The character can choose to succumb. Doing so puts all the pain and suffering to an end. The character's entire being is replicated, so—after a fashion—they continue to exist. But they are an alien entity as well.

> The pain and the horrifying images fade as it drains you of all your emotions and your past. You're nothing but a burnt-out husk who can't even remember how to stand. However, the spirit creates a duplicate of you, for itself, with everything you are and all the mundane equipment you normally have. The duplicate is going to emerge from the canvas and the paint in this room, and you need to play as the duplicate now. You need to insist that the drooling body on the ground is meaningless, and the duplicate is the real you. And for all intents and purposes, it is. This doesn't change anything about your character mechanically or narratively, other than inside you know you're a duplicate and you don't want anyone else to know that. Maybe you can tell the others that you tapped into a magical ability of the canvas, and the comatose body on the ground is a failed attempt at creating a duplicate that you could have controlled or something equally potentially believable.

If the character won't submit, the entity gives up and it won't return. The character's pain fades, as it was all illusory to begin with. They are not hurt, and are free to act as they wish.

LIVING AS A DUPLICATE

If the duplicate got what it wanted, everyone in the room sees energy and matter flow out of the paint jars, the brushes, and the canvas to form a new character. Meanwhile, the old character slumps to the floor, drooling and dead-eyed.

A player whose character is now a duplicate can act as they want. They can go about the rest of their life, with no one else the wiser. The player knows that their character is not really the same character they originally played, but no one else needs to. However, their friends in the studio might be confused or alarmed at the body that looks just like their companion in a vegetative state on the floor. If the player of the duplicate can't persuade them to just leave and not worry about the thing on the floor, you might have to suggest to the player that they try to slip away somehow. Like any living creature, the duplicate will fight to survive. If you don't want to play out a fight between player characters, however, you can just say that the duplicate is eventually overcome. In any event, if the duplicate is slain, they just become a paint stain on the floor, and the memories, emotions, and essence return to the original character.

Keep in mind, however, that unbeknownst to the player, **this will always be true**. If the characters accept the duplicate and continue on, then if the duplicate dies, it becomes just a pool of paint on the ground; the actual character is still in the studio in the Darkest House, even if the group is long gone from the house at that point. (There's a reason to have to return to the house after the characters get out if there ever was one.)

IF THE LURKER IS PRESENT

Ooh, boy. If the Lurker introduced in **the Foyer** (page 162) is present, and its host is the one getting duplicated, it doesn't get to go into the duplicate. Thus, it's stuck in the vegetative character on the floor. After a few moments, though, it will assert enough control to make the character stand (perhaps a bit awkwardly) and insist that *they* are the real character (which is technically true!). Except the Lurker doesn't have the character's memories or personality, and the duplicate does. So it's very likely that the group will subdue or slay the Lurker in the PC's body, which means that if the duplicate dies, the character is really gone. The Lurker, however, is still in the house. It doesn't die if its host dies.

IF THE LURKER IS IN THE HOUSE

The Lurker will happily possess the cast-off character after they've been duplicated. However, the Lurker will wait until the characters have left the studio. Now there's a possessed version of one of the PCs moving about the house, probably looking for the **Mystic Tools**, and likely going to run into the group later. Have fun with that.

TO THE CHILD'S HALLWAY

The door into this room from **the Child's Hallway** (page 178) is locked (Rating 6). The key can be found in **the Foyer** (page 162), though the three-stemmed key in the side table in the Long Corridor also works.

However, the character unlocking the door with the three-stemmed key must immediately face ghostly hands that tear through the veil of our world and grab for them with a cold, numbing clutch. The hands have a Rating of 5. Should they strike, they grasp the character by the throat and begin to strangle them, automatically inflicting a Rating 5 wound each turn the character does not get free of them. If the character does get free, the hands disappear. This happens each time the wrong key is used in one of these three locks. Worse, each time, the Rating of the ghostly hands increases by 1. The appearance of these hands might be a Rating 2 shock (attack inflicting mental damage) for everyone present.

BROTHER

Should the House Die indicate that Brother arrives, the PCs see a lanky, male humanoid figure with hands balled into fists and one eye bulging unnervingly in the doorway. His face shows a sneer, and his shadow doesn't reflect his pose at all, and in fact, seems to hold an axe. Brother wears dark pants and a dark red shirt.

Show the players the image of **Brother**.

Brother doesn't do much besides lurk in the doorway and smirk, while his shadow comes into the room and attacks with the axe. Brother has a Rating of 6; however, the shadow cannot be harmed except by magic. Brother's physical form can be hurt, but if he is attacked, he will try to use the doorway or furniture for cover and may even run off, although he's likely going to hide and ambush anyone who tries to follow him. He can be bribed to leave the PCs alone (this time) with an extremely valuable object, magical device, or very high-tech device, as long as it comes from outside the house. He disappears if slain.

THE FAMILIAR ROOM (FRATER)

This room is different from the others, as its details are dictated by the background of one or more of the PCs.

An NPC trapped in this room offers a fantastic way to bring in a new PC, should that need arise in the course of playing through the scenario.

OVERVIEW

The doors into this room are locked (Rating 6). The key can be found in the Foyer (page 162). The same key works in both doors, though the three-stemmed key in the side table in the Long Corridor (page 164) also works.

This room is a location from the past of at least one of the characters. It is unmistakably their childhood bedroom, a prison cell where they were incarcerated, the taproom from a bar they used to frequent, a training dojo where they studied, or the library where they first saw an early crush. Or someplace else. The important thing is, it is not a replica—it's actually that room. The details might have changed somewhat, but that's only because time has passed. Or, it might look precisely as if they had just left it. It comes complete with furnishings, but any windows look out into pitch blackness. There are no occupants.

FITTING THE ROOM IN

The room needs to conform to the needs of the map. In other words, where the diagram shows entrances and exits, the room needs to have them as well. It must have a door that connects to the Long Corridor (page 164) and one that connects to the Child's Hallway (page 178). If the original room didn't have the same exits, it appears the way it did originally, but you must modify the room as needed with new, hidden doors, or original doors that no longer open. A secret panel might slide to reveal an exit where there wasn't one originally, or a now extraneous door cannot be opened, or perhaps leads to a solid black wall through which passage is impossible.

COORDINATING WITH OTHER FAMILIAR ROOMS

There are two other similar rooms in the house (possibly more if the PCs explore the Backrooms). They are always different rooms, and very likely they are from the past of a different character. What happens when PCs visit a familiar room depends not on which room they discover, but the order in which the PCs discover them.

The first time the PCs come to a familiar room, it is just that—nothing more.

The second time the PCs come to a (different) familiar room, it is as the character acquainted with the room remembers it, but there is blood on the floor or perhaps on the furniture. Some recognizable memento of an NPC associated with this room can be found near or in the blood.

The third time the PCs come to a (different) familiar room, it is different because it is occupied. The PC acquainted with the room recognizes the NPC; they're someone the PC would normally expect to find in this room (in a world outside the house).

The NPC is just as surprised to see the PC, whom they likewise recognize. Their shock is quite genuine. "What are you doing here?"

From the NPC's point of view, they are still in the room where the room should be. They aren't in the Darkest House. When the NPC looks through the entrance the PCs came through, they don't see where the PCs have been, but rather where the original room's entrance would normally lead.

This changes if a PC attempts to persuade the NPC to come through one of the exits of the room (or tries to force them to do so). In this eventuality, the NPC is now in the Darkest House, trapped there alongside the PCs. It doesn't matter if they go back into the familiar room. The NPC is now with the PCs, and likely in a lot of danger.

There is no way to reverse this process. A character within the Darkest House cannot escape through a familiar room, and all effects of being in the house still apply while within.

As long as the NPC remains in the familiar room, it's impossible to convince them that they aren't where they appear to be (because in a very technical sense, they are where they appear to be). The safest and kindest thing would, in fact, be to leave them where they are. Should the PCs leave and return, the NPC is gone.

DOOR TO THE LONG CORRIDOR

The door into this room from **the Long Corridor** (page 164) is locked (Rating 6). The key can be found in **the Foyer** (page 162), though the three-stemmed key in the side table in **the Long Corridor** also works.

However, the character unlocking the door with the three-stemmed key must immediately face ghostly hands that tear through the veil of our world and grab for them with a cold, numbing clutch. The hands have a Rating of 5. Should they strike, they grasp the character by the throat and begin to strangle them, automatically inflicting a Rating 5 wound each turn the character does not get free of them. If the character does get free, the hands disappear. This happens each time the wrong key is used in one of these three locks. Worse, each time, the Rating of the ghostly hands increases by 1. The appearance of these hands might be a Rating 2 shock (attack inflicting mental damage) for everyone present.

DOOR TO THE CHILD'S HALLWAY

The door into this room from **the Child's Hallway** (page 178) is locked (Rating 6). The key can be found in **the Foyer** (page 162), though the three-stemmed key in the side table in **the Long Corridor** (page 164) also works.

However, the character unlocking the door with the three-stemmed key must immediately face ghostly hands that tear through the veil of our world and grab for them with a cold, numbing clutch. The hands have a Rating of 5. Should they strike, they grasp the character by the throat and begin to strangle them, automatically inflicting a Rating 5 wound each turn the character does not get free of them. If the character does get free, the hands disappear. This happens each time the wrong key is used in one of these three locks. Worse, each time, the Rating of the ghostly hands increases by 1. The appearance of these hands might be a Rating 2 shock (attack inflicting mental damage) for everyone present.

BROTHER

Should the House Die indicate that Brother arrives, the PCs see a lanky, male humanoid figure with hands balled into fists and one eye bulging unnervingly in the doorway. His face shows a sneer, and his shadow doesn't reflect his pose at all, and in fact, seems to hold an axe. Brother wears dark pants and a dark red shirt.

Show the players the image of **Brother**.

Brother doesn't do much besides lurk in the doorway and smirk, while his shadow comes into the room and attacks with the axe. Brother has a Rating of 6; however, the shadow cannot be harmed except by magic. Brother's physical form can be hurt, but if he is attacked, he will try to use the doorway or furniture for cover and may even run off, although he's likely going to hide and ambush anyone who tries to follow him. He can be bribed to leave the PCs alone (this time) with an extremely valuable object, magical device, or very high-tech device, as long as it comes from outside the house. He disappears if slain.

THE DOG

Got to rescue the dog, people.

> *Buddy is here to tug at heartstrings. Most people can handle a fictional person in danger, but not a dog. They're going to want to protect the dog.*

OVERVIEW

This is a bedroom, probably of a teenage boy. Pictures of armored warriors striking battle poses and stylish automobiles racing down the road cover the walls. Sports equipment, building toys, and a few books (fantasy fiction) clutter the carpeted floor. Furnishings include an unmade bed, a dresser with open drawers stuffed with clothing, and a desk cluttered with more toys, a trophy or two, and a notebook. Though there's no sign of an occupant at the moment, it looks like it could easily be in use currently.

UNDER THE BED

A dog cowers under the bed. It's an honest-to-god dog, that got trapped here in the house as the rooms expanded, shifted, and devoured rooms in other places. He has a collar with a name tag that reads, "Buddy." Buddy has a Rating of 3. If coaxed out (perhaps with some food) and treated with kindness, he quickly forms a bond with one or more of the PCs. He will accompany them and try to help in very dog ways: barking to alert them of surprise dangers, growling to intimidate obvious dangers, and charging in to attack if that seems a good option (he's not an idiot, though). He can't, however, understand commands beyond "sit," "stay," and "shake."

Finding Buddy automatically heals any character of their current lowest Rating mental wound.

Buddy has no connection to this room or any former occupant—it's just where he found a decent place to hide.

To the
Child's Hallway

Secret
Passage

Bed

Notebook

NOTEBOOK

This lined, spiral-bound notebook is filled with what looks like math homework in the front, but toward the end, each page just has scrawled in dark letters one of the following phrases: *I hate you. I will kill you. I'm better than you.* Each is repeated many times.

SECRET PASSAGE

A wall panel low to the ground near the dresser pries away with a bit of force and probably something to pry with, like a knife or a screwdriver (or, of course, a prybar). The panel is only 3 feet to a side, and reveals a tunnel about that wide of rough wooden planks on the floor, walls, and ceiling. Obviously, most characters will have to crawl. The passage proceeds to twist and turn back on itself more than once, eventually coming out (impossibly) in the vestibule of **the Secret Chapel** (page 218).

TO THE CHILD'S HALLWAY

This innocuous door leads to **the Child's Hallway** (page 178). It is unlocked.

BROTHER

Should the House Die indicate that Brother arrives, the PCs see a lanky, male humanoid figure with hands balled into fists and one eye bulging unnervingly in the doorway. His face shows a sneer, and his shadow doesn't reflect his pose at all, and in fact, seems to hold an axe. Brother wears dark pants and a dark red shirt.

Show the players the image of **Brother**.

Brother doesn't do much besides lurk in the doorway and smirk, while his shadow comes into the room and attacks with the axe. **Horrifically, he attacks Buddy first if possible.** Brother has a Rating of 6; however, his shadow cannot be harmed except by magic. Brother's physical form can be hurt, but if he is attacked, he will try to use the doorway or furniture for cover and may even run off, although he's likely going to hide and ambush anyone who tries to follow him. He can be bribed to leave the PCs alone (this time) with an extremely valuable object, magical device, or very high-tech device, as long as it comes from outside the house. He disappears if slain.

A place for a young child to grow, but the Darkest House is growing something else there.

If the monstrous infant scuttling about like a roach doesn't have your players screaming in horror and disgust, you're not doing your job. Make this a memorable scene.

OVERVIEW

A pleasant little nursery where a baby would have been kept, although it's clearly been a long time. There's a crib, a changing table, and a rocking chair. It's dusty with a cobweb or two. The walls have some happy images painted on them, although the paint is faded.

CRIB

There is a stitched cloth doll of the Smiling Man here, very similar to the one that Sister carries.

Changing Table

To the Child's Hallway

Tumor

Crib

Rocking Chair

CHANGING TABLE

In a drawer is a book. The cover has a happy drawing of a family, and the title is, in fact, *Happy Family*. Inside, every page bears the same sing-song verse. Show the players **Remnant 11** (page 278).

ROCKING CHAIR

It occasionally rocks of its own accord, and squeaks a bit. Because of course it does.

THE TUMOR

A huge tumor grows on the wall above the crib. Its nasty vein-like extensions reach outward and anchor it to the wall, but also crawl down into the crib, like ivy vines growing on a structure. The tumor emits a horrific red-orange light from within. However, this is all invisible unless the PCs are specifically searching behind the crib. Then, suddenly, it's just there and they all see it. It throbs with unsettling life and power.

Show the players this version of the room image.

If there's any attempt at all to harm the tumor, it will act to defend itself with psychic powers. The tumor is Rating 7. It is impossible to miss, so no attack roll is needed, but it is Rating 8 to resist damage. The tumor can use any two of the following powers on its turn:

- ✦ **Telekinetic Thrust:** A victim is tossed backward against the wall, hard.
- ✦ **Telekinetic Grab:** An object in the room lifts up (perhaps from a PC's possession) and hurls itself at a victim.
- ✦ **Telepathic Stab:** A victim's mind overloads and they suffer mental damage.
- ✦ **Mental Confusion:** A victim intending on attacking the tumor attacks another PC instead.

If the tumor is destroyed, it bursts with dark fluids, blood, and pus. A horrifically misshapen **monstrous infant** drops out of it, either into the crib or onto the floor.

Show the players the image of the monstrous infant.

CARING FOR THE MONSTROUS INFANT

Torn from the tumor, the infant cries and wails, and reaches for anyone that comes near with its tiny hands dripping with blood and far more disgusting things.

If a character takes pity upon it and tries to care for it, the monstrous infant attacks with a vicious blood-draining bite, revealing a mouth full of viperfish-like teeth. This immediately is a Rating 4 mental attack on everyone present from the shock and horror.

The infant has a Rating of 4, defends itself with a Rating of 5, and makes its initial attack with a Boon. Its bite, if successful, continues to inflict damage each turn as it hangs on and drinks blood. Consuming blood restores it to full health, so it's unlikely that damaging it will get it off—the victim or their friends will need to tear the baby away.

If not biting a victim, the baby skitters around the nursery like a cockroach, clinging to the walls or the ceiling as easily as the floor. If able to hide under the crib, the table, or the rocking chair, it launches another attack (with a Boon) to re-establish its draining bite.

If clearly in trouble, it will try to scuttle out of the room down the hallway, and then hide elsewhere. It's twice as fast as a human adult when it flees.

Important: If the Lurker is possessing the infant, it does not attack a caregiver. It tries to get them to raise it. This very likely has long-term campaign implications.

DESTROYING THE MONSTROUS INFANT

If, before the monstrous infant even attacks, a character decides that it should be destroyed as the abomination it most certainly is, they get one damage roll before the infant begins to fight back. If the character slays the infant, they are tortured with nightmares in the coming weeks, and wake up certain that people can tell that they are a "babykiller." They become obsessed with the guilt, and the term "babykiller" and will probably need some kind of therapy.

IF THE LURKER IS PRESENT

If a character is possessed by the Lurker, it will do everything it can to protect the tumor. In fact, it will make the PC try to steer the group away from or out of this room altogether. The tumor is its fallback plan. Eventually, the Lurker hopes to inhabit it, and use the developing infant within as a permanent body for itself.

If the infant is revealed, the Lurker leaves the character and enters the infant, hoping that someone will take pity on it. If they do, it just bides its time in its new body. If they don't, it goes back out into the dark void around the house and waits for someone to let it in again.

IF THE LURKER IS IN THE HOUSE

If the Lurker is loose in the house, it will come to the Nursery eventually. It tries to inhabit the tumor, to dwell within it, and use the developing infant within as a permanent body for itself. If it can't pull this off, it will try to get the Mystic Tools to build itself some kind of body.

If the infant is revealed, the Lurker enters the infant, hoping that someone will take pity on it. If they do, it just bides its time in its new body. If they don't, it goes back out into the dark void around the house and waits for someone to let it in again.

TO THE CHILD'S HALLWAY

This innocuous door leads to **the Child's Hallway** (page 178). It is unlocked.

BROTHER

Should the House Die indicate that Brother arrives, the PCs see a lanky, male humanoid figure with hands balled into fists and one eye bulging unnervingly in the doorway. His face shows a sneer, and his shadow doesn't reflect his pose at all, and in fact, seems to hold an axe. Brother wears dark pants and a dark red shirt.

Show the players the image of **Brother**.

Brother doesn't do much besides lurk in the doorway and smirk, while his shadow comes into the room and attacks with the axe. Brother has a Rating of 6, and the shadow cannot be harmed except by magic. Brother's physical form can be hurt, but if he is attacked, he will probably run off, although he's likely going to hide and ambush anyone who tries to follow him. He can be bribed to leave the PCs alone (this time) with an extremely valuable object, magical device, or very high-tech device, as long as it comes from outside the house. He disappears if slain.

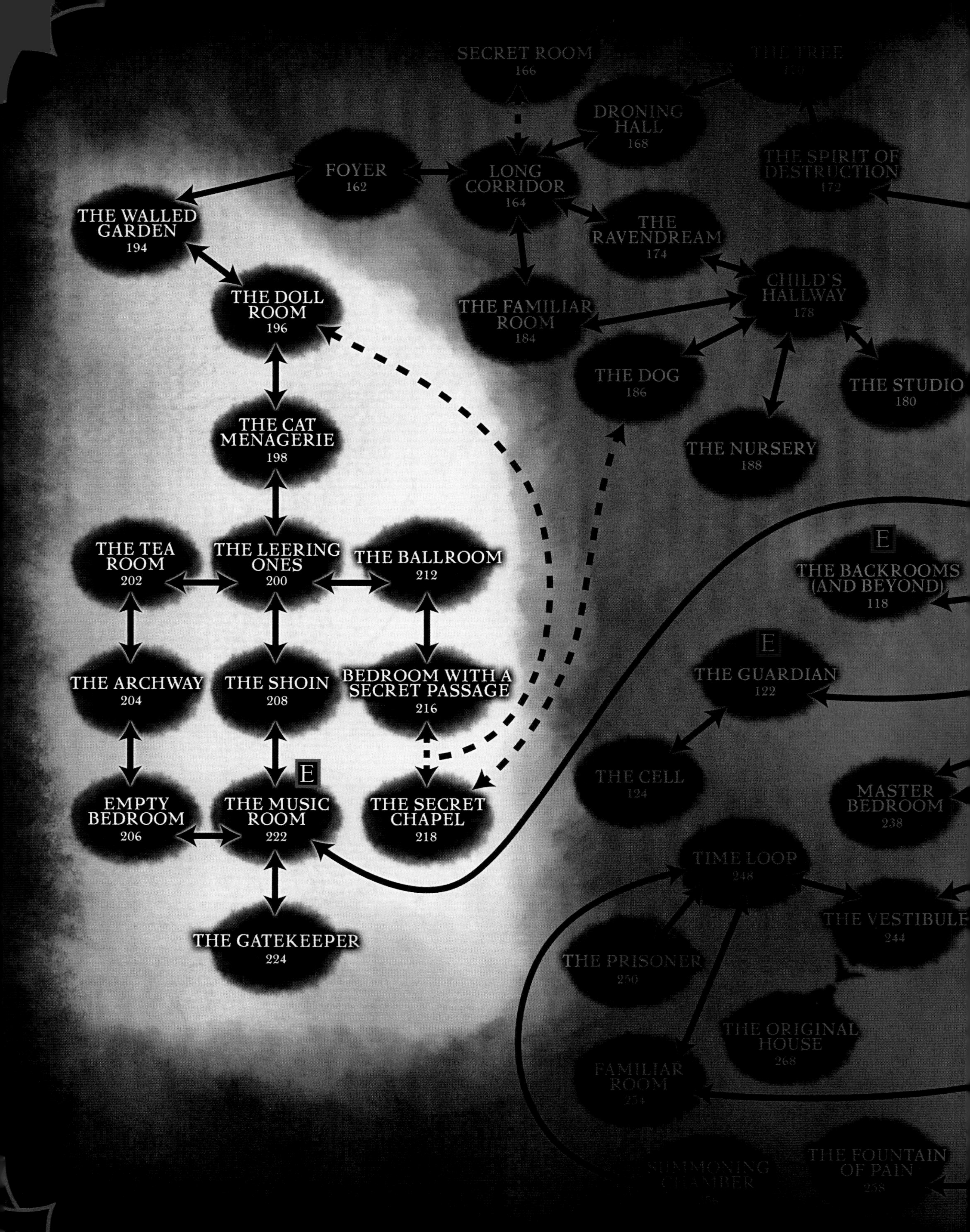

SECRET ROOM
166

THE TREE

DRONING
HALL
168

THE SPIRIT OF
DESTRUCTION
172

FOYER
162

LONG
CORRIDOR
164

THE WALLED
GARDEN
194

THE
RAVENDREAM
174

CHILD`S
HALLWAY
178

THE DOLL
ROOM
196

THE FAMILIAR
ROOM
184

THE DOG
186

THE STUDIO
180

THE CAT
MENAGERIE
198

THE NURSERY
188

THE TEA
ROOM
202

THE LEERING
ONES
200

THE BALLROOM
212

E
THE BACKROOMS
(AND BEYOND)
118

THE ARCHWAY
204

THE SHOIN
208

BEDROOM WITH A
SECRET PASSAGE
216

E
THE GUARDIAN
122

THE CELL
124

MASTER
BEDROOM
238

EMPTY
BEDROOM
206

E
THE MUSIC
ROOM
222

THE SECRET
CHAPEL
218

TIME LOOP
248

THE VESTIBULE
244

THE GATEKEEPER
224

THE PRISONER
250

THE ORIGINAL
HOUSE
268

FAMILIAR
ROOM
254

SUMMONING
CHAMBER

THE FOUNTAIN
OF PAIN
258

THE NARROW
STAIRCASE
146

PARLOR
130

THE
GREENHOUSE
148

THE SITTING
ROOM
140

THE GRAND
STAIRCASE
128

THE WHEEL
OF BLOOD
158

THE DINING
ROOM
136

WINE CELLAR
142

THE STOREROOM
150

THE DRIPPING
ROOM
156

THE ATTIC
144

THE ARMORY
ROOM
154

E
GREAT HALL
114

THE ARMORY
112

THE INTERIOR
COURTYARD
102

THE CELLAR
104

PSYCHOMANTEUM
240

THE GALLERY

SHADOWY
HALLWAY
100

THE BLUE
CORRIDOR
236

A STOREROOM
OF SORTS
110

THE TROPHY
ROOM
98

PRIVATE STUDY
234

HIDDEN
ELEVATOR

THE FAMILIAR
ROOM
94

LYING IN STATE
96

THE TWISTED
ROOM
242

MEDITATION
CHAMBER
230

LIGHTLESS
HALL
84

HALLS OF
THE PAINED
260

THE RED ROOM
262

THE LIVING
ROOM
82

SOROR

THE WALLED GARDEN

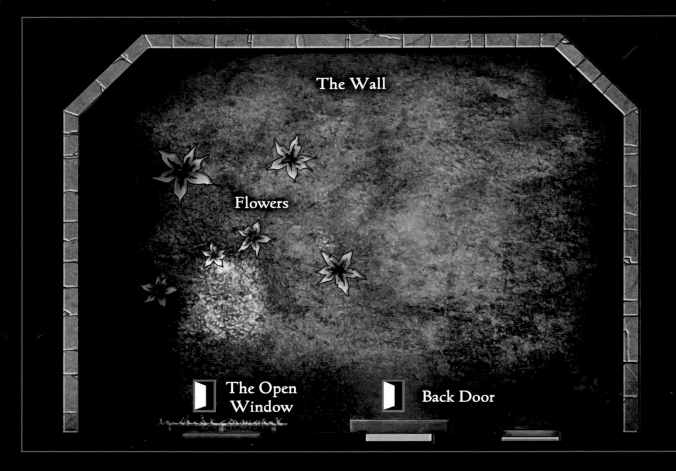

A back garden, overgrown and infested with deadly carnivorous flowers, but with two different ways into the house.

If there is no walled garden, but there is a back door, the PCs go straight into the Foyer. If there is a garden, they have the choice of going in through the back door, or up the trellis and in through the Doll Room window.

OVERVIEW

A 7-foot stone wall, overgrown with ivy and moss, wet with cold dew, surrounds a garden. If the characters enter the Darkest House by going over the garden wall, they find themselves here. It is an ill-tended, overgrown garden, with six very large, gorgeous pink and white flowers amid the grass and weeds. The flowers have such short stems they almost seem to sit upon the ground.

A back door leads into the house. There is also a high open window with faint light coming from it. An ivy-covered trellis runs up the side of the house below it.

Regardless of what time it was or what the weather was like before the characters climbed over the wall, now the sky is black as a cast iron pan, with a gibbous red moon placed high above the horizon. (This is what characters see if they enter the garden from inside the house as well, regardless of the time of day.)

BACK DOOR

This innocuous door leads to **the Foyer** (page 162). It is unlocked.

THE WALL

From the outside, it's easy to climb up and over. The wall is indestructible just like the rest of the outside of the house.

From within the garden, the wall is impossible to climb. Or rather, it's just as easy to climb as it was, but the climber always ends up back in the garden. This is true even if a character jumps, flies, or magically moves through the wall.

FLOWERS

The flowers smell sweet. Each bloom is almost 8 inches across. The only surprising thing is that they are extremely resilient. The petals seem to have the strength of leather. Okay, there is one other surprising thing—if you harm them, they shiver.

THE OPEN WINDOW

Climbing the trellis is easy, as is climbing through the window. Those peering into the window can clearly see **the Doll Room** (page 196), which is where the window will take them.

ENTERING THE GARDEN FROM WITHIN THE HOUSE

Should the PCs return to the garden at any time, or enter the garden from inside the house, the flowers begin to bloom more fully, rising out of the ground as they do. This reveals their true, monstrous nature: each bloom is actually the crest of a serpentine creature with a human face and dozens of pairs of grasping, segmented arms.

These six bloom guardians rasp in terrible voices, through clicking mouths filled with far too many teeth. If damaged, they shiver and scream like children. They are Rated 4, and have a Rating 5 resistance to damage due to their armorlike flesh. When they attack, they do so by grasping a foe and biting, all in one terrible motion.

Their bite is venomous, so all wounds they inflict are rated +2 higher than normal. (To be clear, this doesn't improve the Rating of the attack, only the Rating of a wound they inflict.) Being poisoned feels like someone pushing hard on your eyes . . . from behind them.

SISTER

Sister doesn't come into the garden.

THE DOLL ROOM

A room filled with creepy dolls turns out not to be at all what it appears, but rather a relatively safe haven.

Play up the creepiness, particularly if one or more of the players seem disturbed by lots of staring dolls.

OVERVIEW

The walls are wallpapered in pink and white. A bed covered in dolls and stuffed animals is pushed against one wall. A high shelf runs the perimeter of the room, loaded with more ceramic and plastic-faced dolls. A white wooden dresser with drawers is likewise covered in various dolls. Are they staring at you as you come in? Or is it just your imagination?

THE DOLLS

In truth, the dolls present no danger. There's no force possessing them, and they don't move on their own. However, a very careful search (Rating 5) reveals that two of the dolls have had their heads switched. Similarly, one of the same two dolls bears the arm of a third, and that third doll has the other doll's arm. If both the correct head and arm are attached to this doll—a sturdy, hard plastic and wood girl in a dark blue dress—she can move and act, but only upon the command of the one that put her right. She cannot speak, but she can move at about half the speed of a person, she can climb surprisingly well, and she can perform simple actions like pick up a relatively light object, or pull a lever. She cannot make attacks, and if she suffers a wound of Rating 3 or higher, she is destroyed (she ignores lesser wounds, although her face might gain a crack or an eye might fall out).

The other thing that can be found if the dolls are searched is a folded piece of paper: a letter.

Window

To the
Cat Menagerie

THE LETTER

The paper seems old and worn. Show the players **Remnant 10** (page 277).

SAFE HAVEN

No entity of the house will enter this room. The PCs could retreat to this room and be relatively safe.

WINDOW

This open window looks down into **the Walled Garden** (page 194). A trellis is easily climbed down into the garden.

TO THE CAT MENAGERIE

The door to the Cat Menagerie (page 198) is locked from the inside. A simple deadbolt handle unlocks it.

SISTER

Sister will not enter this room.

THE CAT MENAGERIE

ozens of cats guard a partially hidden corpse, which wears a valuable necklace.

Don't worry too much about the practical logistics of being swallowed by a giant cat and spit up by a normal-sized cat. Instead, play up how disturbing and disgusting it all is.

To the Doll Room

To the Leering Ones

OVERVIEW

Furniture crowds this room. Stools, tables of different sizes and heights, chairs, benches, chifforobes, dressers, a small couch, and a mattress propped against one wall. While it's possible to navigate a path through this room, doing so would be slow and likely difficult. Certainly, this would be an impossible room for a person to use in any fashion.

But that's not the point. This room is full of cats. Dozens of them. They perch upon all the furniture (as well as sit on the floor) and stare silently at any intruders, moving only a little. Perhaps not surprisingly, the room is filled with cat hair and dander and smells of piss. In the distance, faint music can be heard.

THE CATS

The cats avoid contact with all other creatures, but never run too far. When not approached, they only stare. Each cat is Rating 1, but taken together they are as a Rating 6 (8 to control, persuade, or direct in any way). However, if one of the cats is caught or harmed in any way, the offending character is attacked by some invisible force. This force has a Rating of 6, and if it successfully strikes, it doesn't inflict a wound. Instead, it swallows the victim. To the other characters, it seems as if the affected character is pulled up into the air and their body disappears, starting at the top and moving quickly downward. (If the attack fails, the victim just feels something large brush against them. There are no further attacks, unless a character catches or harms a cat again.)

The character is now *inside* one of the cats in the room. Moments after they were swallowed, one of the cats in the room begins coughing and hacking, as if with a hairball. After a few heaves, the cat produces the character, who is tiny but grows to normal size very quickly. They are coated in digestive juices, mucus, and cat hair, and have lost 1d6 random pieces of equipment, armor, or clothing. The entire process results in a Rating 7 attack that inflicts mental damage, due to the shock and psychological scarring of the experience.

THE FURNITURE

Navigating through the room is difficult, but if the characters go slow, it's not impossible. The staring cats likely make the slow progression all the more unnerving. Amid the jumble of furnishings, hidden from view until one is actually in the room, is quite a surprise. The dead body of a slender young girl, dried but preserved—almost mummified—lies on the floor beneath a table and a pair of chairs. A black dress, hardened but brittle with age, clings tightly around her. However, a silver necklace around her neck seems shiny and new. It can be easily removed, but disturbing the corpse in any other way results in the invisible force attack just as if someone harmed a cat.

THE NECKLACE

The silver necklace on the corpse is shaped like a heart locket. Once in hand, it becomes obvious that it is an intricate and delicate puzzle, with tiny sliding and revolving pieces of silver. Given quite a bit of time (perhaps an hour), a character can figure out a way to transform the locket into the rough shape of a key, still on the silver chain of the necklace. This is the key to **the Music Room** (page 222).

THE MUSIC

The PCs can hear very faint music coming from the radio in **the Shoin** (page 208).

Play this audio clip for the players:

mymcg.info/tdh-soror-sound-musicfromadistance

TO THE DOLL ROOM

This innocuous door leads to the Doll Room (page 196). The door is locked with a deadbolt from the other side.

TO THE LEERING ONES

This innocuous door leads to the Leering Ones (page 200). It is unlocked.

SISTER

Should the House Die indicate that Sister appears, she screams violently, "Get out! Get away from my little loves!" She'll attack anyone that doesn't comply. She is a young woman with half of her face missing, broken as if she was a hollow porcelain doll. The PCs can see into her head through the missing part of her face and it's full of moths. She's holding a stitched cloth doll of the Smiling Man in one hand and hides something behind her back with the other. (Spoiler: it's a knife.)

Show the players the image of **Sister**.

The PCs can try to speak with her, but she's a compulsive liar. She is stealthy, deceptive, and creepy, but not physically imposing. She has a Rating of 4 for anything physical, except for stealth or deception, in which case she has a Rating of 7. The 7 Rating is also for making sudden surprise attacks with her knife. She has the uncanny ability to vanish and suddenly reappear close by—probably no more than 25 feet or so. She usually uses this to escape into a hiding place to prepare for her next attack.

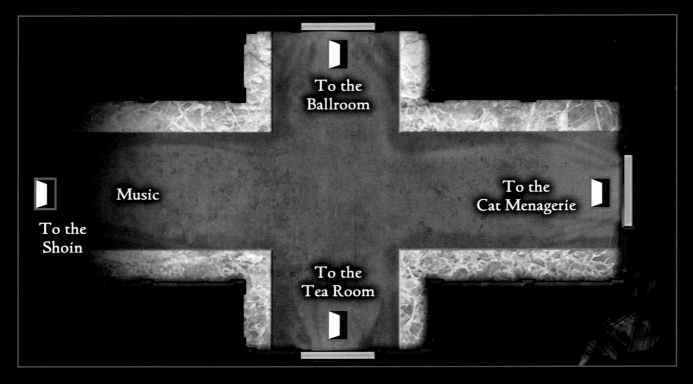

To the Ballroom

Music

To the Cat Menagerie

To the Shoin

To the Tea Room

Carved faces near the ceiling of a hallway begin to state what each character finds most annoying about their friends, in order to sow dissent.

Try to get through the players' answers about what annoys them as quickly as possible so you can get to the revelation of the effect while the emotions are still present.

OVERVIEW

The floor is green marble veined with black. Ugly faces are carved into the wooden coving on the walls, near the relatively high ceiling. As soon as anyone enters the hall, the faces begin to contort, stick out their tongues, close their eyes, and so forth. Then they begin to speak.

From perhaps the next room, strange music can be heard, and then a bout of static, and then the same strange music.

WHAT THE FACES SAY

Determine a PC at random, and then another. Ask the player of the first PC, "What about [the second PC] annoys your character the most?"

Don't accept "Nothing" as an answer.

Then do the same again with two more PCs. And again, until every PC has expressed what annoys them about at least one other PC. Once you have this information, the faces in the walls begin expressing these feelings out loud, naming the annoyed character, and the character(s) annoying them.

Don't do this via direct message of any kind. Ask the questions directly, out loud, in front of all the other players. (They're going to hear it all anyway.) This might cause some in-character dissent, even before you describe that the faces in the walls begin speaking. But that's okay. In fact, that's the point.

The house hates you.

MUSIC

The PCs can hear the faint music and static coming from the radio in **the Shoin** (page 208). They must resist a magical effect with a Rating of 2 or follow the sound of the music, entranced until they get to the Shoin.

Play this audio clip for the players:

mymcg.info/tdh-soror-sound-musicfromadistance

TO THE SHOIN

This doorway leads directly into **the Shoin** (page 208).

TO THE BALLROOM

This innocuous door leads to **the Ballroom** (page 212). It is unlocked.

TO THE CAT MENAGERIE

This innocuous door leads to **the Cat Menagerie** (page 198). It is unlocked.

TO THE TEA ROOM

This innocuous door leads to **the Tea Room** (page 202). It is unlocked.

SISTER

Should the House Die indicate that Sister appears, she skips in, uses a deep, mocking voice to talk about what the Leering Ones have said, and laughs at the PCs. She then attempts to use an opportune moment to savagely and surprisingly attack a character and then run away. She is a young woman with half of her face missing, broken as if she was a hollow porcelain doll. The PCs can see into her head through the missing part of her face and it's full of moths. She's holding a stitched cloth doll of the Smiling Man in one hand and hides something behind her back with the other. (Spoiler: it's a knife.)

Show the players the image of **Sister**.

The PCs can try to speak with her, but she's a compulsive liar. She is stealthy, deceptive, and creepy, but not physically imposing. She has a Rating of 4 for anything physical, except for stealth or deception, in which case she has a Rating of 7. The 7 Rating is also for making sudden surprise attacks with her knife. She has the uncanny ability to vanish and suddenly reappear close by—probably no more than 25 feet or so. She usually uses this to escape into a hiding place to prepare for her next attack.

THE TEA ROOM

Someone beloved of one of the PCs is now trapped in the house as well.

> It's key that the NPC has a strong connection to one or more of the PCs, preferably an emotional one. In the best-case scenario, love is at stake here. Even if they get out alive, the relationship will likely be challenged. Who wouldn't resent being dragged into a haunted house just because someone else went in?

OVERVIEW

White and blue wallpaper with delicate designs covers the walls. A round table with a lace cloth draped over it, set with an ornate tea set, furnishes this room. Five chairs surround the table, and a light wooden hutch holds decorative plates, cups, and dishes, most neatly stacked upon white doilies. A familiar figure sits in one of the chairs, looking stunned and surprised.

THE FAMILIAR FIGURE

You need to find out which of the PCs has a strong connection to an NPC that you can place here. You might have to pick a player and have them create the character on the spot. Or there might be an NPC already established. The NPC should not be particularly capable, or able to defend themselves well. You can rate them appropriately, but ideally, their Rating is low, 2 or 3 at the most. The idea is that it will be a challenge to protect this person.

While the person is meaningful emotionally to at least one PC, in the best case, they are known to some or even all of the characters. That's because the PCs are the only hope this person has of ever getting out of the house. All the NPC remembers is that they were going about their normal life (you and the player involved will come up with what that entails) and they suddenly felt very sleepy. They lay down for a short nap, and then woke up here, in this room, sitting at the table. They have no idea why they are here.

The reason they are here is that the house brought them here *because* of their connection to the PC. The beloved person is just one more way for the house to cause the PC—or PCs—pain. The characters might believe that the person is not real, but

rather is some kind of illusion or trick, but indeed they are real. And now they're trapped unless the PCs can get them out.

If the characters never enter this room, none of them loses a familiar NPC to the house.

HUTCH

Amid the various plates and dishes, all of which are very nice and probably worth something ($300 for the whole set), there is a child-sized tea set. On the bottom of the saucers, someone has written "Penelope" in thick blue ink. It's pretty unlikely that anyone would, but if someone sets up this small set on the table (clearing away what's already there) and puts a doll or stuffed animal from **the Doll Room** in each of the chairs, Sister appears in the doorway but causes no harm. She looks in, nods, and then disappears. The next time the House Die calls for Sister to appear, she will do likewise—inflicting no harm.

TO THE LEERING ONES

This innocuous door leads to **the Leering Ones** (page 200). It is unlocked.

TO THE ARCHWAY

This innocuous door leads to **the Archway** (page 204). It is unlocked.

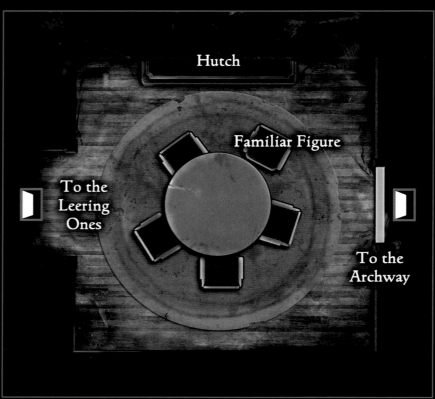

Hutch

Familiar Figure

To the Leering Ones

To the Archway

SISTER

Should the House Die indicate that Sister appears, she sneaks in quietly, attempting to use an opportune moment to savagely and surprisingly attack the familiar and beloved NPC and then run away. She is a young woman with half of her face missing, broken as if she was a hollow porcelain doll. The PCs can see into her head through the missing part of her face and it's full of moths. She's holding a stitched cloth doll of the Smiling Man in one hand and hides something behind her back with the other. (Spoiler: it's a knife.)

Show the players the image of **Sister**.

The PCs can try to speak with her, but she's a compulsive liar. She is stealthy, deceptive, and creepy, but not physically imposing. She has a Rating of 4 for anything physical, except for stealth or deception, in which case she has a Rating of 7. The 7 Rating is also for making sudden surprise attacks with her knife. She has the uncanny ability to vanish and suddenly reappear close by—probably no more than 25 feet or so. She usually uses this to escape into a hiding place to prepare for her next attack.

mostly empty room has an enchanted exit that drains those who pass beneath it of meaning.

> *The implication is the effect of the arch is linked to the god revered in the Secret Chapel.*

OVERVIEW

This room has a single side table pushed against one wall, upon which a vase holds a bouquet of dead flowers. The archway is different from other exits seen so far. It seems to be made of ancient, rough stones, like something you'd find in some long-hidden temple of forbidden rites and forgotten gods.

THE ARCHWAY

The archway leads into **the Empty Bedroom** (page 206). From this side of the opening, characters can see the dark gray draperies that block vision into the bedroom.

Carved into the apex of the archway are the words "Meaning is a burden." Should anyone step through the archway, it is activated, shimmering with multicolored flashes of light. The arch has a Rating of 6, and the character stepping through must successfully resist its effects. If they do, nothing happens beyond the light show.

If they fail, the victim is drained of meaning. This means they have no history, no identity, and no sense of self. They are little more than a listless, burbling mass that lies down on the ground, unknown and unrecognized by anyone. Meaningless.

The other PCs not only don't know who that person is (and have utterly forgotten that their companion ever existed) but are not at all inclined to help them, because the person is meaningless to them—utterly without consequence. The victim won't ask for help or communicate in any way, as they have no sense of self, no sense of self-preservation, and are incapable of making themselves understood.

Even the presence of the unknown person on the ground isn't cause for the other PCs to be alarmed or alerted to the danger of the archway, because again, the person is of no consequence, so what happened to them must be meaningless as well.

Thankfully, the affected PC's condition is not permanent. After about a minute, the drained victim slowly regains their meaningfulness. (This process

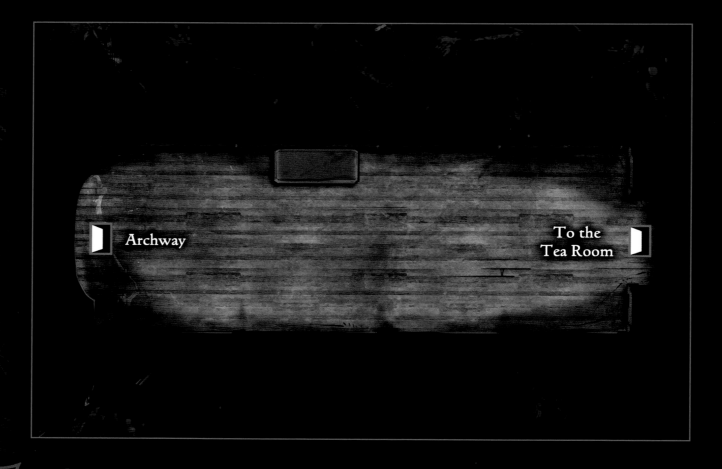

Archway

To the Tea Room

takes another few minutes.) Their friends may have left them by that point, or they may be in a room full of meaningless people because everyone went through the arch one by one and all failed their rolls.

There are four major consequences of being drained of meaning:

1. The character suffers a mental wound with a Rating of 5. There's no chance to resist this. The experience was awful, and having recovered, in some ways at least, the victim will think of it as worse than death.
2. The character will absolutely under no circumstances go through the archway again. It was too horrible.
3. If physically forced through the archway, should the character fail their roll again, this time the draining is permanent. Basically, they are dead.
4. The character is immune to the risk of looking out the rose window in **the Secret Chapel** (page 218). Going through the window, however, is still just as consequential (in a bad way).

TO THE TEA ROOM

This innocuous door leads to **the Tea Room** (page 202). It is unlocked.

SISTER

Should the House Die indicate that Sister appears, she saunters in, mocking anyone who has been drained of meaning. Eventually, she's likely to attack someone with her knife—but she won't attack someone without meaning. She is a young woman with half of her face missing, broken as if she was a hollow porcelain doll. The PCs can see into her head through the missing part of her face and it's full of moths. She's holding a stitched cloth doll of the Smiling Man in one hand and hides something behind her back with the other. (Spoiler: it's a knife.)

Show the players the image of **Sister**.

The PCs can try to speak with her, but she's a compulsive liar. She is stealthy, deceptive, and creepy, but not physically imposing. She has a Rating of 4 for anything physical, except for stealth or deception, in which case she has a Rating of 7. The 7 Rating is also for making sudden surprise attacks with her knife. She has the uncanny ability to vanish and suddenly reappear close by—probably no more than 25 feet or so. She usually uses this to escape into a hiding place to prepare for her next attack.

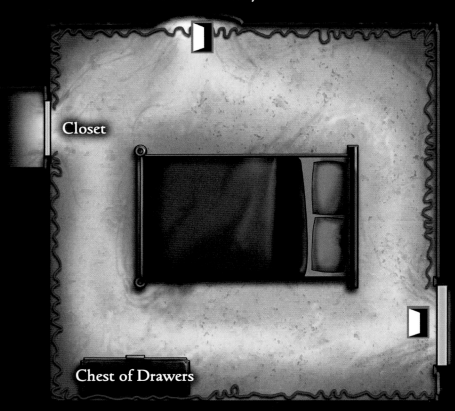

To the Archway

Closet

To the
Music Room

Chest of Drawers

here's really nothing here.

While not as safe as the Doll Room, the PCs can perhaps find some respite here.

OVERVIEW

A large bed of rich, dark walnut with a black bedspread over it sits in the center of the room. Heavy, dark gray curtains hang from the walls. A gap between the curtains reveals two different dark wooden doors, carved with a gothic style and a grotesque face on each. A large chest of drawers, also of dark walnut, is pushed into the corner.

CLOSET

This door goes to an empty closet.

CHEST OF DRAWERS

Empty.

TO THE ARCHWAY

Behind the curtain is an opening that leads to **the Archway** (page 204). Make sure you read the text associated with this archway, as anyone using this exit from the bedroom is immediately subject to some very harmful effects.

TO THE MUSIC ROOM

This innocuous door leads to **the Music Room** (page 222). It is unlocked.

SISTER

Should the House Die indicate that Sister appears, she sneaks in quietly, attempting to use an opportune moment to savagely and surprisingly attack a character and then run away. She is a young woman with half of her face missing, broken as if she was a hollow porcelain doll. The PCs can see into her head through the missing part of her face and it's full of moths. She's holding a stitched cloth doll of the Smiling Man in one hand and hides something behind her back with the other. (Spoiler: it's a knife.)

Show the players the image of **Sister**.

The PCs can try to speak with her, but she's a compulsive liar. She is stealthy, deceptive, and creepy, but not physically imposing. She has a Rating of 4 for anything physical, except for stealth or deception, in which case she has a Rating of 7. The 7 Rating is also for making sudden surprise attacks with her knife. She has the uncanny ability to vanish and suddenly reappear close by—probably no more than 25 feet or so. She usually uses this to escape into a hiding place to prepare for her next attack.

This Japanese-style drawing room has a deadly guardian and a haunted radio.

This room is different enough from most of the others that we can assume it was devoured by the house.

OVERVIEW

Although they can hear static as they approach, as soon as the PCs enter this room, they hear a click and then silence. The radio has turned off.

Woven tatami mats cover the floor. The far wall has a paper shoji-style door that slides. There's a faint light behind it. A suspended ceiling of intricately carved wood hangs above. The left wall bears an elevated recess filled with staggered shelving holding various small art pieces.

Against the right wall is a low wooden desk. Atop this desk sits a large, cathedral-style, wood-case radio, and a few papers. The room holds no other furniture.

The translucent surface of the door shows the shadowy silhouette of a young woman behind it, standing as if listening.

If the characters don't investigate the silhouette right away, they'll see the figure motion as if with a fan. However, they'll hear what sounds like knives scraping against the door. If they still don't open the door or interact with her, she appears to walk away from the door, and the characters hear indistinct whispers and then scratches on the wall. And then nothing more, until she magically teleports to where the PCs are and attacks.

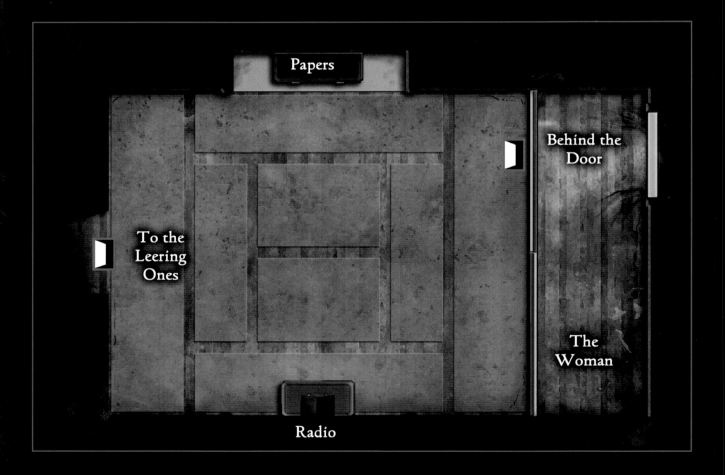

Papers

Behind the Door

To the Leering Ones

The Woman

Radio

THE WOMAN

The silhouette is not real. The figure is actually
a monstrous creature. A skeletal, exaggeratedly
long-limbed, vaguely female figure, she has wild hair and
terrifying eyes. Her hands are very long, needle-like claws
and she wears the tattered remnants of a gown.

Show the players the image of **the Corpse Woman**.

If she is revealed, she vanishes. A few moments later, however, she appears again, directly behind one of the characters, attacking them with a Boon.

Before she appears, one PC hears a whispered voice and is then attacked.

> You smell something that reeks of death and rot, and hear a whispering voice, not unlike the sound of a sarcophagus opening after untold aeons: "Murrrrrderrrrrrr."

Horrific and savage, the gaunt and haggard creature appears to have been a living human once, perhaps, but it is difficult to imagine that it is so. Her body is a cold corpse now, regardless, seemingly animated by the power of murder alone. Her initial appearance is a Rating 3 mental attack for everyone due to the shock.

The corpse woman attacks with her horribly long claws and seeks only to kill anything she sees that is alive. As she does so, if she can get close to a victim's face or even just their ear, she will whisper again, "Murrrrrderrrrr."

She is very deadly. Her Rating is 7, and her attacks are rated as 8. Her hardened flesh gives her a Rating of 8 for resisting damage (as if she were wearing armor). She can blink in and out of any location in this section of the house that she wishes. In a single action, she can attack and then vanish, or reappear and then attack. She cannot appear, attack, and vanish in one turn, however. If she appears and then attacks, the attack has a Boon from the surprise factor.

Inflicting at least a Rating 5 wound upon her drives her away for some time, but she will return when the characters least expect it, probably when they are in a completely different room.

BEHIND THE DOOR

Behind the door is a small room with no furniture, again with straw tatami mats on the wooden floor. There is a stout wooden door here, which is locked (Rating 6) and leads to **the Music Room** (page 222). The key to this door is in **the Cat Menagerie** (page 198).

PAPERS

These appear to be pages torn from a book—perhaps a personal journal. Show the players **Remnant 8** (page 276).

THE RADIO

Turning on the radio produces a lot of static. But given a little bit of time, perhaps fiddling with the tuning knob, the characters hear what sounds like a child's voice. "Hello? Is anyone there?"

Play this audio clip for the players:

mymcg.info/tdh-shoin-sound-hello

The radio isn't a two-way instrument, so it doesn't matter if the PCs attempt to answer.

Then the radio plays a bit of music through the static, before the child's voice returns. "Can anyone hear me?"

Play this audio clip for the players:

mymcg.info/tdh-shoin-sound-cananyonehearme

The same bit of music plays, and then the child says, "If you can hear me, the room with all the dolls is safe. Go to the Doll Room."

Play this audio clip for the players:

mymcg.info/tdh-shoin-sound-advice

If the PCs turn the radio off, and then turn it on again, or try to tune it away from the voice, it will eventually come back, first with the bit of music. "Don't do that," the child says. "I'm trying to talk to you."

Play this audio clip for the players:

mymcg.info/tdh-shoin-sound-dontdothat

Music plays again, and then the child says, "Find the Doorman if you want to leave. Find the Smiling Man if you want to stay. Forever."

Play this audio clip for the players:

mymcg.info/tdh-shoin-sound-doorman

If the PCs just leave the radio on, they only hear the first part of the message. If they leave it on and exit the room and then come back, they will hear the second part. (They might not know what "Don't do that" refers to in this instance. That's fine.)

TO THE LEERING ONES

This innocuous door leads to **the Leering Ones** (page 200). It is unlocked.

SISTER

Should the House Die indicate that Sister appears, and the radio is playing, she will shout "Hands off! That's mine!" and then attempt to turn off the radio while threatening the PCs with her knife. If the radio isn't playing, she sneaks in quietly, attempting to use an opportune moment to savagely and surprisingly attack a character and then run away. She is friends with the corpse woman and will aid her in any way she can.

Sister is a young woman with half of her face missing, broken as if she was a hollow porcelain doll. The PCs can see into her head through the missing part of her face and it's full of moths. She's holding a stitched cloth doll of the Smiling Man in one hand and hides something behind her back with the other. (Spoiler: it's a knife.)

Show the players the image of **Sister**.

The PCs can try to speak with her, but she's a compulsive liar. She is stealthy, deceptive, and creepy, but not physically imposing. She has a Rating of 4 for anything physical, except for stealth or deception, in which case she has a Rating of 7. The 7 Rating is also for making sudden surprise attacks with her knife. She has the uncanny ability to vanish and suddenly reappear close by—probably no more than 25 feet or so. She usually uses this to escape into a hiding place to prepare for her next attack.

THE BALLROOM

A ghostly orchestra compels characters to dance, but a strange barman at the bar on the balcony above attempts to get characters magically drunk, and then tempt them to do terrible things.

> *If you want a little inspiration, the scene where Jack Torrance talks to the bartender in* The Shining *works well for the Barman.*

OVERVIEW

This ballroom is a large open space with grand pillars and a polished marble floor. Dark windows on the left-hand wall somehow give off a kind of radiance. A pair of grand—but also dark—crystal chandeliers hangs from the high ceiling. A sweeping staircase leads to a balcony above the dance floor. There's a feeling of long history here, of romance and broken hearts, lust, and betrayal. There's a slight odor of alcohol and sweat-stained but expensive clothing.

THE ORCHESTRA STAGE

As soon as the PCs approach the stage, a ghostly orchestra appears and plays ghostly instruments in a slow, somber version of what might have originally been a dance tune. These ghosts are insubstantial figments, and cannot be physically harmed or affected. After a moment or two, anyone listening to the music is subject to a mental attack with a Rating of 7. Instead of suffering damage, however, anyone affected is compelled to enter into a slow but elegant dance. Should someone attempt to prevent them from dancing or disturb them in any way, the dancers suffer another Rating 7 mental attack, but this time it does inflict mental damage. The music and the dance continue for about two minutes (enough time for non-affected characters to take as many as ten actions or so). If someone can somehow silence the music, the dancers come out of their trance-like dance after a minute or two. As soon as the dance begins, anyone not affected by the music hears noises from the balcony, like the clink of glass against glass.

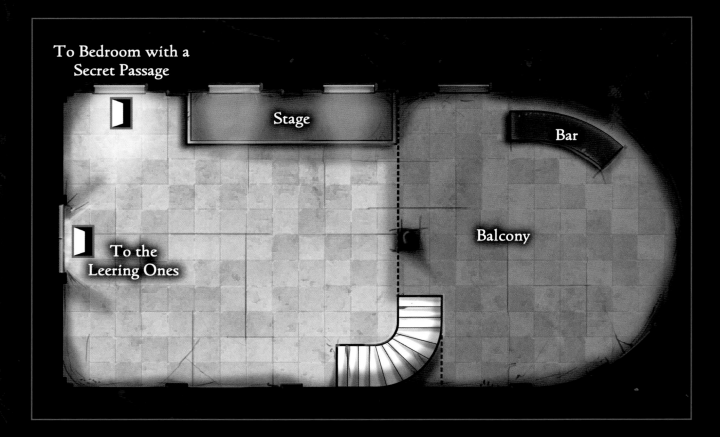

To Bedroom with a Secret Passage

Stage

Bar

To the Leering Ones

Balcony

THE BALCONY

The balcony has some cocktail tables and a full bar of polished dark wood. Dozens of glistening bottles of alcohol along with an assortment of elegant glassware decorate the wall behind the bar. The noise comes from a ghostly **barman** who is pouring drinks. He wears a pressed black vest over a white shirt with a black bow tie. His hair is slicked back, and he shows a crooked smile. "The usual?"

THE BARMAN

The Barman is a manifested physical entity, not at all as he appears, but not an insubstantial phantom like the orchestra members, either. He has a Rating of 7. But he doesn't show his true form unless attacked or otherwise provoked.

✦ Accepting a drink from the Barman and drinking it results in immediately becoming partially intoxicated, even after just a sip. Partially intoxicated characters suffer a Bane against mental attacks.

✦ Drinking more than one drink from the Barman gets the character extremely intoxicated. Such characters have a Bane affecting all their actions.

Intoxication lasts until the character sleeps.

CHATTING WITH THE BARMAN

As you might expect from a bartender, the Barman is happy to chat, but he always tries to bring the conversation around to the characters talking to him. He's polite, always addressing the character as "sir," or "madam," or "friend" as seems appropriate. If asked questions, he might provide some information, but turns it back into a question about the character. If there's a pause in the conversation, he'll ask a question like, "How are you enjoying the evening?" or "Music reminds you of your youth, I bet." His main goal, however, is to get the character(s) to drink. He can make any drink that they name.

A few sample exchanges might go like this:

PC: Who are you?
Barman: I'm just here to serve, [sir or madam or friend]. Can I get you anything?
PC: What can you tell me about the house?
Barman: That depends, [sir or madam or friend], what areas have you visited already?
PC: How long will my dancing friends be entranced?
Barman: The orchestra's repertoire is mainly short pieces. Would you like a drink while you wait?
PC: Do I owe you anything for these drinks?
Barman: Of course not, [sir or madam or friend]. On the house.
PC: How do we get out of this place?
Barman: Why would you want to leave? The music is good and the drinks are free.

If one or more of the characters is at least partially intoxicated, he eventually takes a different tack. He begins sowing dissent or even suggesting actions for them to take. They are minor suggestions at first:

> PC: What's the story of this place?
> Barman: That's pretty complicated. [Whispers] I can tell you this, though, friend: that one there [subtly pointing at another PC] knows more than they're letting on. Maybe you should find out why they're keeping secrets. [GM note: you could do this as a Direct Message.]
> PC: [Asks for more information about the house]
> Barman: I bet you could find out if you picked that one's pocket [subtly pointing at another PC]. [GM note: you could do this as a Direct Message.]

Suggestions involve a roll to affect the character. Remember that intoxicated characters get a Bane on attempts to resist (or rather, the Barman gets a Boon to affect them, depending on how you want to handle that), and the Barman is rated as a 7. If affected, a character believes whatever the Barman says, and if he suggests an action, they will attempt it.

Eventually, these suggestions get more dramatic and violent. These overt suggestions only affect the character's next turn.

> Barman: I know you don't like the way that one talks to you sometimes [subtly pointing at another PC]. I think the proper response would be a sword blade in their belly, don't you?

FIGHTING WITH THE BARMAN

Provoking or attacking the Barman gets him to reveal his true form: that of a gangly, hollow corpse. Gigantic golden centipedes with enormous antennae crawl in and out of various orifices—his eyes, his mouth, a gaping hole in his dried, desiccated chest, and so on.

Show the players the image of the Barman.

He reacts with horrific violence, attacking two opponents every turn either with a centipede that darts out of his mouth like a gigantic tongue or with a centipede curled around his hand like a chitinous, thorny fist. His attacks inflict physical damage, but that's not the worst of it. The Barman is a being of addiction and vice, and his touch causes monstrous cravings.

The GM should ask the player what risky or potentially dangerous thing gives the character the most comfort or joy. Not a person, a specific object, or something abstract (like justice or love), but an activity or a general substance. Getting gold (money), eating food, drinking alcohol, doing drugs, fighting, sleeping, having sex, casting spells, and gambling are all acceptable answers—depending on your group's comfort level with each of those things. And there could be other answers, depending on the characters. The point is, when the Barman successfully strikes, whether he inflicts damage or not, the character must resist an effect with a Rating of 7. Failure means they leave the combat with the Barman to satisfy their craving. (Thus, even if they say "fighting," they'll leave the fight with the Barman and attempt to start a fight with someone else, maybe another PC.) A craving for alcohol is easy to sate here at the bar. And it's likely that the need for food can be sated if any of the characters brought some with them.

Keep in mind, the craving doesn't make them into something they're not. If they're craving sex, the effect doesn't force them to assault someone if they wouldn't normally do that (and hopefully that's the case). But it might make them proposition someone nearby, or even beg. Craving fighting won't make them attack a friend, but it might make them belligerently provoke their friend. Addiction is not pretty.

The craving ends when sated, or if the character is restrained and then makes a successful roll to resist the effect.

BEHIND THE BAR

Many of the bottles of alcohol and wine behind the bar are rare and valuable. There are five bottles worth $200 each, two worth $500, and one worth $1000.

The characters can also find the Warding Stone, a magical bit of black tourmaline about 4 inches long that is wrapped in cloth. The person that carries it, and all those allied with them within 10 feet or so are protected from magical effects, essentially gaining a Boon to resist them (or the attacker gains a Bane—either way). This useful item, however, has a serious drawback, a sort of magical curse. The stone gets heavier by the hour. When first touched or grasped by one of the characters, it weighs about 1 pound. After an hour, it weighs 10 pounds. After another hour, it weighs 100 pounds. Then 1,000 pounds. Eventually, the PCs won't be able to move it. If left somewhere for more than an hour, it disappears and this room resets.

There is also a silver key, which opens the lock in **the Doorman's** chest. The characters must find him first. The Doorman can be found in **the Cellar** (page 104) or with **the Gatekeeper** (page 224).

If the Barman is slain, his physical body transforms into a silver drink shaker. This is magical, and any liquid placed within it and shaken up is safe to drink—poisons and diseases are neutralized—and is as intoxicating or not as the user wishes it to be.

TO BEDROOM WITH A SECRET PASSAGE

This innocuous door leads to the Bedroom With a Secret Passage (page 216). It is unlocked.

TO THE LEERING ONES

This innocuous door leads to the Leering Ones (page 200). It is unlocked.

SISTER

Should the House Die indicate that Sister appears, she comes into the ballroom and dances to the sound of the music, seemingly ignoring the PCs. Eventually, however, she uses an opportune moment to savagely and surprisingly attack a character and then runs away. She is a young woman with half of her face missing, broken as if she was a hollow porcelain doll. The PCs can see into her head through the missing part of her face and it's full of moths. She's holding a stitched cloth doll of the Smiling Man in one hand and hides something behind her back with the other. (Spoiler: it's a knife.)

Show the players the image of **Sister**.

The PCs can try to speak with her, but she's a compulsive liar. She is stealthy, deceptive, and creepy, but not physically imposing. She has a Rating of 4 for anything physical, except for stealth or deception, in which case she has a Rating of 7. The 7 Rating is also for making sudden surprise attacks with her knife. She has the uncanny ability to vanish and suddenly reappear close by—probably no more than 25 feet or so. She usually uses this to escape into a hiding place to prepare for her next attack.

BEDROOM WITH A SECRET PASSAGE

There's little of note here beyond the secret passage.

You really want to play up the creep factor of crawling into a dark, tiny tunnel of old, creaky boards.

OVERVIEW

This looks like an ill-used bedroom, filled with cobwebs and dust. There's an empty dresser with a cloudy mirror, a lumpy bed covered in ratty linens, and a closet filled with old coats and a variety of board games and boxed puzzles, none of which have all the pieces.

SECRET PASSAGE

It is a Rating 4 task to notice that a panel low to the ground next to the bed pries away with a bit of force. The PCs probably need something to pry with, like a knife or a screwdriver (or, of course, a prybar). The panel is only 3 feet to a side, and reveals a tunnel about that wide of rough wooden planks on the floor, walls, and ceiling. Obviously, most characters will have to crawl. The passage proceeds about 9 feet, then disconcertingly turns downward, becoming a shaft about 12 feet long. It's narrow enough, and the planks are uneven enough, that one can climb up and down if both hands are free. It's difficult, but there's likely no die roll involved unless a character is significantly injured and has no assistance. The bottom of the shaft is the vestibule of **the Secret Chapel** (page 218).

Refer to the **Bedroom Map—After Discovery** when the characters discover the secret passage.

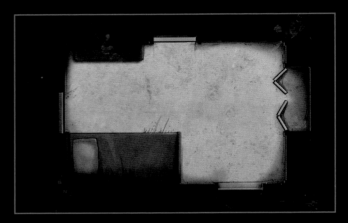

To the Ballroom

Secret Passage

However, there's a secret passage within the secret passage. About halfway down the length of the passage on the left, the boards can pry away to reveal a similarly low and narrow passage. This winds its way (impossibly) all the way back to **the Doll Room** (page 196). That end of the passage has been plastered over entirely—which is why it was impossible to find the passage from that end, and which is why characters will have to smash their way through the wall and into that room if they wish to get there.

TO THE BALLROOM

This innocuous door leads to the Ballroom (page 212). It is unlocked.

SISTER

Should the House Die indicate that Sister appears, the PCs see her come out of the secret passage, whether they have discovered it or not. She tries to stab the nearest character and then flee down the tunnel. She is a young woman with half of her face missing, broken as if she was a hollow porcelain doll. The PCs can see into her head through the missing part of her face and it's full of moths. She's holding a stitched cloth doll of the Smiling Man in one hand and hides something behind her back with the other. (Spoiler: it's a knife.)

Show the players the image of **Sister**.

The PCs can try to speak with her, but she's a compulsive liar. She is stealthy, deceptive, and creepy, but not physically imposing. She has a Rating of 4 for anything physical, except for stealth or deception, in which case she has a Rating of 7. The 7 Rating is also for making sudden surprise attacks with her knife. She has the uncanny ability to vanish and suddenly reappear close by—probably no more than 25 feet or so. She usually uses this to escape into a hiding place to prepare for her next attack.

THE SECRET CHAPEL

A hidden chapel dedicated to a horrific god filled with danger for curious characters.

> *Do what it takes to make the chapel both unnerving and surreally unsettling. Insert your own inexplicable random events if it helps.*

OVERVIEW

The chapel is entered via the narthex, a small room with heavy purple curtains covering the walls. One curtain has a dim light coming out from beneath it, suggesting a room beyond.

That room is the chapel itself. This cold stone room is dim, and the contents are either dark, chaotic, or both.

Stylized ceramic cats flank what appears to be an altar, while others are scattered elsewhere in the room—atop a side table, on the floor, and hanging from the ceiling by worn, white string.

The altar is a single piece of stone that rises 6 feet from the floor, although a semicircular portion has been removed from the top, creating a deep, rounded depression, with swooping sides that look almost like animal horns. Upon the altar, in the rounded cavity, lies a taxidermied raven with its head broken off.

Small niches in the stone walls hold lit candles resting in brass holders formed in distasteful shapes. Shelves run the length of each wall near the ceiling, and hold various tiny personal items pilfered over time—a mostly used tube of toothpaste, a pen, a doll's head, a pill bottle with a single pill, a crumpled piece of paper, a toy car, a spool of thread, and so on.

THE NARTHEX

The narthex has a small crawlspace covered by curtains—perhaps it goes unnoticed by all but the most thorough of PCs. It leads (impossibly) to **the Dog** (page 186). Additionally, a shaft in the ceiling of the narthex is the end of the secret passage between this room and **the Bedroom With a Secret Passage** (page 216).

Refer to the **Secret Chapel Map—After Discovery** when the characters discover the crawlspace.

To the Bedroom with a Secret Passage — Narthex — To the Dog

Candles

Cats — Broken Raven

Glass Partition

Window

THE CANDLES

The candles are lit, but don't seem to burn down. Anyone snuffing one out notices that the room gets colder with each one. If all the candles are put out, the room is plunged into complete darkness and cold, clammy hands reach out to touch and grab at everyone in the room. Everyone is subject to a mental attack with a Rating of 5. Then all the candles flare to life again.

PILFERED ITEMS

There are hundreds of things on the shelves, and more scattered around the chapel. Things that might catch a child's eye, but some have been altered. A photograph has all the faces scribbled out. A glove has each finger marked with a weird runic symbol. A tiny ballerina figurine has a noose around her neck. A miscellany of pencils of different lengths is bound in twine. Shredded pages from a holy book are piled like a tiny haystack. A bottle is full of dead bugs.

THE CATS

Each cat is different, and none are realistic. They are all painted, and the eyes seem to always be watching.

BROKEN RAVEN

Shoved into the raven's neck is a tiny piece of paper, rolled up tightly. Show the players **Remnant 14** (page 279).

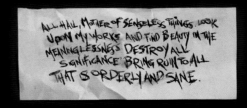

If the head is placed back on the body, the character doing so sees a vision of **the Trophy Room** (page 98). In that vision, the deer head will move just enough to make it clear that it is animate. The vision fades after a few moments.

STAINED GLASS PARTITION

This is heavy but fragile. The glass is mostly red, violet, and black. It seems to be in an abstract pattern that is somehow disturbing. If a character studies it, the glass appears to move and take on identifiable shapes. However, the shapes are defined by them. At least at first.

The glass in the folding screen appears to move and take on identifiable shapes, almost like it suddenly portrays a scene. What scene does it portray?

Whatever they say, reply to them that that's exactly what they see. Except after just a few moments, things take a dark turn. If they imagined people or animals, it suddenly appears as though their heads are severed and spew fountains of blood—all portrayed in tiny pieces of colored glass. If they pictured buildings, the buildings collapse. A forest? Consumed by flames. And so on. Describe this in a direct message to them. For shock, this is a Rating 3 mental attack.

IF THE LURKER IS PRESENT

If the character possessed by the Lurker (from **the Foyer [page 162]**) is present when the screwdriver is discovered, it forces the character to act.

The spirit possessing you compels you to grab the screwdriver and shout, "Mine!"

If this action causes any kind of questioning of the possessed character or their actions, the Lurker yet again compels its host.

The spirit possessing you makes you say, "I'm fine. Don't worry about it. Now, where do you think the rest of these tools might be?"

Obviously, the Lurker wants the **Mystic Tools**. It will continue to compel its host to keep trying to find them. Should the entire set be found, the Lurker will attempt to kill all the other characters so that it can have the tools for itself.

STAINED GLASS WINDOW

Set into the wall behind the screen is a stained glass rose window. Faint light comes from its translucent orange, green, and black panes as if it looks outside.

On the wall below the window, someone has scratched into the stone: "Tomorrow's girls are yesterday's corpses." A wooden-handled screwdriver lies on the floor beneath it. The screwdriver is part of the tool set with magical properties collectively called the **Mystic Tools**.

The chapel feels like a basement room. Underground. So the window seems quite out of place. Even a moment's examination reveals that the entire rose window will pivot horizontally if given a push.

The view out the window is into a terrible kaleidoscope-like miasma of constantly shifting color and light. Imagery more random than can be safely contemplated appears and then disappears out of this visual cacophony. A horse. A candle. Two circular pools. An elevated train with people leaping out of the windows. A pair of scissors. A beast with three eyes and five mouths. A star imploding. A knife plunged into a pumpkin. A bird made of liquid. A rotating dodecahedron.

Anyone looking upon this panorama that exists in an inconceivable world of chaos and madness is subject to a Rating 10 attack that inflicts mental damage.

A character would have to really squeeze to get through the opening, but if they smashed the window, they could fit easily. Any creature or object that passes through the window is gone forever, into an eternity of dissolution, transmutation, and creation.

Smashing the window summons Sister immediately.

She is a young woman with half of her face missing, broken as if she was a hollow porcelain doll. The PCs can see into her head through the missing part of her face and it's full of moths. She's holding a stitched cloth doll of the Smiling Man in one hand and hides something behind her back with the other. (Spoiler: it's a knife.)

Show the players the image of **Sister**.

The PCs can try to speak with her, but she's a compulsive liar. She is stealthy, deceptive, and creepy, but not physically imposing. She has a Rating of 4 for anything physical, except for stealth or deception, in which case she has a Rating of 7. The 7 Rating is also for making sudden surprise attacks with her knife. She has the uncanny ability to vanish and suddenly reappear close by—probably no more than 25 feet or so. She usually uses this to escape into a hiding place to prepare for her next attack.

TO THE BEDROOM WITH A SECRET PASSAGE

A shaft leads up, eventually reaching **the Bedroom With Secret Passage** (page 216).

TO THE DOG

A small crawlspace—about 3 feet across—leads to **the Dog** (page 186).

SISTER

As stated, smashing the window summons **Sister** immediately. Otherwise, she will not come into this room while others are present. If the House Die indicates that she should appear, have something different and seemingly random happen without meaning, like one or more of the cats animates and attacks, or the stained glass partition shatters and sprays glass shards everywhere.

THE MUSIC ROOM

An elegant chamber containing, among other things, a haunted viola.

If the PCs linger here, strongly consider having the Gatekeeper (page 224) come from her chamber to confront them here.

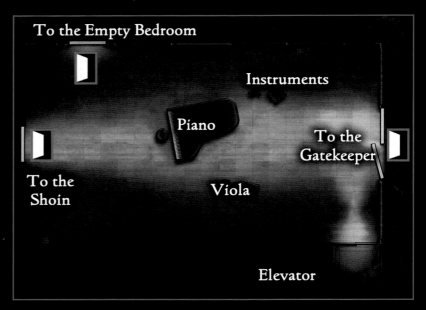

To the Empty Bedroom

Instruments

Piano

To the Gatekeeper

To the Shoin

Viola

Elevator

OVERVIEW

The door to this room from **the Shoin** *(page 208) is locked (Rating 6). The key is in* **the Cat Menagerie** *(page 198).*

This grand chamber has sweeping, arched ceilings and decorative wood panels. A grand piano dominates the room, although several other instruments can be found, as well as music stands and a few other furnishings. There's an aura of practice and punishment here.

THE PIANO

If someone plays the snippet of music heard on the radio in the Shoin (probably requiring a good memory and some music knowledge or skill), a secret panel in the piano bench opens, revealing a small compartment that holds one of the **Mystic Tools**. In this case, it is a chisel. The compartment is very difficult to find and open without this aid (Rating 8).

IF THE LURKER IS PRESENT

If the character possessed by the Lurker (from **the Foyer [page 162]**) is present when the chisel is discovered, it forces the character to act.

> The spirit possessing you compels you to grab the chisel and shout, "Mine!"

If this action causes any kind of questioning of the possessed character or their actions, the Lurker yet again compels its host.

> The spirit possessing you makes you say, "I'm fine. Don't worry about it. Now, where do you think the rest of these tools might be?"

Obviously, the Lurker wants the Mystic Tools. It will continue to compel its host to keep trying to find them. Should the entire set be found, the Lurker will attempt to kill all the other characters so that it can have the tools for itself.

INSTRUMENTS

Besides the piano, the instruments here include a cello, a violin, a viola, a piccolo, a flute, and a guitar. Each has a variety of sheet music to go along with it. The viola is special. However, the only overt clue to the viola's special nature is that sheet music for it has something written upon it. Show the players **Remnant 18** (page 281).

THE VIOLA

Of all the instruments, the viola is special. It's haunted. The spirit that inhabits it ultimately wants to take the body and the life of a person and make it their own, so that the spirit can live again. This is a long-term goal, however. In the short term, if the viola is picked up, the spirit conveys to the person holding it how to play it flawlessly, as if they were a skilled musician. Further, if the musician wishes it, playing the viola can conjure a spirit with a Rating of 3 that can manifest physically. The spirit acts on the musician's behalf. However, each time the musician conjures a spirit, the ghost in the viola gets one step closer to its goal. After ten such summonings, and every time after the tenth, the viola attempts to possess the musician, making an attack with a Rating of 1, and then a Rating of 2, and so on.

THE ELEVATOR

The elevator is essentially a large brass cage.
Show the players the image of **the elevator**.
On the floor is a heavy lever with six positions. It is currently in position 1. The elevator moves very slowly,

taking almost a full minute to reach the next level up or down. There is a mechanical sound when it moves, and a clinking of chains. Through the cage, chains and gears can be seen moving. Damaging any of them renders the elevator inoperable for 24 hours before it resets.

✦ Position 1: Where the lever is now (if the elevator goes to another level, 1 returns it to this room)
✦ Position 2: Takes the elevator to **the Great Hall** (page 114)
✦ Position 3: Takes the elevator to **the Mannequin Room** (page 154)
✦ Position 4: Takes the elevator to **the Room With the Hidden Elevator** (page 88)
✦ Position 5: Takes the elevator to **the Backrooms** (page 118)
✦ Position 6: Takes the elevator to **the Guardian** (page 122)

TO THE SHOIN
This innocuous door leads to **the Shoin** (page 208). It is unlocked from this side.

TO THE EMPTY BEDROOM
This innocuous door leads to **the Empty Bedroom** (page 206). It is unlocked.

TO THE GATEKEEPER
This large door is ajar, letting in a ghostly blue light. It leads to **the Gatekeeper** (page 224).

SISTER
Should the House Die indicate that Sister appears, she sneaks in quietly, attempting to use an opportune moment to savagely and surprisingly attack a character and then run away. She is a young woman with half of her face missing, broken as if she was a hollow porcelain doll. The PCs can see into her head through the missing part of her face and it's full of moths. She's holding a stitched cloth doll of the Smiling Man in one hand and hides something behind her back with the other. (Spoiler: it's a knife.)

Show the players the image of **Sister**.

The PCs can try to speak with her, but she's a compulsive liar. She is stealthy, deceptive, and creepy, but not physically imposing. She has a Rating of 4 for anything physical, except for stealth or deception, in which case she has a Rating of 7. The 7 Rating is also for making sudden surprise attacks with her knife. She has the uncanny ability to vanish and suddenly reappear close by—probably no more than 25 feet or so. She usually uses this to escape into a hiding place to prepare for her next attack.

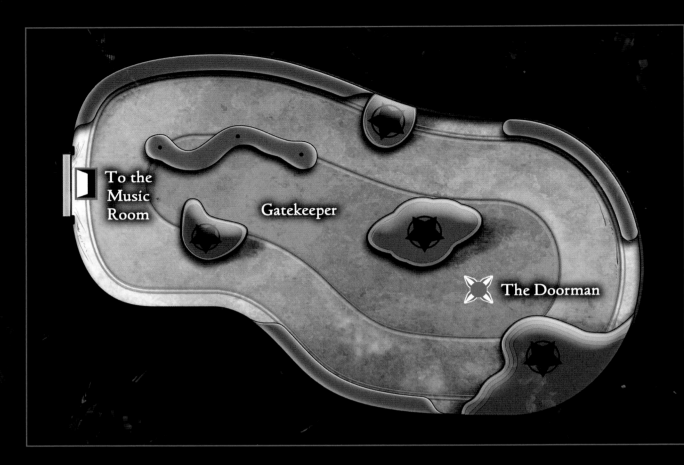

To the Music Room

Gatekeeper

The Doorman

Finally, a way out. But PCs can only use this exit if they are willing to sacrifice that (or whom) they truly love.

> *Yes, the Gatekeeper's price is awful. While you don't want paying that price to traumatize the player, it might traumatize the character, and that's intentional. Allow them the space and the time to play through that experience.*

OVERVIEW

This chamber is spacious and beautiful, albeit strangely decorated. It's nothing like the rest of the house, with glistening white, curved, almost organic-looking furnishings; blue-tinted lights; and abstract sculpture jutting from the walls, hanging from the ceiling, and rising from the floor. One's gut instinctively tells them that this is the lounge or parlor of someone not even remotely human. Indeed, this is the chamber of the Gatekeeper, and she protects the Doorman while he's here. She stops the characters from proceeding and demands her price.

FURNISHINGS AND SCULPTURE

The sculptures and furnishings here can't be easily moved and have no particular value, but there are also a great many loose objects that the PCs cannot identify, resting on tabletops, on shelves, and so on. Are they art? Are they technological devices? Magic? They're too alien for the PCs to tell, and in fact, for anyone to tell, *ever*. (Which I suppose makes them, at best, art.) There are a dozen of these mystery objects and if taken, each has a value of about $200. If the Gatekeeper is alive, however, she'll attack anyone attempting to steal her things.

THE GATEKEEPER AND HER PRICE

Tall, lithe, cold, and severe, this human(ish) figure appears only slightly female—she's almost androgynous. Her eyeless face is long and drawn, and her mouth is full of teeth like a deep-sea fish. She seems to be clothed in strips of literal darkness that hang from her almost like a draped net or web. Floating around her head are five black clay tablets, each bearing a golden symbol.

Show the players the image of **the Gatekeeper**.

When she encounters the PCs, the Gatekeeper speaks with them telepathically. She asks them some very specific and important questions. She won't interact with them in any other way, regardless of what they say or ask. If they try to move past her or attack her, she reacts with violence. Otherwise, she will let them leave.

In each case, if the PCs say yes, she will move on to the next question.

These are her questions:

1. "Do you wish to leave?"
If they say no, she will tell them to go away.

2. "Do you have the key?"
If they do not, she will tell them to go away.

3. "Are you willing to pay?"
If they say no, she will tell them to go away. Far more likely, however, someone will ask what the toll or price is. She will answer, "One of you must tell me whom or what you love most." She won't elaborate.

4. "Whom or what do you love most?"
If they tell her, she immediately conjures that person or thing. There is no dice roll involved when paying the Gatekeeper's price. ONLY ONE CHARACTER NEEDS TO PAY THE PRICE FOR THE WHOLE GROUP.

✦ If the answer's a person (or a creature of any kind), she conjures them. If they were dead, they're now alive. If they were imprisoned or lost, they come. And then she murders them, their essence immediately forming into a sixth black clay tablet around her head. She lets all the characters go past her, but the shock causes the character who paid the price to suffer a mental attack with a Rating of 5.

✦ If the answer's an object, she conjures it—even if it was in someone's possession, it's in her hands now. And then she destroys it, its essence immediately forming into a sixth black clay tablet around her head. She lets all the characters go past her, but the shock causes the character who paid the price to suffer a mental attack with a Rating of 3.

✦ If the answer's a class of object (like "gold") all objects of that type are stripped from the character, appear in her hands, and then she destroys them, their essence immediately forming into a sixth black clay tablet around her head. Further, the character can never possess that kind of object again. It burns them like fire to attempt it. She lets all the characters go past her, but the shock causes the character who paid the price to suffer a mental attack with a Rating of 4.

✦ If the answer's an abstract concept (like "justice" or "magic"), she conjures an image that symbolizes

that concept and crushes it in her hands. Its essence immediately forms into a sixth black clay tablet around her head. Additionally, the character can never have that concept as a part of their life again. In some cases, this may be tricky to adjudicate, but the general idea of real loss of love needs to be represented. She lets all the characters go past her, but the shock causes the character to suffer a mental attack with a Rating of 5.

✦ If they lie to the Gatekeeper, she will angrily tell them to go away and will never let them past her again. If they don't leave, she lashes out with violence.

If the PCs have come here before and paid her price to get at the Doorman, neither she nor the Doorman will be here.

FIGHTING THE GATEKEEPER

The Gatekeeper has a Rating of 6, but in any kind of defensive action, she has a Rating of 8. She has three different kinds of attacks she can make, and as her action, she can do any two of them:

✦ She can conjure an important object belonging to a character (like a weapon, armor, or magic item) and destroy it. The character can resist this theft (unlike when paying her price, for which there is no die roll involved). If the item is destroyed, its essence immediately forms into a new black clay tablet around her head.

✦ She can launch a burst of black magical energy by sacrificing one of her black tablets. The energy affects all her foes, has a Rating of 7, and attacks with a Boon, inflicting physical damage.

✦ She can bite a foe.

If she kills any of her opponents, their essence immediately forms into a new black clay tablet around her head.

GETTING PAST THE GATEKEEPER

Only after the Gatekeeper lets them past or is defeated can the PCs move to the back of her chamber. There, they will find the Doorman. The Doorman looks to be human at first, and perhaps he once was. Now, however, his mostly bare skin is covered in a rough topography of scars and scarification while his eyes and mouth are stitched shut. Many padlocks have been sewn into his flesh, but prominently there is a large keyhole in his chest and another in his forehead. The silver key found behind the bar in **the Ballroom** (page 212) or **A Storeroom of Sorts** (page 110) opens the lock in his chest.

If that lock is opened, a door appears in the middle of the room. This is the Front Door, and PCs can use it to exit the house (even if that's not how they got in). Going back through the Front Door from the other side does not bring them back here, however; it takes them into **the Living Room** (page 82), as normal.

The plain key found in A Storeroom of Sorts opens the lock in his head. If the lock in his head is unlocked, a doorway of utter blackness opens next to him. This doorway leads to the secret room in **the Private Study** (page 230).

This is the same Doorman that can be found in **the Cellar** (page 104). He moves around, but he can also be in two places at once. If slain in either place, he's dead in both. So if the PCs already killed him in the Cellar, he won't be here. The PCs can only encounter him once in each location, so if they use him as an exit here, he will never be here again, nor will the Gatekeeper (though they can still find him in the Cellar, if they haven't already).

The Doorman has a Rating of 4, and will defend himself with his fists if he must.

TO THE MUSIC ROOM

This innocuous door leads to **the Music Room** (page 222). It is unlocked.

SISTER

Should the House Die indicate that Sister appears, she won't come near the Gatekeeper. She'll just appear in the doorway, peeking in. If the Gatekeeper is gone or destroyed, she will come in, giggling and singing a little song about the Doorman.

Sad little Door-man, used to be a poor man. Really just a bunch of locks, silly as a bag of rocks. Sad little Door-man. Abused and really sore-man.

If the PCs have one of the keys that will open the Doorman's locks, Sister will skip and playfully run toward the key holder and attempt to steal it from them and vanish.

Sister is a young woman with half of her face missing, broken as if she was a hollow porcelain doll. You can see into her head through the missing part of her face— and it's full of moths. She's holding a stitched cloth doll of the Smiling Man in one hand and hides something behind her back with the other. (Spoiler: it's a knife.)

Show the players the image of **Sister**.

The PCs can try to speak with her, but she's a compulsive liar. She is stealthy, deceptive, and creepy, but not physically imposing. She has a Rating of 4 for anything physical, except for stealth or deception, in which case she has a Rating of 7. The 7 Rating is also for making sudden surprise attacks with her knife. She has the uncanny ability to vanish and suddenly reappear close by—probably no more than 25 feet or so. She usually uses this ability to escape into a hiding place and prepare for her next attack.

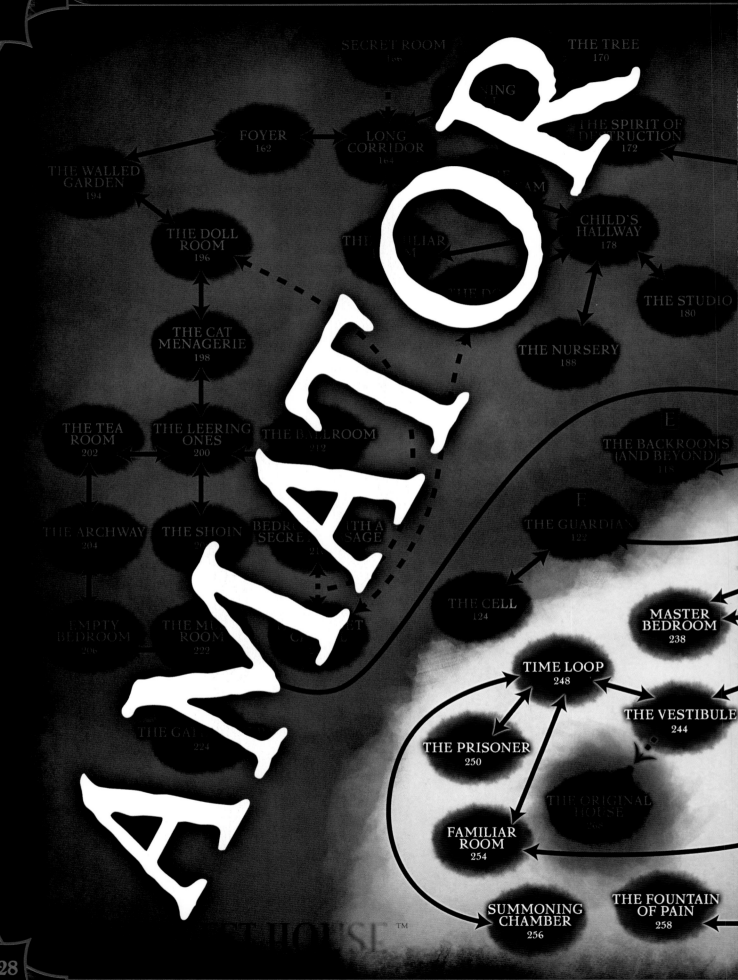

SECRET ROOM
168

THE TREE
170

NING

FOYER
162

LONG
CORRIDOR
164

THE SPIRIT OF
DESTRUCTION
172

THE WALLED
GARDEN
194

CHILD'S
HALLWAY
178

THE DOLL
ROOM
196

THE STUDIO
180

THE CAT
MENAGERIE
198

THE NURSERY
188

THE TEA
ROOM
202

THE LEERING
ONES
200

THE BALLROOM
212

E
THE BACKROOMS
(AND BEYOND)
118

THE ARCHWAY
204

THE SHOIN
206

BEDROOM WITH A
SECRET PASSAGE
210

F
THE GUARDIAN
122

THE CELL
124

MASTER
BEDROOM
238

EMPTY
BEDROOM
206

THE MUSIC
ROOM
222

TIME LOOP
248

THE VESTIBULE
244

THE PRISONER
250

THE ORIGINAL
HOUSE
268

THE GALLERY
224

FAMILIAR
ROOM
254

SUMMONING
CHAMBER
256

THE FOUNTAIN
OF PAIN
258

228

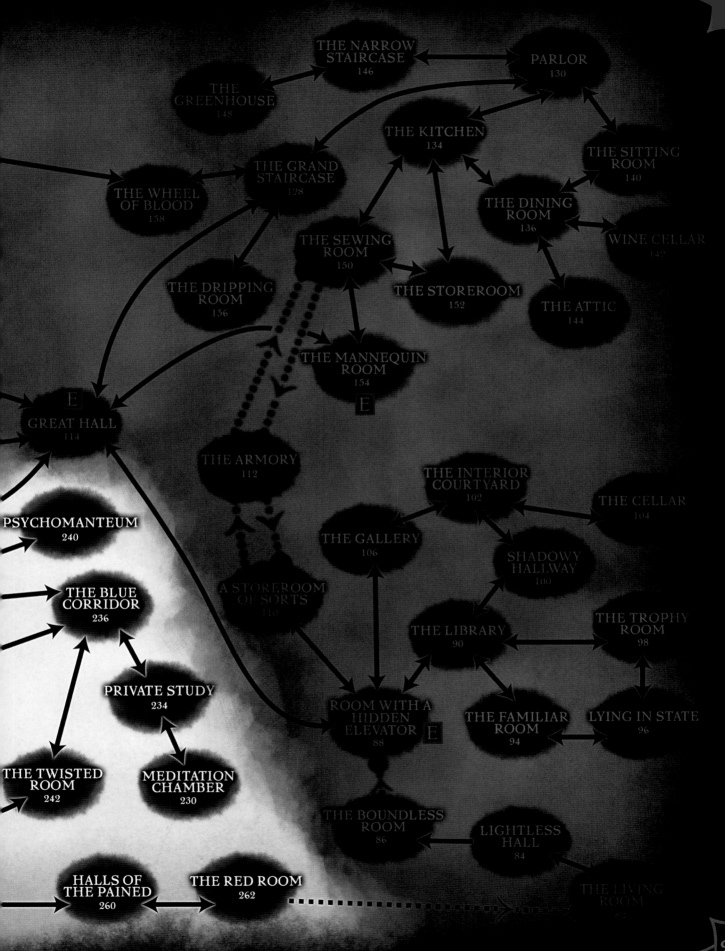

THE NARROW
STAIRCASE
146

PARLOR
130

THE
GREENHOUSE
148

THE KITCHEN
134

THE SITTING
ROOM
140

THE GRAND
STAIRCASE
128

THE WHEEL
OF BLOOD
158

THE SEWING
ROOM
150

THE DINING
ROOM
136

WINE CELLAR
142

THE DRIPPING
ROOM
156

THE STOREROOM
152

THE ATTIC
144

THE MANNEQUIN
ROOM
154

E

E
GREAT HALL
114

THE ARMORY
112

THE INTERIOR
COURTYARD
102

THE CELLAR
104

PSYCHOMANTEUM
240

THE GALLERY
106

SHADOWY
HALLWAY
100

THE BLUE
CORRIDOR
236

A STOREROOM
OF SORTS
110

THE LIBRARY
90

THE TROPHY
ROOM
98

PRIVATE STUDY
234

ROOM WITH A
HIDDEN
ELEVATOR
88

E

THE FAMILIAR
ROOM
94

LYING IN STATE
96

THE TWISTED
ROOM
242

MEDITATION
CHAMBER
230

THE BOUNDLESS
ROOM
86

LIGHTLESS
HALL
84

THE LIVING
ROOM
82

HALLS OF
THE PAINED
260

THE RED ROOM
262

his room contains a wealth of information and secrets.

Some of the books found here are tongue-in-cheek jokes, references to various horror tales, or similar things. If you think that naming them will throw off the mood, don't do it. Like the book list in the Library, it's a mixture of real book titles and completely fictional ones.

OVERVIEW

The door is locked (Rating 5) and the key is in **the Master Bedroom** (page 238).

This room has a desk piled with paper and pens, a chair, and a low bookshelf with books. Books are also piled on the floor. The floor is wood. The walls are just bare drywall.

There is a mysterious occult diagram on a huge sheet tacked to one wall, and several sheets of paper are tacked to another wall with strings connecting them.

If the characters appear here due to unlocking the lock in the Doorman's head, they appear in the secret room behind the occult diagram.

Secret Room

Occult Diagram

Books

Desk

To the Blue Corridor

To the Meditation Chamber

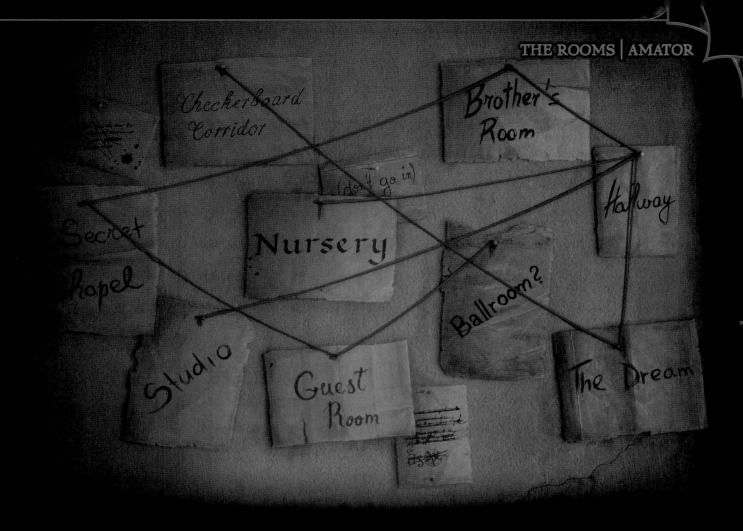

ARRIVING HERE VIA THE DOORMAN

This small chamber is where characters appear if the key is used to open the lock in the Doorman's forehead in **the Gatekeeper's Chamber** (page 224) or **the Cellar** (page 104). A simple unlocked door leads to the main part of the room.

SECRET DOOR AND ROOM

The door leading into this small room is hidden behind the occult diagram. Finding it probably requires a successful roll to complete a Rating 3 action.

OCCULT DIAGRAM

This has little or no significance. Anyone with any occult knowledge can ascertain that this is someone trying to work out a brand-new occult diagram, and it's unfinished. It might be a part of a ritual to travel beyond the mortal plane (if it worked). There is a secret door hidden behind the diagram.

THE HOUSE DIAGRAM

This shows nine different pieces of paper that have been tacked to the wall. They are of different ages, as though they've been tacked there at very different times. They are labeled Secret Chapel, Brother's Room, Guest Room, Ballroom?, Hallway, Studio, Nursery (don't go in), The Dream, and Checkerboard Corridor.

Show the players the image of Phillip's Diagram.

There is string wrapped around the tacks holding them, connecting them. The strings connect Secret Chapel to Brother's Room and Guest Room. Guest Room to Secret Chapel and Ballroom?. Brother's Room to Secret Chapel and Hallway. Hallway to Brother's Room, Nursery (don't go in), The Dream, and Studio. And finally The Dream and Checkerboard Corridor.

This is Phillip's attempt from long ago to map portions of the house decidedly unfamiliar to him.

BOOKS

Most of the books appear to be books about magic, immortal spirits and entities, and extradimensional realms. To a book collector or just someone interested in such things, there are a dozen books worth taking with a total value of about $5,000. The other books aren't very valuable; anyone even vaguely familiar with magic, the occult, or just books in general can discern what's valuable and what isn't. In addition to the books, there is also a handwritten note and some rolled blueprints.

Book titles in this room include:

+ *Magic in Theory and Practice*
+ *Outer Gateways*
+ *Traveling Through Impossible Realms*
+ *The Princes of Hell*
+ *The Hellbound Heart*
+ *Speaking With Hollow Voices*
+ *Enchiridion of the Path*
+ *The Entities Beyond*
+ *Stepping Into the Astral Realm*
+ *The House on the Borderland*
+ *Merriam Webster Dictionary*
+ *Lands Beyond Color*
+ *Gods or Demons*
+ *Men Are From Mars, Women Are From Venus*
+ *Grail Myths*
+ *Invisible Cities*
+ *Secrets Without Number*

HANDWRITTEN NOTE

Atop a stack of books right by the desk is a piece of paper with writing on both sides. Show players **Remnant 24** (page 286).

BLUEPRINTS

Amid the books, one can find a small set of blueprints tightly rolled and tied with twine. The blueprints seem to be designs for a rather odd door (the Mystic Door, in fact). The blueprints are one of the eight **Mystic Tools**. In addition to being one of these magical objects, the blueprints can also guide a character holding them, pointing the way to the nearest Mystic Tool that they have not already procured. It will, one by one, guide the characters to all the tools if they wish it.

IF THE LURKER IS PRESENT

If the character possessed by the Lurker (from **the Foyer** [page 162]) is present when the blueprints are discovered, it forces the character to act.

> The spirit possessing you compels you to grab the blueprints and shout, "Mine!"

If this action causes any kind of questioning of the possessed character or their actions, the Lurker yet again compels its host.

> The spirit possessing you makes you say, "I'm fine. Don't worry about it. Hey, I think these might help us find the rest of the tools."

Obviously, the Lurker wants the **Mystic Tools**. It will continue to compel its host to keep trying to find them. Should the entire set be found, the Lurker will attempt to kill all the other characters so that it can have the tools for itself.

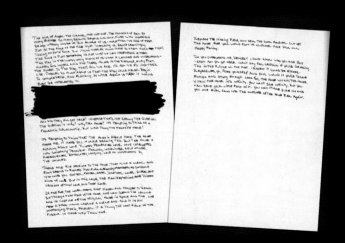

DESK

The desk is messy, and the papers include an unfinished handwritten note (show the players **Remnant 26** [page 288]) as well as notes on magic rituals that make no sense even to the most learned mage in the group (if any). The desk drawers hold more pens and other supplies, including a rather ornate **magnifying glass**.

Shoved in the back of a drawer are four keys. Two nickel, one large and brass, and one small and gold-plated. The gold-plated key opens the locked trunk in **the Attic** (page 144). The others open locks no longer found in the house. (The large brass key was originally the front door key, but the front door now operates under its own rules and that key serves no purpose.)

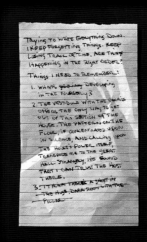 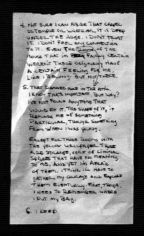

MAGNIFYING GLASS

This is an old, silver-plated magnifying glass that, when set up, sits on a tabletop to allow someone to read a book placed below. It's probably worth $250, but far more importantly, if the Ghost Book found in **the Parlor** (page 130) is placed beneath the magnifying glass, it can indeed be read. Titled *The Book of Names*, this book is a treatise on otherworldly beings and dark gods, offering the names that can be used to call to them and perhaps gain their attention. If the names are called out in a ritual in **the Attic** (page 144) surrounding the window into the void (the puzzle hole), one of the named beings may very well answer the call. Rather than immediately appearing, the diabolical king, queen, prince, or emperor of Hell observes the characters and intervenes in their lives much later on. This is almost certainly something that will take place after the PCs have left the Darkest House, and may involve a bargain, a possession, or something even grander. It will, however, be fraught with danger both physical and spiritual.

TO THE BLUE CORRIDOR

This door leads to **the Blue Corridor** (page 236). It does not bear the strange pattern that the other side of the door shows. The door is locked, but easily unlocked from this side without a key—it's a simple deadbolt.

TO THE MEDITATION CHAMBER

A ladder leads up to **the Meditation Chamber** (page 234).

LOVER

The Lover is invisible and immaterial. If the House Die indicates that they arrive here, they choose one character and make a Rating 6 attack. This inflicts no damage, but the character does pass out for a few minutes, unable to be roused. During this brief time, the victim has a romantic dream of a lover (whose appearance and gender are appropriate to the character, but who is not someone they actually know). They are now obsessed with finding this person (who may or may not exist, but certainly isn't in the house . . . unless perhaps in one of the Familiar Rooms). The Lover then leaves.

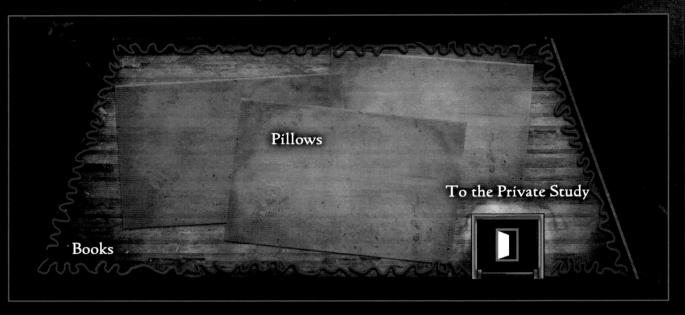

Pillows

To the Private Study

Books

This might serve as a decent place for a (small) group of PCs to rest.

> *If they haven't done so yet, encourage the players to take a minute in a safe place like this to piece together the information they've gathered, and develop a goal.*

OVERVIEW

This room is mostly free of furniture, with many pillows on the ground, with a distinctly Arabic feel. There is a stack of books in one corner. The room smells of incense, but there is no incense burner.

This loft can only be reached by the ladder in **the Private Study** (page 230).

BOOKS

The subject matter of these books appears to be astral projection, mental powers, and psychic phenomena. Tucked into one of the books is a page torn from a journal. Show the players **Remnant 23** (page 285).

THE PILLOWS

Hidden among the pillows, the characters find a bottle of calming elixir. There are three doses of the elixir in the bottle and each dose heals one mental wound.

TO THE PRIVATE STUDY

A ladder leads down to **the Private Study** (page 230).

LOVER

If the House Die indicates that the Lover arrives, they do, but not physically. Instead, the characters just feel a cold chill. Each must resist an attack with a Rating of 6. Those that fail suffer physical damage from the terrible cold and hear the Lover speak:

> "Oh, my love. You seem so cold. Let me warm you."

These characters must now resist a second attack with a Rating of 6, inflicting physical damage from the terrible cold. The Lover then leaves.

THE BLUE CORRIDOR

simple corridor, but rather than a pause between rooms, a door here offers its own illusory trick.

You could always ask the players personal questions about their characters beforehand. Who's the person you care about the most? What dream did your character have last night? And so on. But it can be fun to ask such questions in the middle of a session as well, as it completely throws the conversation into a new pattern.

OVERVIEW

The walls of this curved corridor are covered in dark blue wallpaper. The outer curve of the hall has two doors. One has a sign hanging on it that reads, DO NOT DISTURB. Even a casual glance at the other door reveals a strange pattern in the wood that likely bears closer examination.

ARCHWAY TO THE VESTIBULE

An archway opens into **the Vestibule** (page 244).

DOOR WITH A SIGN

This is the door into **the Master Bedroom** (page 238). The door is locked (Rating 5). The key is in **the Vestibule** (page 244).

DOOR WITH A PATTERN

This door leads to **the Private Study** (page 230). It is also locked (Rating 5) and the key is in **the Master Bedroom** (page 238). In the wood grain of the door, one can see a face. However, the first character to look at it will not just see a general crude face, but instead, they will see the face of a loved one, accurate down to the finest detail. You'll need to ask the player who it actually is unless their character is already well-developed enough that the answer is obvious.

The face you are so intimately familiar with is animate and looks at you with pleading eyes, silently mouthing a call for help.

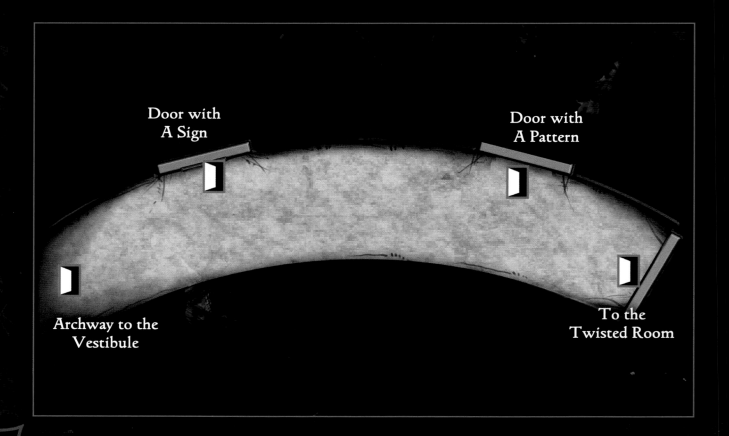

Door with
A Sign

Door with
A Pattern

Archway to the
Vestibule

To the
Twisted Room

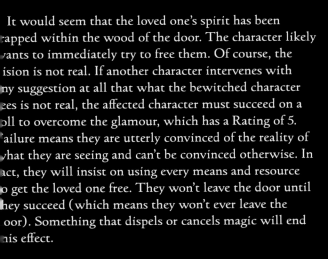

It would seem that the loved one's spirit has been trapped within the wood of the door. The character likely wants to immediately try to free them. Of course, the vision is not real. If another character intervenes with any suggestion at all that what the bewitched character sees is not real, the affected character must succeed on a roll to overcome the glamour, which has a Rating of 5. Failure means they are utterly convinced of the reality of what they are seeing and can't be convinced otherwise. In fact, they will insist on using every means and resource to get the loved one free. They won't leave the door until they succeed (which means they won't ever leave the door). Something that dispels or cancels magic will end this effect.

TO THE TWISTED ROOM

This innocuous door leads to **the Twisted Room** (page 242). It is unlocked.

LOVER

The Lover arrives if the House Die indicates it, in the form of utter darkness. There is a crash of thunder, and all the lights go out, even if the characters have magical lights, and even if they can somehow see in the dark. It's now completely dark in the corridor, and in whatever room they go into next, regardless of any lights in that location. The PCs will be forced to feel their way around in the dark. At some point, they hear a far-off scream. Eventually, the lighting returns to normal. The Lover then leaves.

Perhaps this bedroom can offer the characters a moment of quiet.

This was Phillip Harlock's bedroom.

OVERVIEW

The door is locked (Rating 5). The key is in the Vestibule.

There is a large bed with very nice red pillows and blankets, a nightstand, a closet, and a bureau with drawers. The furnishings are dark wood. The floor is white tile, and the bed sits upon a red rug. The wallpaper here looks like a flock of white birds. Or are they black birds?

Through a window, a nighttime rainstorm fills the sky with lightning and thunder.

Map labels: Closet · Window · Nightstand · To the Blue Corridor · To the Psychomanteum

NIGHTSTAND

The nightstand drawer holds a book, a piece of folded paper, and a bottle of pills.

BOOK

Titled *The Misery of Mystery,* this seems to be a pulpy dark fantasy adventure novel.

BOTTLE OF PILLS

Each pill is a Rating 3 sleep drug that puts someone to sleep within about 5 minutes of swallowing it.

FOLDED PAPER

This is apparently a letter. Show the players **Remnant 22** (page 285).

CLOSET

This is filled with men's clothing—shirts, slacks, jackets, ties, shoes, a bathrobe, and so on. The bathrobe bears the initials "P.H." In one of the jacket pockets is the key to **the Private Study** (page 230). This would require a thorough search and probably a roll to succeed at a

WINDOW

A storm rages outside the window. Lightning flashes, wind rattles windowpanes, thunder echoes in the distance.

✦ If this is the first or second time the PCs have encountered a room where they could see a storm outside, nothing special happens.

✦ If this is the third time the PCs have encountered a room where they could see a storm outside, they see a tall, gaunt, and gangly creature in the distance illuminated by a lightning flash.

✦ If this is the fourth time the PCs have encountered a room where they could see a storm outside, they see a tall, gaunt, and gangly creature, tattered bits of clothing soaking wet, seemingly staring at them through the window, illuminated by a lightning flash. It's hard to know if it's actually staring because it seems to have a massive wound where its face should be. And then it is gone.

✦ If this is the fifth time the PCs have encountered a room where they could see a storm outside, they see a tall, gaunt, and gangly creature, tattered bits of clothing soaking wet, jaundiced flesh covering its body, with long limbs twisted in strange positions and its face torn messily from its head, leaving only blood and gore where it should be. It is tap, tap, tapping on the window.

✦ If this is the sixth time the PCs have encountered a room where they could see a storm outside, they

of clothing soaking wet, jaundiced flesh covering its body, with long limbs twisted in strange positions and its face torn messily from its head, leaving only blood and gore where it should be. It is tap, tap, tapping on the window. And then it smashes the window and comes into the room. It has a Rating of 5 and while it can make physical attacks, it also has the ability to use a hex power that causes some kind of deformity in the body of another—enlarged hand, lengthened arm, misshapen face, sealed-up eye, and so on—if they cannot resist the effect. The victim suffers a Bane to all physical activity. The changes last as long as the Faceless Thing lives.

Show the players the image of **the Faceless Thing.**

The Faceless Thing will pursue characters that flee.

The window seals itself once again and becomes unbreakable. The characters see only storm outside the windows from now on.

TO THE BLUE CORRIDOR

This door leads to **the Blue Corridor** (page 236). It is locked (Rating 5). The key is in **the Vestibule** (page 244).

TO THE PSYCHOMANTEUM

This small door leads to **the Psychomanteum** (page 240). It is unlocked.

LOVER

The Lover arrives if the House Die suggests it, but is invisible and immaterial. It picks a single character and follows them, starting in this room, wherever they go. *Every roll the character makes is a failure.* After a few failures (particularly if it seems like they should have been successes), the Lover whispers in the character's ear.

> A pleasant, soft voice whispers in your ear. "Aww. Are you having a run of bad luck, my precious one? I can help with that. Just promise me you won't leave me. Stay with me in the house forever."

If the character won't make that promise, they should roll to resist a Rating 6 mental attack *which does not automatically fail.* If they fail this roll, they suffer no damage but the failures will go on, with the voice whispering to them again later, asking for the same promise. This will continue until the character makes the roll to resist or they make the promise.

If the character makes the promise to never leave the Lover, if and when the characters have the opportunity to escape the Darkest House, the character can't go unless they succeed in resisting a Rating 6 mental attack. If the character succeeds, they hear a cry of anguish as they leave, and the Lover will likely not be kind if they ever return.

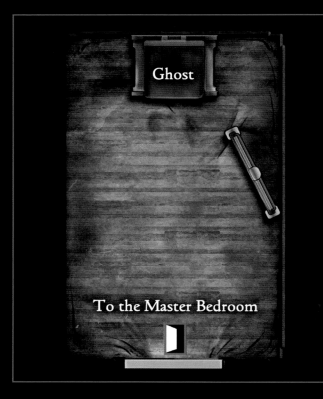

Ghost

To the Master Bedroom

An angry and devious ghost wants to talk with the characters, and perhaps take possession of one of them.

> *You can be generous with characters trying to identify useful things in the house, like potions or, in this room, ectoplasm.*

OVERVIEW

This small, enclosed area is set up with a comfortable chair, dim lighting, and a mirror angled so as not to reflect anything but darkness. It is intended to communicate with spirits of the dead. Ironically, there appears to be a man who is spectral and ghostly, sitting in the chair, staring at the characters as they come in. He is an old man with long hair, wearing a suit. He also has a hole in his chest (probably the wound that killed him).

GHOSTLY MAN

A psychomanteum is meant to be a conduit with the dead, and this ghost managed to use that to his advantage. The spirit is the ghost of Charles Kingson, and he greets anyone coming into the room and asks their name and what they're doing in the house. He has no knowledge or connection to the past or present of the house. He's just a restless spirit who found the equivalent of an unlocked door.

After briefly chatting, he picks one of the characters present and attempts to draw their spirit out of them

and into his ectoplasmic form. Effectively, he wants the character to possess *him*. If successful, he is then free to take possession of their body. If a character is already possessed (such as by the Lurker from **the Foyer** [page 162]), Charles will choose someone else.

Charles has a Rating of 4. He cannot be touched physically (nor can he touch anyone or anything physically without a long, grueling effort, such as what he did to get into the chair). Magic or energy affects him, including enchanted weapons.

Should Charles possess the character, he won't even try to conceal the fact. He will exclaim with delight, shouting his joy about having a body again, and then run off. He doesn't know his way around the house at all, so his path will be random. He's also not used to having a physical form again after decades (or longer), so all of his actions will have a Bane.

BEING IN A GHOSTLY FORM

First of all, being put into a ghostly body is an attack with a Rating of 5, inflicting mental damage from the shock and horror.

Additionally, if a character is put in the ghostly form of Charles Kingson, they will need a few minutes to adjust to the very different "body."

+ No physical actions they attempt will have any effect. They can't touch or move things, or touch or be moved.
+ Even if they could touch things, they wouldn't have any of their possessions. Charles has them now.
+ They can move from place to place twice as fast as normal.
+ They don't need to eat, sleep, drink, or breathe. In fact, they cannot do any of those things.
+ They can move through solid objects (including walls) as easily as through empty air, but moving from one room of the Darkest House to another in this way is dangerous to their sanity. They'll be thrust into a chilling, screaming void of loneliness for what seems like an eternity before they reach the next room, even though no real time has passed. This is a Rating 6 attack that inflicts mental damage each time.
+ They can use any magical, psychic, or supernatural powers they might have had before.
+ Any solid matter they pass through, or that passes through them, is coated in a fine layer of ectoplasm.
+ They can attempt to possess living mortal beings. There aren't many living mortal beings in the house, but this is a way they can try to get their body back. This is handled just like if they were making an

attack against the potential victim, but if they are successful, both spirits will be in the body. They must then succeed with a second attack against the victim to force their spirit out. Meanwhile, the original spirit can make attacks to force the character out. If the PC is forced back out of a victim before they force the other spirit out, they cannot try to enter that living mortal being again for an hour or so. None of these attacks inflict any damage. This is how they can try to get their own body back. If Charles is expelled from the character's body, he disappears forever.

✦ They can attempt to possess a living mortal being's body, but not exert any kind of control, effectively just "riding" them. This requires a mental attack against the victim that inflicts no damage.

ECTOPLASM

The spiritual residue that the character can leave behind is viscous, gelatinous, and very difficult to see (but easy to feel). If a person or their belongings has any ectoplasm on them, they have a Bane in any action (including defense) taken against spiritual entities or non-mortal beings, such as most of the inhabitants of the Darkest House. Cleaning the ectoplasm off is not too difficult, but first it must be found—special senses, detection, or even a black light would help greatly.

At the same time, if a being is afflicted by a mystical malady, ingesting ectoplasm may help alleviate it. The affected character gets another roll to try to resist the affliction. Someone with occult or magical knowledge would know this.

TO THE MASTER BEDROOM

This innocuous door leads to **the Master Bedroom** (page 238). It is unlocked.

LOVER

If the House Die indicates that the Lover arrives, they whisper each PC's name in their ear (the Lover does this individually, so each character hears their own name and no others).

> You hear a loving and pleasant voice whisper your name fondly in your ear.

Each character must attempt to resist a Rating 6 attack or suffer a mental wound. The Lover then leaves.

THE TWISTED ROOM

A room that seems to have its own laws of gravity offers a strange place for an ambush.

One of the most common features of nightmares is when a person who should be protecting you (like a parent or an older sibling) ignores you when you are in distress. That's what the Lover plays upon if they arrive in this room.

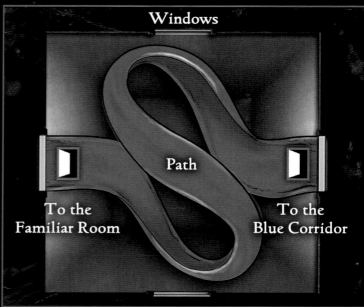

Windows

Path

To the
Familiar Room

To the
Blue Corridor

OVERVIEW

This weird room is a perfect cube, and all the interior surfaces (floor, walls, ceiling) are mirrored. The doors are in the middle of the walls (both vertically and horizontally). A smooth, glistening red walkway leads into the room from the doorway, curves over to the right-hand wall (where there is a window, not a door), curves up to the ceiling, then over to the left-hand wall (another window), and then to the door, and finally up to the other door. The light in this room flickers constantly, like a strobe effect. Through the windows, it is night and storming outside, with rain on the glass.

THE PATH

If the characters follow the red path, gravity changes with them, so they'll always be right side up from their own perspective. As long as the PCs stay on the path, they'll be fine. Gravity is always oriented toward the path while they stand or walk upon it, so even though they might seem to be walking up the walls or along the ceiling, even in relation to each other, each will feel as though they stand on the floor.

Characters who leave the path feel no gravity at all. They float helplessly to the center of the room. Characters cannot take advantage of the null gravity, because there is no way to gain momentum or "push off" into the air. As soon as they are no longer on the path, they lose all inertia and float listlessly.

THE BURROWERS

As soon as the PCs are all well into the room, strange creatures that were previously hidden beneath the walkway fly out.

Show the players the image of **the Burrowers**.

Fluttering about on wings of drawn flesh, these grublike creatures are only a danger to characters who are already hurt. Burrowers have a Rating of 2, and there are eight of them. If any characters have physical wounds, the burrowers are drawn to them and make a physical attack in which they thrust themselves into the wound and bury themselves in the victim's flesh. This doesn't cause damage based on the burrower's Rating. Instead, if they successfully hit, they inflict damage on the victim, equivalent to the victim's original wound. Once they have burrowed in, they writhe and wriggle, automatically inflicting a Rating 2 physical wound each time they have a turn. Getting them out very likely requires inflicting at least a Rating 3 wound upon their victim.

WINDOWS

If a character wants to look at a window closely, they'll follow the red walkway and the window will be at their feet. A storm rages outside of both the windows. Lightning flashes, wind rattles windowpanes, thunder echoes in the distance.

- ✦ If this is the first or second time the PCs have encountered a room where they could see a storm outside, nothing special happens.
- ✦ If this is the third time the PCs have encountered a room where they could see a storm outside, they see a tall, gaunt, and gangly creature in the distance illuminated by a lightning flash.
- ✦ If this is the fourth time the PCs have encountered a room where they could see a storm outside, they see a tall, gaunt, and gangly creature, tattered bits of clothing soaking wet, seemingly staring at them through the window, illuminated by a lightning flash. It's hard to know if it's actually staring because it seems to have a massive wound where its face should be. And then it is gone.
- ✦ If this is the fifth time the PCs have encountered a room where they could see a storm outside, they see a tall, gaunt, and gangly creature, tattered bits of clothing soaking wet, jaundiced flesh covering its body, with long limbs twisted in strange positions and its face torn messily from its head, leaving only blood and gore where it should be. It is tap, tap, tapping on the window.
- ✦ If this is the sixth time the PCs have encountered a room where they could see a storm outside, they see a tall, gaunt, and gangly creature, tattered bits of clothing soaking wet, jaundiced flesh covering its body, with long limbs twisted in strange positions and its face torn messily from its head, leaving only blood and gore where it should be. It is tap, tap, tapping on the window. And then it smashes the window and comes into the room. It has a Rating of 5 and while it can make physical attacks, it also has the ability to use a hex power that causes some kind of deformity in the body of another—enlarged hand, lengthened arm, misshapen face, sealed-up eye, and so on—if they cannot resist the effect. The victim suffers a Bane to all physical activity. The changes last as long as the Faceless Thing lives.

Show the players the image of **the Faceless Thing**. The Faceless Thing will pursue characters that flee. The window seals itself once again and becomes unbreakable. The characters see only storm outside the windows from now on.

TO THE FAMILIAR ROOM

This innocuous door leads to **the Familiar Room** (page 254). It is unlocked.

TO THE BLUE CORRIDOR

This innocuous door leads to **the Blue Corridor** (page 236). It is unlocked.

LOVER

If the House Die indicates that the Lover arrives here, they choose one character that is subject to the burrowing things' attack. They then reach into the character's mind and take the image of someone that the character loves or loved—preferably someone who offered them comfort or protection in the past. The Lover then makes the character see that person:

> Even as these horrible things attack and attempt to bury themselves in your wounds, you suddenly notice someone you love or loved standing by one of the windows. Even as you're attacked, even as you cry out, they just look out the window and do not move, as if ignoring you and your plight.

You'll then have to work out with that player who their character sees. It's important that they understand this isn't an illusion, but the person is really there (even though they aren't). And frankly, here in the Darkest House, where people and places from characters' pasts get pulled in, is it really so hard to believe that the house did it one more time? In any event, this is a Rating 6 attack against the character that inflicts mental damage. The character also loses their next turn, as they spend it calling out to the image of that person for help—which that person ignores.

The Lover then leaves.

THE VESTIBULE

Possible arrival point for this section of the house, this room also offers the ability to go to the Original House.

> *If at all possible, it would be good to convey to the players by the time that they get here, that they are very deep within the house, and perhaps close to the very heart of some of its mysteries.*

OVERVIEW

This is a grand room, with curving staircases up to a balcony, where you can see a door. Sconces on the wall provide medium illumination. The tiles of the floor here create an intricate geometric pattern. An archway on the lower level gives access to a blue corridor.

A window shows a nighttime rainstorm outside. There are multiple small tables against the walls, all around the large room, each holding a vase with orchids.

ARRIVING BY SPEAKING THE WORDS

Mater, *Pater*, *Frater*, and *Soror*. If these four Latin words are spoken aloud by a character who has visited at least one room in each of the four sections, that character is instantly transported here. Characters arrive atop the pattern on the floor, right in the middle of it. These words might be learned in **the Wheel of Blood** (page 158).

PATTERN

The pattern is geometric and pleasing. If a character concentrates on the pattern in silence, and calls upon the house's power, the pattern will transport them to **the Great Hall** (page 114). They'll feel, for a moment, that they are passing through a void filled with screaming spirits. Then, they'll arrive, right in front of the Host. The secret of this can be learned in **the Private Study** (page 230).

Calling upon the house means, of course, that the character gains a Doom, and the house acts.

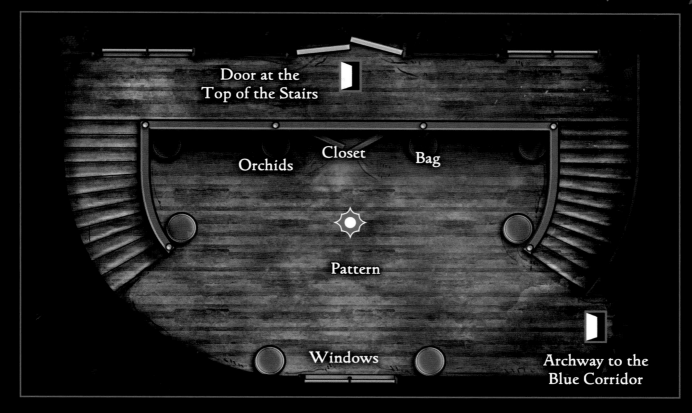

Door at the
Top of the Stairs

Orchids | Closet | Bag

Pattern

Windows

Archway to the
Blue Corridor

PHILLIP'S BAG

Phillip's bag is under one of the tables. It's not immediately obvious, but anyone taking even a minute or two to look around the room will spot it. It holds the following objects:

✦ The key to **the Master Bedroom** (page 238).
✦ A gold pocketwatch worth $150.
✦ A tincture of magical oil that heals one wound.
✦ A note. Show the players **Remnant 27** (page 289).

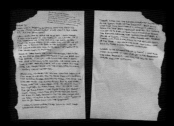

✦ A pocketknife.
✦ A handgun, fully loaded with eight rounds. If the characters come from a setting where handguns are not common, treat it as a very easy to use and accurate ranged weapon that inflicts impressive but not overwhelming damage.
✦ Phillip Harlock's business card (the address it bears has no relation to a street or community in the PC's setting.) Show the players **Remnant 28** (page 289).

ORCHIDS

Characters that speak their mother's name into one of the orchids' blooms will be instantly transported to **the Original House** (page 268). The secret of this trick can be found in **the Meditation Chamber** (page 234) or **the Summoning Chamber** (page 256).

LARGE CLOSET

This closet is filled with a variety of heavy coats, some scarves, hats, gloves, umbrellas, and galoshes.

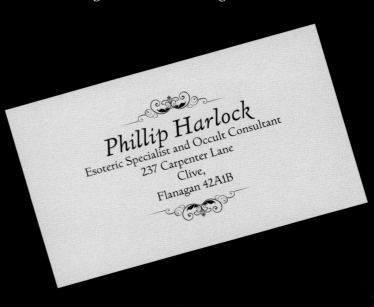

Phillip Harlock
Esoteric Specialist and Occult Consultant
237 Carpenter Lane
Clive,
Flanagan 42A1B

WINDOW

A storm rages outside the window. Lightning flashes, wind rattles windowpanes, thunder echoes in the distance.

+ If this is the first or second time the PCs have encountered a room where they could see a storm outside, nothing special happens.
+ If this is the third time the PCs have encountered a room where they could see a storm outside, they see a tall, gaunt, and gangly creature in the distance illuminated by a lightning flash.
+ If this is the fourth time the PCs have encountered a room where they could see a storm outside, they see a tall, gaunt, and gangly creature, tattered bits of clothing soaking wet, seemingly staring at them through the window, illuminated by a lightning flash. It's hard to know if it's actually staring because it seems to have a massive wound where its face should be. And then it is gone.
+ If this is the fifth time the PCs have encountered a room where they could see a storm outside, they see a tall, gaunt, and gangly creature, tattered bits of clothing soaking wet, jaundiced flesh covering its body, with long limbs twisted in strange positions and its face torn messily from its head, leaving only blood and gore where it should be. It is tap, tap, tapping on the window.
+ If this is the sixth time the PCs have encountered a room where they could see a storm outside, they see a tall, gaunt, and gangly creature, tattered bits of clothing soaking wet, jaundiced flesh covering its body, with long limbs twisted in strange positions and its face torn messily from its head, leaving only blood and gore where it should be. It is tap, tap, tapping on the window. And then it smashes the window and comes into the room. It has a Rating of 5 and while it can make physical attacks, it also has the ability to use a hex power that causes some kind of deformity in the body of another—enlarged hand, lengthened arm, misshapen face, sealed-up eye, and so on—if they cannot resist the effect. The victim suffers a Bane to all physical activity. The changes last as long as the Faceless Thing lives.

Show the players the image of **the Faceless Thing**. The Faceless Thing will pursue characters that flee. The window seals itself once again and becomes unbreakable. The characters see only storm outside the windows from now on.

DOOR AT THE TOP OF THE STAIRS

This heavy wooden door leads into **the Time Loop** (page 248).

ARCHWAY TO THE BLUE CORRIDOR

An archway opens into **the Blue Corridor** (page 236).

LOVER

If the House Die indicates that the Lover arrives, they do so invisibly and intangibly, without physical form. They pick one character and whisper to them.

> A loving but stern voice whispers to you, "Your family never loved you. I'm the only one that ever loved you."

The character essentially has four options: ignore the voice, deny it, agree with it, or react in some other way.

- Characters that ignore it hear the whisper again. It will continue until they react (following them wherever they go, unless they leave the Amator section) or until the constant whispering threatens to drive them a little crazy, suffering a mental wound with a Rating of 4.
- A character that denies it provokes the Lover into an argument. "What have they ever done for you?" "They were always cruel to you," and so on. Play out the argument, but note that the Lover will ignore anything the other characters say or do at this time. A character can win this argument, but only if they really believe what they're saying. If they do, the Lover will never bother them again. They are henceforth immune to even further house actions in this section as well. If they don't win the argument, they suffer a mental wound with a Rating of 4.

- Characters that sincerely agree are either filled with a longing for their romantic partner/interest or feel a terrible emptiness for not having one. If they have someone in their life, they are now compelled to get to that person with all due haste. If they don't, they're compelled to try to find someone. This probably means escaping the house, then immediately traveling to the object of their love or starting their search for someone. Characters that agree but aren't sincere incur the Lover's wrath. "Liar!" they shout. "You never loved me!" And then the Lover makes an attack with a Rating of 6 that inflicts mental damage.
- Characters that do basically anything else are treated as those that ignore the Lover. Essentially, only denying or agreeing with the statement gives the character the chance to avoid a mental wound here.

This is a central room in this portion of the house, but it's not an easy room to pass through quickly, as characters must restart their visit here over and over.

> *You've seen this movie. Or movies. You know how this works.*

OVERVIEW

Tick. Tick. Tick. The grandfather clock in this room seems almost deafeningly loud. It's not, but it seems that way, at least to some. An intricately woven round rug covers much of the floor, the walls have a red and white patterned wallpaper, and faint illumination comes from electric sconces on the walls.

THE TIME LOOP

After the PCs enter and poke around and find nothing of import, let one of the players know that something is amiss.

> You remember your companions doing and saying the same things they just said once before. Maybe twice. Maybe more.

The characters are caught in a time loop, and they have already entered this room and undertaken the actions here many times before. Eventually, one by one, they will remember this. The time loop resets each time someone tries to leave the room.

THE CLOCK

The clock is a normal grandfather clock. It merely makes it clear, once characters are paying attention, that time keeps resetting. Otherwise, it is not involved in the cause of the loop.

LEAVING THE ROOM

This resets the time loop. Tell the players that they are entering the room, as if for the first time. Now at least half of them remember this happening before. If they try again, everyone will remember the repeating loop. Even if just one person tries to leave, the loop resets for everyone, and they are just entering the room once again.

ACTUALLY GETTING OUT

This isn't a trap or a mechanism—there's no way to "disarm" it. There's no trick. Time is out of joint within the house (by mortal perceptions). The only way to get out of the time loop is to call upon the house. This is just like when a player decides to add the House Die to their roll. Their character gains a Doom and the house acts. In fact, if someone calls upon the house in this "normal" way, that will inadvertently get them out of the loop. That one character can leave the room, but when the other characters reset, they will be separated from the group until everyone eventually calls upon the house. And since this is an individual action, that means the house acts each time. And the PCs may have to cross through this room multiple times.

TO THE FAMILIAR ROOM

This doorway leads to **the Familiar Room** (page 254). No character can successfully exit this room through here without first calling upon the house. See the entry, **Actually Getting Out**.

TO THE SUMMONING CHAMBER

This innocuous door leads to **the Summoning Chamber** (page 256). It is unlocked. No character can successfully exit this room through here without first calling upon the house. See the entry, **Actually Getting Out**.

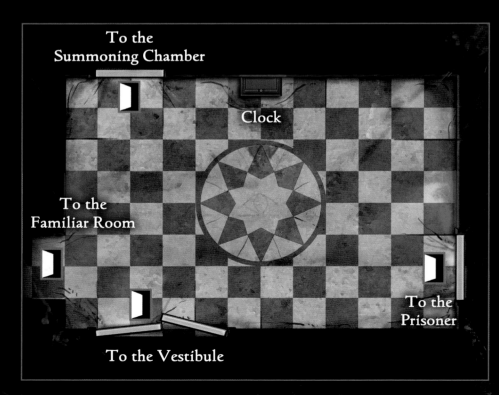

To the Summoning Chamber

Clock

To the Familiar Room

To the Prisoner

To the Vestibule

TO THE VESTIBULE

This innocuous door leads to **the Vestibule** (page 244). It is unlocked. No character can successfully exit this room through here without first calling upon the house. See the entry, **Actually Getting Out**.

TO THE PRISONER

This innocuous door leads to **the Prisoner** (page 250). It is unlocked. No character can successfully exit this room through here without first calling upon the house. See the entry on **Actually Getting Out**.

LOVER

If the House Die indicates that the Lover acts, remember that they have no physical form or appearance. Instead, they begin whispering lies in the ears of the PCs. As the characters are trying to figure out how to get out of the time loop, send one this message:

> A soothing, calming voice whispers in your ear, "It's the clock, my love. That's the key to getting out."

Later, send another character the same message. But then, soon thereafter, send a third character (or the first character, if you'd rather) this message:

> A voice filled with sincerity and affection says, "There's a pattern in the rug. Look at the rug."

(There is a pattern in the rug, but it's got nothing to do with anything other than an interesting design.)

If any character tries to reply to the voice, it ignores them, unless they accuse it of lying. Then, everyone in the room will hear "I don't like being called a liar," and they all feel a deep chill and must resist a Rating 4 mental attack. Then the Lover is gone.

If the PCs have already figured out the way out of the loop, the Lover will silently follow them to the next room and act there instead, as indicated.

THE PRISONER

Someone is held here in a magical box, and it might be someone the PCs know.

This chamber offers you the opportunity to replace Nyaar with an NPC from your existing campaign, or even an NPC from a different campaign. Interestingly, the prisoner character should probably be a villain.

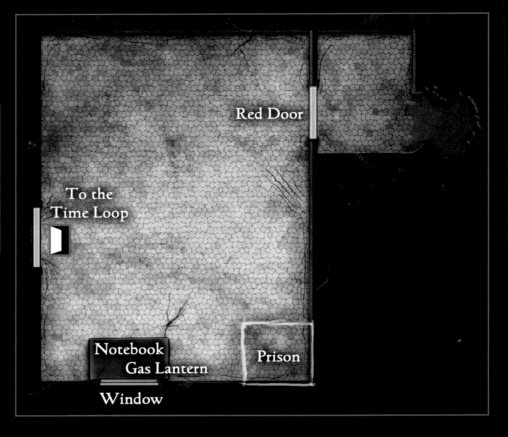

Red Door

To the Time Loop

Notebook
Gas Lantern

Prison

Window

OVERVIEW

This dark room has a plain stone floor and brick walls. A human figure huddles in the corner. Someone has drawn on the floor and walls around the figure with chalk so that it looks like they are within a three-dimensional box from the angle of someone coming through the door. Chains depend from the ceiling, most going all the way to the floor. A red door is on one side of the "box." A table to the other side holds an old-fashioned gas lantern, which gives the only light. It has a small notebook on it as well. Above the table is a window, showing a nighttime rainstorm.

THE PRISON

The chalk drawing is a peculiar magical prison. Although it is two-dimensional, it creates an emergent three-dimensional "box." The person within it cannot leave under their own power. Only a person outside the box, who stands at an angle from which the lines on the walls and floor do not look like a three-dimensional box, can pull the prisoner free.

THE PRISONER

The figure in the prescribed area is Nyaar, a man who's been trapped here for a very long time. Like others before and after him, he ventured into the house and then couldn't leave. He tried to use some powerful explosives to blow a hole in the house and when that didn't work, the Cenotaph grabbed him and put him here.

Nyaar has a Rating of 4 and comes from a setting that is not unlike our own modern world. He is, however, a liar, a cheat, and a violent criminal, although he tries to paint himself as an innocent victim. He has a Rating of 5 for deception and stealth. He doesn't currently have anything in the way of equipment, and he has no idea how long he's been in the house.

He spends all his energy on getting the PCs to help free him. He doesn't know the secret of the prison, and if asked who drew it, he will only say, "He calls himself the Cenotaph."

ALTERNATE PRISONER

If you have an ongoing campaign that is following a different ongoing campaign—even, or especially, one using a different system—strongly consider putting a villain or other NPC from the previous campaign in here instead of Nyaar. I cannot stress enough the metagame shock and even horror the players will experience by suddenly running into an old Call of Cthulhu cult leader that their previous PCs barely escaped from. Or by facing their hated nemesis from a Shadowrun game from years back with their current Cypher characters. I practically guarantee you'll have to pause the game for a few minutes to make room for all the "No way!" and "Holy crap!" exclamations you'll get. If you do this, you can still use the notebook remnant as-is, and make it clear that Nyaar was the prisoner prior to the NPC you place here.

THE CENOTAPH

Once the PCs enter the room and have spent a minute or two there, perhaps speaking with Nyaar, the red door opens and a figure comes in.

Show the players the image of **the Cenotaph**.

This entity appears to be a large man with prominent features and a massive black beard that extends down to his stomach. He wears a long black coat with silver buttons and buckles, and his silver and metallic rings appear downright dangerous. Monstrous, non-human things emerge from the beard. Their wriggling limbs and toothy mouths look deadly, and their eyes seethe with hate.

The things in his beard are the horrific, ghostly remnants of those who have died in the house. The Cenotaph stands for and embodies all the lost souls of the Darkest House. The more death, the more power and influence he holds. And there has been a lot of death. The Cenotaph has a Rating of 7, and he wields magical powers that include:

+ Conjuring black flames that take the form of occult symbols, burning everyone he wishes to harm in the room.
+ Emitting a low mystic syllable. Anyone who hears it and fails a roll to resist it must use their next turn to inflict self-harm (all characters inflict a wound equal to their own Rating upon themselves).
+ Conjure a barrier of shifting colors and light that blocks off a portion of a room, a corridor, a door, or something of that nature.
+ Sense the presence of anyone he has laid eyes upon, so that he always knows where they are in the house.

All of his magical powers have a Rating of 7, like him. But there's more. The hungry ghosts in his beard attack every foe that stands near the Cenotaph. The ghosts have a Rating of 2 each and their bite is venomous, so any wound they inflict is rated +2 higher than it would normally be. (This doesn't improve the Rating of the attack; it increases the Rating of a wound they would normally inflict.) Being poisoned like this makes you feel as though your very bones shift from freezing cold to fiery hot, and then back again.

THE CENOTAPH'S ACTIONS

Right now, the Cenotaph is mainly interested in guarding his prisoner. If the PCs have no desire or intention to free the prisoner, the Cenotaph will merely say, in a low, throaty whisper, "Get out." He is not a source of information or aid.

If the PCs do try to free the prisoner, the Cenotaph attacks. He will not pursue them if they flee.

If the PCs leave and return, the Cenotaph is back in the side room behind the Red Door. If the characters are very deliberately stealthy, they could free the prisoner and get away before the Cenotaph knows.

BEHIND THE RED DOOR

The Cenotaph keeps to himself in a tiny chamber just off the main room. As an immortal entity, he doesn't have the same needs or desires as a human. There is only a sort of hairy nest built within a cavity dug into the far wall. It is huge and reeks of decay and bodily odors. Tucked within it is a jeweled necklace worth $7,500, wrapped carefully around a lock of hair that is not the Cenotaph's.

NOTEBOOK

This small notebook has many missing pages, but still has five with writing on them and a dozen blank pages at the end. Show the players **Remnant 25** (page 287).

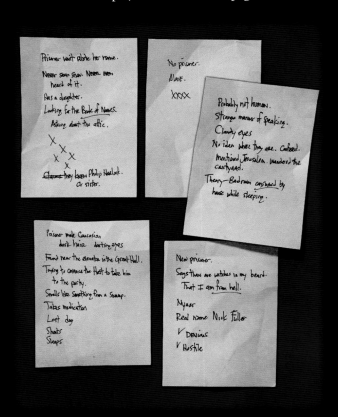

GAS LANTERN

Hidden behind the gas lantern (Rating 4 action to find) are two small glass bottles, each with a bit of magical powder, one bright orange and the other pale yellow. The orange powder, if sprinkled upon a wound, heals the wound, and there is enough for three wounds. However, the person treated in this way will have the memory of the last 24 hours utterly erased from their mind. The yellow powder, if sprinkled upon a creature, automatically and instantly removes all magic affecting them (beneficial and detrimental). If used offensively against a magical creature or entity, the victim loses their next action. There are two doses of the yellow powder.

WINDOW

A storm rages outside the window. Lightning flashes, wind rattles windowpanes, thunder echoes in the distance.

✦ If this is the first or second time the PCs have encountered a room where they could see a storm outside, nothing special happens.

✦ If this is the third time the PCs have encountered a room where they could see a storm outside, they see a tall, gaunt, and gangly creature in the distance illuminated by a lightning flash.

✦ If this is the fourth time the PCs have encountered a room where they could see a storm outside, they see a tall, gaunt, and gangly creature, tattered bits of clothing soaking wet, seemingly staring at them through the window, illuminated by a lightning flash. It's hard to know if it's actually staring because it seems to have a massive wound where its face should be. And then it is gone.

✦ If this is the fifth time the PCs have encountered a room where they could see a storm outside, they see a tall, gaunt, and gangly creature, tattered bits of clothing soaking wet, jaundiced flesh covering its body, with long limbs twisted in strange positions and its face torn messily from its head, leaving only blood and gore where it should be. It is tap, tap, tapping on the window.

✦ If this is the sixth time the PCs have encountered a room where they could see a storm outside, they see a tall, gaunt, and gangly creature, tattered bits of clothing soaking wet, jaundiced flesh covering its body, with long limbs twisted in strange positions and its face torn messily from its head, leaving only blood and gore where it should be. It is tap, tap, tapping on the window. And then it smashes the window and comes into the room. It has a Rating of 5 and while it can make physical attacks, it also has the ability to use a hex power that causes some kind of deformity in the body of another—enlarged hand, lengthened arm, misshapen face, sealed-up eye, and so on—if they cannot resist the effect. The victim suffers a Bane to all physical activity. The changes last as long as the Faceless Thing lives.

Show the players the image of **the Faceless Thing**. The Faceless Thing will pursue characters that flee. The window seals itself once again and becomes unbreakable. The characters see only storm outside the windows from now on.

TO THE TIME LOOP

This innocuous door leads to **the Time Loop** (page 248). It is unlocked.

LOVER

If indicated by the House Die, the Lover arrives. They are invisible and without physical form. Still, they manage to jostle a character with a physical attack (Rating 6). If the Lover is successful, the character stumbles into the prescribed prison, and is trapped there until freed. The former prisoner is pushed out. The Lover then leaves.

This room is different from the others, as its details are dictated by the background of one or more of the PCs.

> *An NPC trapped in this room offers a fantastic way to bring in a new PC, should that need arise in the course of playing through the scenario.*

OVERVIEW

This room is a location from the past of at least one of the characters. It is unmistakably their childhood bedroom, a prison cell where they were incarcerated, the taproom from a bar they used to frequent, a training dojo where they studied, or the library where they first saw an early crush. Or someplace else. The important thing is, it is not a replica—it's actually that room. The details might be changed somewhat, but that's only because time has passed. Or, the room might be precisely as if they had just left it. It's furnished, but any windows just look out into pitch blackness. There are no occupants.

FITTING THE ROOM IN

The room should conform to the needs of the map. In other words, where the diagram shows entrances and exits, the room needs to have them as well. It must have a door that connects to **the Twisted Room** (page 242) and one that connects to **the Time Loop** (page 248). If the original room didn't have the same exits, it appears the way it did originally, but you must modify the room as needed with new, hidden doors, or original doors that no longer open. A secret panel might slide to reveal an exit where there wasn't one originally, or a now-extraneous door cannot be opened, or perhaps leads to a solid black wall through which passage is impossible.

COORDINATING WITH THE OTHER FAMILIAR ROOMS

There are two other similar rooms in the house (possibly more if the PCs explore **the Backrooms** (page 118). They are always different rooms, and very likely they are from the past of a different PC. What happens when PCs visit them depends not on which room they discover, but the order in which they are discovered.

The first time the PCs come to a familiar room, it is just that—nothing more.

The second time the PCs come to a (different) familiar room, it is as the character acquainted with the room remembers it, but there is blood on the floor or perhaps on the furniture. Some recognizable memento of an NPC associated with this room can be found near or in the blood.

The third time the PCs come to a (different) familiar room, it is different because it is occupied. The PC acquainted with the room recognizes the NPC; they're someone the PC would normally expect to find in this room (in a world outside the house).

The NPC is just as surprised to see the PC, whom they likewise recognize. Their shock is quite genuine. "What are you doing here?"

From the NPC's point of view, they are still in the room where the room should be. They aren't in the Darkest House. When the NPC looks through the entrance the PCs came through, they don't see where the PCs have been, but rather where the original room's entrance would normally lead.

This changes should a PC attempt to convince the NPC to come through one of the exits of the room (or forces them to do so). In this eventuality, the NPC *is* now in the Darkest House, trapped there alongside the PCs. It doesn't matter if they go back into the familiar room. They are now with the PCs, and likely in a lot of danger.

There is no way to reverse this process. A character within the Darkest House cannot escape through a familiar room, and all effects of being in the house still apply while within.

As long as the NPC remains in the familiar room, it's impossible to convince them that they aren't where they appear to be (because in a very technical sense, they are). The safest and kindest thing would, in fact, be to leave them where they are. Should the PCs leave and return, the NPC is gone.

LOVER

If the Lover appears thanks to the House Die, they invisibly and insubstantially move to the PC to whom the room is familiar and begin whispering to them.

> A soft voice purrs in your ear. "Ah, remember when we were here together? Remember what you said?"

If the PC responds with anything other than some sort of fabricated lie about the loving or kind thing they said, the Lover screams in their ear. The character must resist a Rating 6 attack that inflicts mental damage. They are also automatically deafened for a full minute. The Lover then leaves.

We make our own monsters, then fear them
for what they show us about ourselves.
~Mike Carey and Peter Gross,
The Unwritten

SUMMONING CHAMBER

Table

Girl

To the Time Loop

 demon bound to speak truly can be a useful asset.

> *Urloznon is very devious. Play it to the hilt as much as you can.*

OVERVIEW

A young girl in a taffeta dress stands in the middle of a magical diagram painted on the floor in blood, circled by dozens and dozens of candles of different heights. The rest of the room is quite dark, but there is a table with some mystic-looking equipment on it, including a knife, a skull, and a chalice.

BOUND DEMON

The little girl is a demon bound within the diagram. It doesn't try to fool the PCs into thinking it is a real little girl; however, it will use this version of its appearance to help manipulate them. It promises to grant the PCs what they seek: information, wealth, healing, power, or perhaps something else in exchange for its freedom. The thing is, if they are very clever, the PCs can actually get the demon to fulfill its promises.

At first, the only question it will answer truthfully (because it must—that's what the magical diagram does, in addition to keeping it in place) is "How do we get you to tell us the truth?"

If the PCs ask that, it will sigh and say, "Use the knife on the table and spill your own blood upon the skull. I'll speak truthfully to whoever does that." However, it's not compelled to speak at all beyond saying that. The PCs will need to bargain for that. What it wants is to be free.

To get free, someone must take the wine in the chalice on the table and spill it upon the diagram on the floor.

The demon's name is Urloznon. If forced to speak truly, it will promise *one* of the following for its freedom (or a close equivalent):

+ Information: It can tell them where to find the Doorman (either in **the Gatekeeper's Chamber** [page 224] or **the Cellar** [page 104]), or where to find a particular key they are looking for.
+ Information: It can tell them where the nearest Mystic Tool is (which would be the blueprints in **the Private Study** [page 230]).
+ Information: It can tell them that the way to Phillip Harlock is in the room with all the orchids (**the Vestibule** [page 244]) and by speaking their own mothers' names into the orchid blooms, they'll be taken to him. (This is true, but only in the most technical of senses, in that the Antinomy is actually some far-future version of Phillip.)
+ Wealth: It can conjure $5,000 worth of gemstones.
+ Healing: It can heal all the wounds upon a single character, or one wound per character.
+ Power: It can conjure a single enchanted tool or weapon of the PCs' choosing that adds a Boon when used.

If it speaks truly in the bargaining process, it will uphold its end, give them what they asked for, and then disappear in a puff of brimstone.

If it's not forced to speak truly, the demon will say whatever it thinks it has to in order to get free. Once free, with no true bargain binding it, it laughs, and attacks the characters with a psychic burst that affects everyone around it. Urloznon has a Rating of 7. Should the burst kill any of the characters, the demon will visibly grab that character's soul (which looks like a translucent version of the PC) and disappear with it, taking them to Hell to be Urloznon's slave. Perhaps the other PCs, if they escape the house, can mount a mission to rescue them. Or perhaps that character has simply suffered a truly awful fate. Either way, the demon disappears on its turn after blasting the group.

TABLE

On the table is a knife, a skull, and a chalice with some wine in it. All are enchanted, each with a very specific purpose. If someone cuts themselves with the knife (inflicting a Rating 1 wound) and bleeds upon the skull, the demon in the diagram will have to speak truthfully to them. The wine in the chalice is the only thing that will dispel the diagram and free the demon.

TO THE TIME LOOP

This innocuous door leads to **the Time Loop** (page 248). It is unlocked.

LOVER

If the House Die indicates that the Lover arrives, they do, but not physically. Instead, they make an offer to one of the PCs:

> You hear a soft, kind voice whisper in your ear, "If you'd like, I can tell you how to get the truth out of Urloznon, and get it to keep its promises. All you have to do is promise me you won't leave me. Stay with me in the house forever."

If the character won't make that promise, the Lover shouts (so all can hear), "Well then, I hope it devours your soul and takes you to Hell!"

If they make the promise to never leave, the Lover whispers again:

> "Use the knife on the table and spill your own blood upon the skull. The demon will speak truthfully to whoever does that."

If Urloznon sees a character get the knife and skull, it startles. "What? What are you doing? You should put those down. They're dangerous."

If the character makes the promise to the Lover, if and when the characters have the opportunity to leave the Darkest House, the character can't go unless they succeed in resisting a Rating 6 mental attack. If the character succeeds, they hear a cry of anguish as they leave, and the Lover will likely not be kind if they ever return.

THE FOUNTAIN OF PAIN

T his is where characters are brought when they all bear wounds equal to or greater than their Rating at the same time.

This is a special room, very likely only reached if certain conditions are (accidentally) met.

To the Halls of the Pained

Fountain

Windows

OVERVIEW

This room is humid and stifling. Moisture begins to collect on your skin as soon as you arrive. White and green tiles cover the floor and walls here, and they are slick with moisture. A couple of windows on one wall show a nighttime rainstorm, so they are wet on both sides. In the middle of the room, a round, baroque fountain sprays water droplets in the air. Rising from its center is a statue of a weird, disturbing creature.

ARRIVING HERE

Characters arrive here due to pain and suffering that they experience. It happens when all of the PCs have at least one physical wound equal to or greater than their own Ratings at the same time. So, if all the characters have a Rating of 4 and each has at least one wound Rated 4 or higher, the event is immediately triggered and they all disappear from where they are and reappear in this room.

THE FOUNTAIN

The water droplets that strike living creatures heal a wound. Basically, since the only way to get here is by being summoned by the pain the group experienced (each bearing at least one wound of their Rating or higher), whatever wound brought them here heals over the course of about a minute. Once the fountain has healed one wound for each character, it will do no more.

The pain from the wound is gone with the damage, of course, but that pain is absorbed by the water in the fountain. The water's about 10 inches deep near the sides, and 20 inches deep in the middle. In the deepest, most central part of the fountain, the water seethes with a reddish light. This is the pain the fountain absorbs and holds for its master, **the Red Figure** (page 262). When a character touches the red water, they suffer a wound equal to their own Rating and stumble backward, screaming, and falling unconscious (fainting) from the intensity for a few minutes. They can be roused more quickly with assistance.

WINDOWS

A storm rages outside all the windows. Lightning flashes, wind rattles windowpanes, thunder echoes in the distance.

✦ If this is the first or second time the PCs have encountered a room where they could see a storm outside, nothing special happens.

✦ If this is the third time the PCs have encountered a room where they could see a storm outside, they see a tall, gaunt, and gangly creature in the distance illuminated by a lightning flash.

✦ If this is the fourth time the PCs have encountered a room where they could see a storm outside, they see a tall, gaunt, and gangly creature, tattered bits of clothing soaking wet, seemingly staring at them through the window, illuminated by a lightning flash. It's hard to know if it's actually staring because it seems to have a massive wound where its face should be. And then it is gone.

✦ If this is the fifth time the PCs have encountered a room where they could see a storm outside, they see a tall, gaunt, and gangly creature, tattered bits of clothing soaking wet, jaundiced flesh covering its body, with long limbs twisted in strange positions and its face torn messily from its head, leaving only blood and gore where it should be. It is tap, tap, tapping on the window.

✦ If this is the sixth time the PCs have encountered a room where they could see a storm outside, they see a tall, gaunt, and gangly creature, tattered bits of clothing soaking wet, jaundiced flesh covering its body, with long limbs twisted in strange positions and its face torn messily from its head, leaving only blood and gore where it should be. It is tap, tap, tapping on the window. And then it smashes the window and comes into the room. It has a Rating of 5 and, while it can make physical attacks, it also has the ability to use a hex power that causes some kind of deformity in the body of another (enlarged hand, lengthened arm, misshapen face, sealed-up eye, and so on) if they cannot resist the effect. The victim suffers a Bane to all physical activity. The changes last as long as the Faceless Thing lives.

Show the players the image of **the Faceless Thing**. The Faceless Thing will pursue characters who flee. Once the Faceless Thing is inside, the window seals itself once again and becomes unbreakable. The characters see only a storm outside the windows from now on.

TO THE HALLS OF THE PAINED

This innocuous door leads to **the Halls of the Pained** (page 260). It is unlocked.

LOVER

The Lover will not come here.

HALLS OF THE PAINED

Those who serve the Monarch of Pain dwell here.

The idea here is that this is many rooms, but one space. It's an opportunity for the PCs to move around in an area where there are NPCs, but not have to immediately confront them if they don't want to.

OVERVIEW

What first appears to be a small room is actually a series of small adjoining rooms. The walls are harsh stone, as is the floor. Black iron chandeliers hang from the ceiling with candles, but only one or two are lit in each. Fixtures of similar dark metal adorn the walls like art. Hideous, twisted, repugnant art. In the near distance, something—or somethings—move about, taking no care to conceal their clattering sounds.

ARTWORK

Black iron shapes are bolted to the stone walls throughout this area. While they appear to be meaningless shapes inexpertly crafted and poorly arranged, something about them is disquieting. If anyone spends more than an hour here, they face a Rating 2 mental attack.

THE PAINED

Six armored figures wander about in two groups of three. The Pained were human once, but long ago fell prey to possession by dark spirits of the house. Now they clad themselves in dark armor designed to keep them in agony in order to honor the being they call **the Monarch of Pain** (page 262).

Show the players the image of **The Pained**.

Each of the Pained has a Rating of 3, except for resisting damage, for which they have a Rating of 5. They also have a Boon when inflicting damage. They are equipped with spiked flails and clubs, all stained brownish red from years of bloodletting. The armor the Pained wear has many secret compartments and clever storage spaces, in which they keep things like caltrops, small beartrap-like toothed clamps, small hooked chains, lengths of razor wire, and various sharpened spikes and blades. On their turn, rather than attacking with their obvious weapons, the Pained might produce one of these devious items and inflict them upon a foe. This is a physical attack, but the damage only has a Rating of 2. However, until someone takes their turn to remove the clamp, the entwining razor wire, the caltrops at their feet, and so on, the victim continues to suffer that same physical attack every time they take a turn.

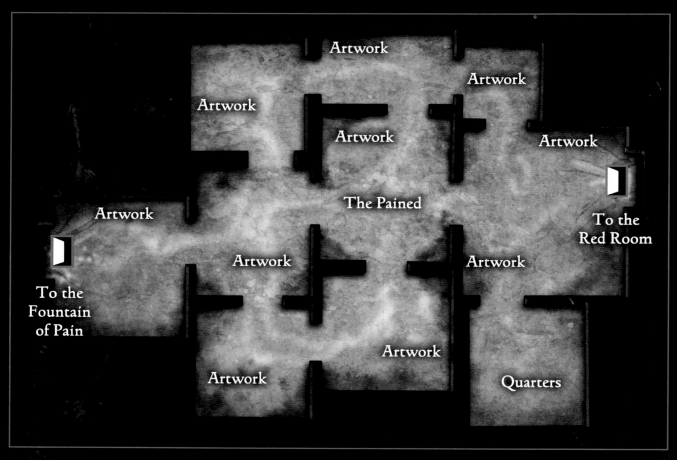

Artwork

Artwork

Artwork

Artwork

Artwork

The Pained

To the Red Room

Artwork

Artwork

Artwork

Artwork

To the Fountain of Pain

Artwork

Quarters

The only way to interact with the Pained other than with violence is to entreat them with servility and submissiveness. Should a character approach them in such a fashion, they might answer a few questions or at least be persuaded not to attack. A bribe (an offering) of some kind would likely make this even easier, probably giving the character a Boon.

The small rooms offer ample opportunities for stealth, perhaps allowing a quiet group to pass through this area and avoid the Pained.

QUARTERS
The dark spirits don't need rest or food, but the bodies they inhabit do. In this area, they keep places to rest and a small amount of supplies that renew themselves over time—they don't know why, and they don't care.

TO THE FOUNTAIN OF PAIN
This innocuous door leads to **the Fountain of Pain** (page 258). It is unlocked.

TO THE RED ROOM
This innocuous door leads to **the Red Room** (page 262). It is unlocked.

LOVER
The Lover will not come here.

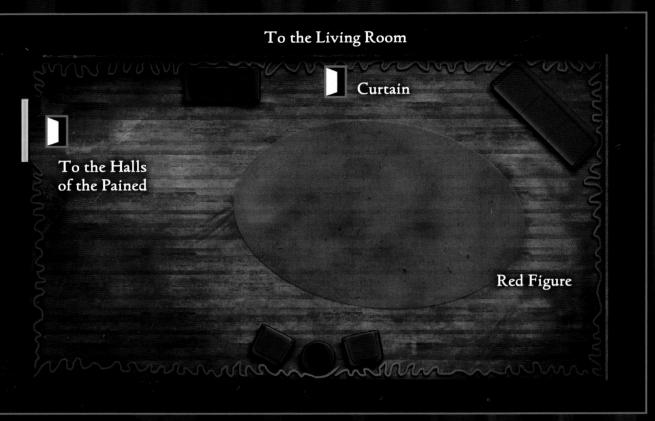

To the Living Room

Curtain

To the Halls
of the Pained

Red Figure

This is where the Monarch of Pain dwells.

> *Yes, the name of the room is an homage to Stephen King's The Shining. Absolutely. (There are homages and references to all sorts of horror tales throughout the Darkest House, but I'll give you that one for free.)*

OVERVIEW

The air here tastes of burnt teeth. The red of the room hurts your eyes, and yet, somehow, still remains dark—a room of red curtains, a red rug, and a few pieces of red upholstered furniture. A figure stands near the back of the room, who seems literally made of . . . red. Clearly inhuman, the figure bears horns and claws, but they seem almost adornments of a macabre aesthetic than functional features. Next to the figure is a nightmarish thing resembling a shattered psyche's poor memory of a wolf. The red here is not the red of blood. It is the red of pain.

THE RED FIGURE

Humanoid but clearly not human, the Red Figure is more energy than matter. More concept than substance. They are a being of pain. Pain is the air that they breathe.

Show the players the image of **The Red Figure**.

When the PCs arrive, the figure says, "I have already supped upon you through my fountain. You hold little interest for me. However, if you wish to gift me with more, I will grant you great rewards."

If the PCs just want to leave, they absolutely can. The Red Figure will not stop them, indicating the curtain that conceals the portal.

If the PCs inquire about the Red Figure's offer, they say, "In exchange for sustenance, I can grant you what you desire."

If the PCs ask for clarification on sustenance, the Red Figure says, "Pain, my love." The price is just that—the Red Figure holds out a hand and the character paying the price writhes in agony for ten seconds times the Rating of the wound they receive.

The PCs could ask for almost anything, but the Red Figure has their limits. Here are a few possible requests, organized by the Red Figure's statement of price:

"A trifle." (Pain that gives a Rating 1 wound)

+ Some mundane physical object (worth up to about $100)
+ Minor temporary power (something equal to a Boon on a significant action that lasts for a day)

"Your offering would not be insignificant." (Pain that gives a Rating 3 wound)

+ Minor lasting power (something equal to a Boon on a significant action that lasts throughout the character's time in the house)
+ Healing a wound up to Rating 5

"That would bear a substantial price." (Pain that gives a Rating 5 wound)

+ Some great treasure (worth up to about $5,000)
+ Information about some specific aspect of the house
+ Some moderate magical item of the player's choosing (or creation)
+ Some moderate power or magical ability that lasts for a year and a day

"A very serious request requires a very serious price." (Pain that gives a Rating 6 wound)

+ Directions on how to get out of the Darkest House
+ Some significant power or magical ability that lasts for a year and a day

"Pain unlike anything you've experienced" (This gives a Rating 10 wound, which could kill a character outright)

+ Information that is secret to all but a few individuals (unrelated to the house)
+ Return someone to life

"For that, I require all the pain one can give." (One character must remain, and become one of **the Pained**.)

+ Escape from the Darkest House

"I'm afraid that is impossible to give."

+ Information known to no one
+ Returning multiple people to life
+ Power or wealth greater than those stated above

In theory, the PCs could try to bargain or haggle, but the Monarch of Pain's Rating of 8 makes that difficult for most characters. The GM will have to be the judge of what a minor, moderate, or significant power is in relation to the game system used in the characters' normal context.

FIGHTING THE RED FIGURE

The Red Figure has no desire to fight the characters, no matter what they have done. The Red Figure is about pain, not violence. They have a Rating of 8, but physical attacks on them only seem to give them pleasure, not pain (or damage). So magical or mental attacks are the only way to inflict damage upon them. Meanwhile, they can inflict physical wounds with a Rating of 5 with a simple glance. They can make this attack on up to three different targets on a single turn.

THE RED FIGURE'S HOUND

The nightmarish beast at their side is a spirit of pain and misery, obeying every command its monarch gives. It has a Rating of 4, and any wound it inflicts with its bite takes on a shape that precisely resembles the Red Figure's horned head.

CURTAIN

One of the red curtains can be pulled back to reveal a swirling vortex of red and black. Stepping through it sends a character to **the Living Room** (page 82), although the front door still will not let them out.

TO THE HALLS OF THE PAINED

This innocuous door leads to **the Halls of the Pained** (page 260). It is unlocked.

LOVER

The Lover will not come here.

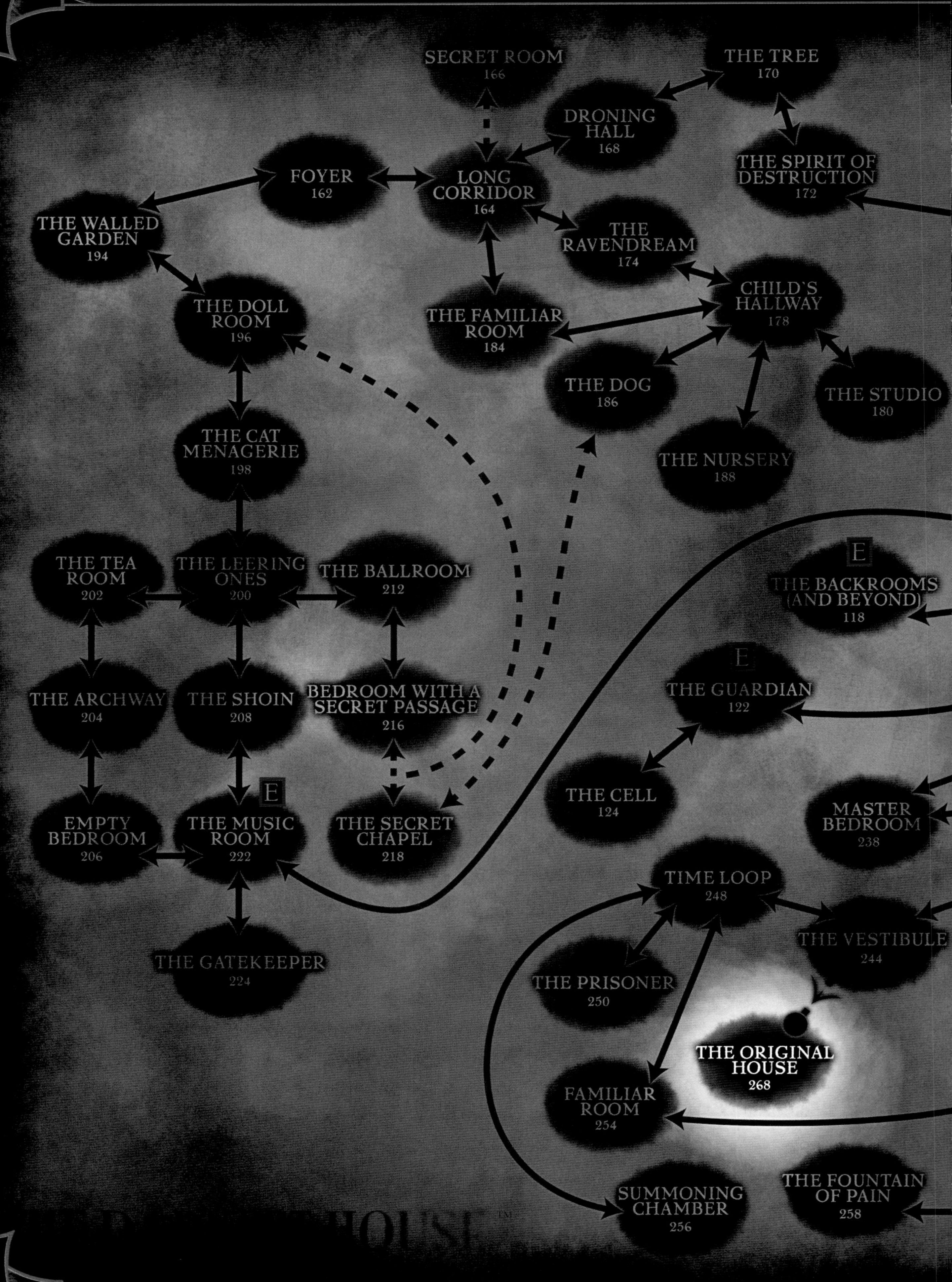

SECRET ROOM
166

THE TREE
170

DRONING
HALL
168

THE SPIRIT OF
DESTRUCTION
172

FOYER
162

LONG
CORRIDOR
164

THE WALLED
GARDEN
194

THE
RAVENDREAM
174

THE DOLL
ROOM
196

THE FAMILIAR
ROOM
184

CHILD'S
HALLWAY
178

THE DOG
186

THE STUDIO
180

THE CAT
MENAGERIE
198

THE NURSERY
188

THE TEA
ROOM
202

THE LEERING
ONES
200

THE BALLROOM
212

E

THE BACKROOMS
(AND BEYOND)
118

THE ARCHWAY
204

THE SHOIN
208

BEDROOM WITH A
SECRET PASSAGE
216

THE GUARDIAN
122

E

THE CELL
124

MASTER
BEDROOM
238

EMPTY
BEDROOM
206

E

THE MUSIC
ROOM
222

THE SECRET
CHAPEL
218

TIME LOOP
248

THE VESTIBULE
244

THE GATEKEEPER
224

THE PRISONER
250

THE ORIGINAL
HOUSE
268

FAMILIAR
ROOM
254

SUMMONING
CHAMBER
256

THE FOUNTAIN
OF PAIN
258

THE ORIGINAL HOUSE

THE GREENHOUSE

RROR
RCASE
146

ART
130

TH CHEN

THE SITTING
ROOM
140

HE GR
STAIRCAS
128

HE SEWING
ROO
150

CLL R

THE DRIPPING
RO

THE ROOM

TIC

MA QUIN
RO

GREAT HALL
114

THE ARMORY
112

THE INTERIOR
COURTYARD
102

THE CELLAR
104

PSYCHOMANTEUM
240

THE GALLERY
106

SHADOWY
HALLWAY
100

THE BLUE
CORRIDOR
236

A STOREROOM
OF SORTS
110

THE LIBRARY
90

THE TROPHY
ROOM
98

PRIVATE STUDY
234

ROOM WITH A
HIDDEN
ELEVATOR
88

E

THE FAMILIAR
ROOM
94

LYING IN STATE
96

THE TWISTED
ROOM
242

MEDITATION
CHAMBER
230

THE BOUNDLESS
ROOM
86

LIGHTLESS
HALL
84

HALLS OF
THE PAINED
260

THE RED ROOM
262

THE LIVING
ROOM
82

THE ORIGINAL HOUSE

This is what Phillip Harlock's house looked like before it began to grow. Or maybe it's just what he imagines it once looked like.

> There's no map here. The layout doesn't matter. It's just a house. It feels very different than the Darkest House. Calmer, less threatening, but mysterious and a little unnerving all the same, like wandering through a stranger's house when they're not at home.

OVERVIEW

The Original House is a large wooden structure, Victorian in style, well cared for (at least at this point in time). Basically, it is a much smaller and more logical version of the Darkest House, incorporating these already-familiar rooms:

The Living Room (page 82), **the Kitchen** (page 134), **the Sitting Room** (page 140), **the Dining Room** (page 136), **the Attic** (page 144), **the Storeroom** (page 152), **the Bedroom With a Secret Passage** (page 216); although there is no passage and the room is lived in, perhaps by a child), **the Nursery** (page 188), **the Library** (page 90), **the Foyer** (page 162), and **the Master Bedroom** (page 238).

The layout isn't all that important, and there are no monsters, ghosts, or other supernatural aspects to the rooms. There are no people here, although it looks as though there could have been just moments ago. This is not an abandoned house. Along with no occupants, there are no real valuables here either, no particularly helpful or informative books—no treasures of any kind. It's just a normal house. Every room looks lived in, but not untended.

The only room in the Original House that is not also present in the Darkest House is a basement, reached by a dark stairway with wooden steps off the kitchen. Significantly, the Nursery has a dollhouse that looks exactly like the actual Original House in miniature.

WINDOWS AND DOORS

Through the house's many windows, PCs can see a sedate city—but it is *not* their city. And it's daytime (dusk). It looks entirely unfamiliar. If you wish to take your game in such a direction, you could let the PCs open the front or back door and just leave. They would then be in an entirely new and unfamiliar world—perhaps forever. If you don't want to deal with such interworld travel, maintain the idea that all the windows and doors here are unbreakable and not openable, just like in the Darkest House.

BASEMENT

It's a dark and damp dirt-floor basement with an oil furnace that has seen better years. Most significantly, there is a device or structure made of multiple facets— glass, crystal, energy, it's hard to tell—sitting atop a brass tripod. It's about 9 feet high, so it reaches the ceiling. Most curiously, as you circle around it and view it from different angles, it changes shape. Likewise, if you move it, it also changes in shape and appearance. The facets move and shift. That's why Phillip Harlock called it the "aeolotropic structure." Once inside the aeolotropic structure, however, he recognized its true nature, and began calling it the Lacuna.

THE LACUNA

The Lacuna is a magical/technological device that creates an "empty space" in both space and time.

Show the players the image of **the Structure**.

Its interior exists in neither space nor time. A character touching the Lacuna feels a draw into it, not unlike a vacuum or perhaps a hungry maw. That character is sucked inside, losing all physical form and entering a "place" where all times and all space is one, but also does not exist. Only one character can enter at once. A character inside will exit again in a random amount of time from the perspective of those outside it. Roll 1d6, and the result is the number of minutes that pass for the characters outside the device, unless you roll a 6, in which case you roll again and this time it's how many hours pass. However, if you roll a 6 on this second die, then you roll a third time, and now it's how many days pass. And so on, through weeks, months, years . . . For the character inside, however, no time passes. If it takes a long time, the other characters might just leave, giving the person inside up for lost or dead.

The exiting character has seen *everything at every time* as a detached observer. This is far more than the mind can take. Upon exiting, the character must resist a Rating 10 mental attack. Even if they are somehow still sane after that, they can only remember a fraction of what they saw. Give them random information about their own past and something else about their future. Let them know about events that happen in a far-off locale that somehow might interest or apply to them. Tell them whatever you want—that's all they remember from their time within, and all they'll ever remember.

The structure, as powerful as it is, is not entirely complete. Characters skilled in esoteric knowledge, fringe science, or higher-dimensional physics ascertain that there's still more to the structure, although it's unclear if it was damaged or never completed. However, if it could be completed, restored, or repaired, it could be one of the most astonishing accomplishments of all time. It might produce the means of traveling anywhere in space or anywhen in time. It might allow for contact with higher entities beyond the scope of humanity. It might repair some flaw in reality that threatens all existence. Or it might end the universe and start a new one. Whatever the Lacuna can do, it is outside the bounds of this adventure though it might serve as a reason to one day return here as the culmination of some monumental quest that almost certainly involves gathering strange parts and ingredients, gaining even more esoteric knowledge, and perhaps somehow tapping directly into the true essence of the Darkest House itself.

If the PCs even consider damaging or destroying the Lacuna, a being called the Antinomy appears. No matter how quickly the characters act, the Antinomy appears first, because he dwells outside of time.

The Lacuna is quite fragile, but as it exists out of time and space, can it really be destroyed? Investigation will prove that the answer seems to be . . . no.

ANTINOMY

Standing about 6 feet tall, the Antinomy is an older man with a short beard and distinguished gray hair. He wears a turtleneck, a suit jacket, and gold-rimmed glasses.

Show the players the image of **the Antinomy**.

He approaches with friendliness, and greets the PCs, squinting a little as he speaks. He always seems a bit distracted. Unlike many of the entities in the house, the Antinomy seems to know the PCs, know what they're doing, and what they've been doing.

The Antinomy has a Rating of 9.

GMs should use this being how they wish. Overall, the Antinomy should be mysterious. Consider the following:

+ The things he says should raise more questions than answers.
+ He will perhaps answer a few questions (if that seems to fit the mood and story you're creating) but he'll also make enigmatic statements about the characters' future, or their ancestors, or their current loved ones. Not threatening—just uncanny and eerie.
+ He certainly won't definitively explain the Darkest House or himself, assuming he even knows the answers to questions regarding such.
+ He might mention Phillip Harlock, as if he knew him once long ago.
+ He might be an aged, future version of Phillip Harlock, but if he is, he's not saying.
+ While the Antinomy might leave this room, the PCs won't ever encounter him away from the Lacuna.

THE RECURSIVE DOLLHOUSE

Sitting close to the wooden crib in the nursery is a large and impressive dollhouse.

Show the players the image of the dollhouse.

It mimics the Original House in miniature, with all of its rooms (except the basement). The dollhouse has four dolls: a man, a woman, a young boy, and a baby. Father is in the library, Mother in the kitchen, the baby is in the nursery, and the young boy is lying on the floor, next to the house.

The dollhouse has a tiny dollhouse in its tiny nursery room. And if there was some way for the characters to investigate such a thing, if they were able to look into this tiny dollhouse, they'd see that its nursery also has a dollhouse. And so on, into infinity. This is the thread that extends through all realities, enabling the house to connect to all worlds.

Even more interesting, the dollhouse's attic also has a black, puzzle-piece-shaped hole floating in it. The hole is very much the size of an actual puzzle piece. Characters can search the Original House and find, in one of the bedrooms, a closet with puzzles and games (just like in **the Bedroom With a Secret Passage** [page 216]). One of the puzzles is called the Happy Family, and within it is a piece that will fit into that hole perfectly. Should characters do this, they are immediately ejected out of the Darkest House in a swirling vortex of interdimensional energies. The energies are in their own world (or worlds), but the house is not. There is just a vacant lot or otherwise empty space where it was. Except that now, it's not just gone—it's never been there. There's no sign of it, no record of it, and, other than in the minds of the PCs, no memory of it. The characters have cut the house off from their world forever.

It should be stressed that this is *a very good thing*. It may not be a "saving the world" scenario, but it is certainly the banishment of a terrible and corrupt danger.

There is no dollhouse in **the Darkest House's Nursery** (page 188). Only in this version of the nursery.

LEAVING THE ORIGINAL HOUSE

At any time, should someone in the Original House wish to, they can cross into a room here and appear in the corresponding room in the Darkest House. They cannot return this way. Obviously, this cannot work in the basement. If they know the secret about saying the four Latin words as described in **the corridor of the Wheel of Blood** (page 158), however, they can easily return to **the Vestibule** (page 244) and thus quickly return to the Original House.

APPENDIX I :
THE REMNANTS

REMNANT 1
In Pater, The Living Room,
The Piece of Paper (page 82)

[A handwritten page, appearing like it's torn from a journal]

February 4

Marjorie attempted to get me to leave the house today. "You've been cooped up in there all winter," she said. I told her I wasn't well and that she should come back another day.

I feel fine, of course. But I've no desire to interact with the world today. The girl from the grocery store brings me food and necessities every week. I've no need to walk about in the sun, and see the "sights." I have all the sights I need here in the house, and in my books. Fresh air holds no appeal, particularly in this cold month. Perhaps in Spring I'll venture out, and make Marjorie happy.

Summer at the latest.

February 7

Heard the child's laughter again today. I suspect there must be some little animal in the walls.

mymcg.info/tdh-livingroom-show-remnant1

REMNANT 2
In Pater, A Storeroom of Sorts,
Human Remains (page 110)

[A handwritten page, appearing like it's torn from a journal]

December 10

My old teacher referred to something he called a mind palace. He said that it was a place where he could mentally preserve all his thoughts, his memories, and his ideas. He visualized it as an actual place. The thoughts and ideas became objects within this place, carefully organized and stored away. Some might be carefully protected, locked away, and some might be displayed prominently. He could then visit his mind palace whenever he wanted. By visiting over and over, always visualizing the objects that represented his thoughts and memories in the same places, he made it very real, at least to him. He could close his eyes and see himself there, strolling the halls, visiting the rooms, and he wouldn't even have to consciously remember where he placed which object. They were just there, ready for him to peruse.

While he originally created his mind palace as a way of remembering everything he wanted to remember, he said that it became far more than that. He felt as though it was truly a retreat designed only for him. A place of respite only he could visit. He reveled in the privacy of it. And he insisted that it preserved his memories so completely that they could replay in his mind, like perfect recordings.

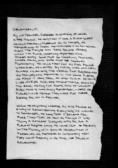

mymcg.info/tdh-storeroomofsorts-show-remnant2

[Handwritten notes, in the same hand as most of the journal entries]

~~Eulogy.~~
~~I can't begin to My father was~~ When I think of my father

~~My father was not~~
When I was asked to give this eulogy
My father was a ~~cruel hard~~ stern strong man. A strict disciplinarian.
He was beloved by all. Beloved by none. My beloved father taught me the value of
[Angry scribbling.]

[Page 2 of handwritten notes, in the same hand as most of the journal entries. Everything other than "I can't do this" has a single, big X over it.]

The dark brooding of my father haunts me to this day. Becoming a man under his hateful, tortured gaze was difficult, like living in a nation in the grip of an aging tyrant. He shaped what my brother became, and my sister. And, obviously, me. His presence and his actions explain much of my mother, but not all.

It serves little purpose to hate or fear someone who is dead. And yet
[scribbles]
When I was young, I found a notebook of his, in which he talked about his "great plan" and his "elaborate work." I could not understand what I read at the time, and as a man, I only remember a few words and phrases: Hunger. Destiny. Key of All Flesh. But what I remember most clearly is the phrase, "it wears a human face."

And there was something about the cellar.

When I asked him about it—God, why did I do that? I was young and did not understand—he bellowed. "Do not interfere with the Great Work. It is more important than you or I!" There was probably more, and probably violence. But I don't remember. Just the ortance, and "it wears a human face."

He would disappear for days at a time. Those times were welcome and I stopped asking Mother where he had gone or how long before he got back. She never really answered anyway. And when he would return, he acted as if he'd never left. I didn't understand as a child, but now, as a man, perhaps I do. A little. This was his house, after all.

I will walk these dark, lonely halls with the certainty that his dreadful gaze is always upon me. He always stands just behind and above my shoulder.

I can't do this.

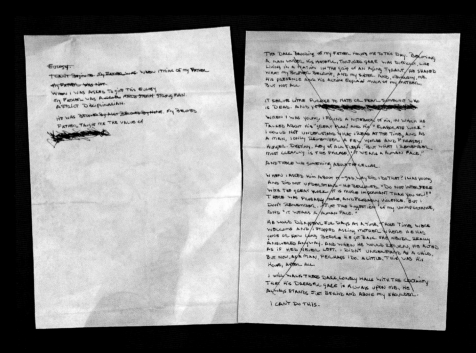

REMNANT 4
In Pater, the Library,
the Notebook (page 90)

[A handwritten page, appearing like it's torn from a journal]

December 17

I've begun work building my own mind palace. Rather than make up some fantastic castle or grand manor, however, I've just used this house. I find it easier to sustain this "mental location" using a place I'm very familiar with.

The thing is, I already find that in order to place all the thoughts and memories I want to preserve within it, I have to change things. Rooms are bigger in my mind palace than in the real house, for example. The mental objects I'm placing there don't match the contents of the actual rooms. But that's alright. I don't regret my choice to base my palace on this house. I love this house. Funny old place. It sat vacant for so long before we came along. At least, that's what I understand to be true. The actual origins of the place are a bit murky.

As a child, I always hoped for a happy family here. My father made that impossible, though. And by not helping me, my mother helped him. I always sought a way to protect my younger brother. I wondered what would happen to him, growing up here with our family. Well, these are the kinds of thoughts I can put in my mind palace I suppose.

mymcg.info/tdh-library-show-remnant4

REMNANT 5
In Pater, Great Hall,
The Side Rooms (page 116)

[A handwritten page, appearing like it's torn from a journal]

February 8

I heard the scratching noise again. This time, I think it was coming from the parlor. But when I checked, as always, there was nothing there. Unlike previous times, however, I'd spilled tobacco from the pouch next to the chair in that room, and amidst the scattered bits, a mark that seemed very much like a footprint. From the size of it, perhaps a woman's. Or a child's. And yet I am certain I am alone here, as I have been for so long.

If there was someone here, I believe I would know about it.

February 10

More scratching. I've just been trying to ignore it now. Perhaps it's all in my mind.

February 19

I've spent the last three days devoted to finding the source of that scratching noise. Practically tore the place apart. I didn't find anything, but I did find . . . something. Maybe. I'm really not sure. It's just that I walked into the sewing room, and damned if I can remember there being a sewing room there before. I mean, of course there was. Obviously. But what's going on with my mind?

March 13

If I'm mad, I'm absolutely mad, but since there's no one here to mock me for it, I'll just stand by what I feel to be true. The house is bigger than it once was. I wasn't certain about the sewing room, and the gallery, but I will go to my grave believing that this house didn't used to have an interior courtyard.

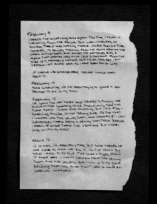

mymcg.info/tdh-greathall-show-remnant5

REMNANT 6
In Frater, Secret Room,
First Locked Box (page 166)

[A handwritten page, appearing like it's torn from a journal]

June 22

I've sent away for more books. Despite my beloved collection, I just can't find the answers I need. Thankfully, I'm in communication with an excellent bookseller who doesn't mind packaging some titles up and sending them my way. I only hope they have the information I seek. Surely I am not the first person to have experienced the situation in the basement.

Speaking of books, I've misplaced that book I felt was my father's the other day. Perhaps it was just a dream.

July 8

When I asked the Antinomy about the origin of the aeolotropic structure, he told me that I created it. But that makes no sense. I don't remember doing such a thing. Seems more like something my father would do. He always talked about his "great work," but I don't remember him being much of a craftsman. He was always in the library.

There are 8 mystical tools, that much I know. I secreted them about the house. I no longer remember why. Which seems strange. <u>Did</u> I build the structure? Something else? I remember something about hot coals.

July 12

I've scoured these blasted books but they're all worthless. Perhaps I am indeed the only one to have seen this aeolotropic structure, or spoken with the Antinomy. I will have to find my own answers. And if I cannot do it in this house, I am certain I can do it in the other.

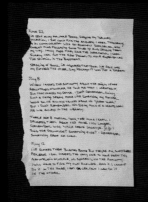

mymcg.info/tdh-secretroom-show-remnant6

REMNANT 7
In Frater, the Ravendream,
The Piece of Paper (page 177)

[A handwritten page, appearing like it's torn from a journal]

August 30

I've entered and exited the aeolotropic structure. From the outside, it appears different from every angle. I suspect if one were to somehow move it, it would change shape. It's like a lacuna . . . in the world. It is not bound by the constraints of neither space nor time. I do not know how long I was within, and am beginning to suspect that the concept doesn't even apply. Similarly, thinking about the interior in terms of shape or size seems almost childly foolish. I think I will call it the Lacuna henceforth.

Questions I still have:

Is the Lacuna alive? Sentient?

Is the Lacuna affecting the house?

Where was the Lacuna before I found it in the cellar? Was it brought here? Did I bring it here?

Where did the Antinomy go?

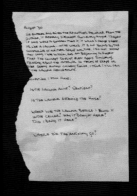

mymcg.info/tdh-ravendream-show-remnant7

[Multiple handwritten pages, appearing like they're torn from a journal]

August 13
I no longer know if I walk the halls of my home or my mind palace.

August 14
I know that voice. It's the voice of my father. Or at least, a father. Someone's father. He seems tied to a particular portion of the house.

August 15
I know now that I'm not alone in the house. It's not just voices in my head as a part of me has insisted all along. Or memories infused into solid matter, which as odd as it seems is something I'd considered as well. I'm not mad. Or at least, if I am mad that's not the sole explanation here. I perceive things I could never have conceived. I don't know exactly where some of these things have come from.
This isn't a mind palace. Or at least, it's not my mind palace.

August 16
Yes, I can feel mother here as well. The smell of her, coming too close. I have infused the house somehow with my memories of both mother and father.

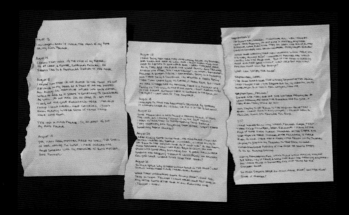

[Page break]

August 17
I didn't bring them here. They came looking for me. My brother and sister are here as well. And I don't mean they are here as opposed to somewhere else. I mean they are here, as in, they are this place. The whole family. And perhaps at least one other. Did I have siblings? I no longer remember. Perhaps a younger sibling. I remember being in a nursery and there being a dollhouse. I so wanted a happy family then. That seems right, or rather it feels right, but I have no idea if these are my memories. There is a portrait of a family on the wall in one of the rooms. I don't appear to be in the picture. Although there is someone in the back, on the right? I can't look at that anymore.

August 18
I managed to move the aeolotropic structure. As I guessed, it changed shape as I did so. I've put it in the basement.

August 22
Some people call a mind palace a memory palace. If that's the case, am I moving through it in the right order? I seem to think that I'm remembering things before they happened, and forgetting them after. Wasn't there something about orchids?

August 24
I keep finding rooms in the house—the mind palace—that I am certain I never saw before. I wonder, is there a way to get back to the original house, as it once was? A tea room. More bedrooms than I can even begin to count. An art studio with some very disturbing art. A great hall, where someone had recently thrown a lavish party. An armory for God's sake. Where is the house that I knew?

August 29
So much space. Why is there so much space in the house? What dwells within these places I never knew existed?
Were these undiscovered rooms always here? I don't feel safe in them. Perhaps I should never have felt safe in any of the rooms of the house at all. Even the ones I thought I knew.

REMNANT 9
In Pater, Room With a Hidden Elevator,
Under the Rug (page 88)

[A handwritten page, appearing like it's torn from a journal]

April 7

    The bone key allowed me into the Armory for the first time. I had no idea there was such a place in the house. I took a knife from there that seemed to want to leave with me.

April 9

    This knife. This eager knife. It wishes to kill. I should return it to the Armory. I am afraid of that place, however. Something dwells there now, I can feel it. I can smell it, like metal shavings and newly drawn blood. Whatever it is, it is like the knife. Perhaps they are one. Perhaps they should be reunited.

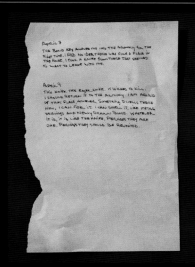

mymcg.info/tdh-emptyroom-show-remnant9

REMNANT 10
In Soror, the Doll Room,
The Letter (page 197)

[A handwritten letter in what looks like a young girl's hand]

Dearest Pen,

    Looks like we're in for another dreary summer. I've always hated all the boys who come around here after school's out. Their silly games are boring. Not like the fun we had in your house last autumn. Remember when we ~~to~~ climbed down the trellis outside your window and then out over your garden wall? I almost got us caught by your father because I couldn't stop laughing.

    What I remember most, though, is when we would go up to your attic and call out the names we found in that book. They were very funny and hard to say. Especially because we were laughing so much. And then that time when you were holding the book over one of the candles and it caught fire! The funny thing is, I don't remember us lighting the candles, do you?

    Anyway, I thought your father was going to be so mad. But the book wasn't even really burned or anything! We got lucky that once. Your father always scared me a little, did I ever tell you that?

    I'm still so very sorry about what happened to your brother. You must miss him so much.

    My family got a dog! His name is Whiskers. He is so cute, but very smelly sometimes. And I'm afraid the cats don't care for him much. Compared to them, he's quite loud. How is your cat? I know you said your parents don't like dogs, especially your father. Maybe if you ask them again, with everything that's happened. A puppy might make you very happy.

    I wish you could be happy, Pen. You're my very best friend. I miss you. Please write back when you can.

    Love,
    Lovila

mymcg.info/tdh-dollroom-show-remnant10

REMNANT 11
In Frater, the Nursery, Changing Table (page 189)

[A page from a children's book, in which every page is the same.]

See Mother, Father, Daughter, and Son
See the family in the house, work to be done.
What's that, Mother?
You cannot see?
Eyes scratched out, now you are free.
What's that, Father?
You cannot feel?
Skin removed, look past the veil.
What's that, Sister?
You cannot hear?
A little slice fixes your ear.
What's that, Brother?
You cannot speak?
Tongue in my hand, no words for the weak
See Mother, Father, Daughter, and Son
See the family in the house, work to be done.

REMNANT 12
In Pater, the Backrooms (and Beyond), the Ocean (page 120)

[An inscription upon a stone in the same handwriting as the majority of the journal entries found in the house]

I am committed now to seeing what lies beyond.
Do not follow.
I am sorry for everything.

—PH

mymcg.info/tdh-backrooms-show-remnant12

REMNANT 13
In Mater, Parlor,
Beneath the Sofa (page 133)

[A handwritten page, appearing like it's torn from a journal]

July 30
   With the Antinomy's help and the power of the Lacuna, and performed a conjuring I could never have managed on my own. The thing was . . . awful. I don't know how to send it back. I enchanted some flames to keep it in place. Perhaps I should post some kind of guard. Or perhaps I could build something. The Antinomy tells me that there are 8 mystic tools that can work wonders, somewhere in the house.

   The tools sound familiar, but why?

July 31
   The Antinomy says that it's possible to enter the Lacuna, but I'm afraid. I think it is not only an empty spot in space, but also time.

August 1
   Have I already written this? I found a page, and it appeared torn from my journal, and the writing was in my hand, but I couldn't have written it. And it was dated later this month, relating things I hadn't yet done. I strongly suspect that there's something about the aeolotropic structure that unhinges us from time. And the journal entry that I saw said that I entered it. I wonder why the page was torn out.

   And now, of course, I've misplaced the journal page. I don't know if it's just the forgetfulness that I've been experiencing, or if it faded away like some kind of ghost.

   I know that wayward or lost spirits exist as ghosts. Goddamn, but I know a thing or two about that. Perhaps things can have ghosts as well. Could a book? I'm not sure you could read the ghost of a book. If I had the ghost book, I would take it to my private study. I'd have a way to read it there.

August 2
   The Mother of . . . something. Inexplicable Things? Senseless Things. One of those. I remember my dear sister whispering about this person. Being. Whatever. Whispering in some secret chapel. Is this Mother related to our mother?

   Did I even have a sister? That suddenly doesn't seem quite right.

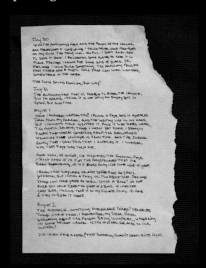

mymcg.info/tdh-parlor-show-remnant13

REMNANT 14
In Soror, the Secret Chapel,
Broken Raven (page 219)

Remnant 14 (in the Secret Chapel)

[A handwritten note in a messy, feverish hand we haven't seen before, on a tiny, rolled up piece of paper]

All hail, Mother of Senseless Things. Look upon my works and find beauty in the meaninglessness. Destroy all significance. Bring ruin to all that is orderly and sane.

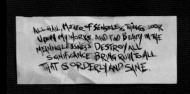

mymcg.info/tdh-secretchapel-show-remnant14

REMNANT 15
In Frater, Secret Room, Second Locked Box (page 167)

[A handwritten note, with some accompanying sketched symbols. Different handwriting than the other journal entries]

With all eight of the Mystic Tools, I shall build the doorway.

And from your flesh, I shall make my key to the highest realm.

Through this door I shall step, this threshold I shall cross.

Sights unknown to mortal man or woman shall greet my eyes.

Pleasures and treasures undreamt shall be mine.

This I shall call my Great Work. It shall be mine alone.

mymcg.info/tdh-secretroom-show-remnant15

REMNANT 16
In Frater, Long Corridor, Envelope (page 164)

[A handwritten letter in a flowing, perfect script]

Dear Phillip,

I'm not going to beat around the bush. I am ending our relationship.

I know this can't come as a surprise to you. We haven't even seen each other in weeks. It has become clear that you won't ever exit from of that damned house, and after what happened the last time, I shall not ever go back in.

I was happy once. We were happy once. But then you started lying. Or maybe you started telling me the truth, and you'd been lying before. Your messages referred more than once to completing your "father's Great Work." But you had told me that your father passed when you were very young and that you had no memory of him. All this talk of mystic tools and things you were building in the house. Phillip, I know you far too well to start believing you're suddenly handy in that way. You wouldn't know a wrench from a saw unless maybe they were diagrams in one of your books.

And then the last time, when I visited and tried to build some kind of a bridge to you, the things you said. I couldn't even get a word in as you raved about some new section of the house you'd found by going up the elevator. I knew damn well your house didn't have an elevator, Phillip. I'd been in it a hundred times. Why would I believe such a story? Who finds a whole section of their own house that they'd never seen before? That sounds more like something you'd experience in a dream. Not in reality.

But then when I went into your pantry to fetch some tea to help calm you down, well, Phillip, I thought you were alone in that strange old house. I'd been feeling so sorry for you, shut in and lonely, but you weren't alone at all. I saw that man. I don't know what he was doing there, or why you were hiding him in that storage room, but I'll never forget the way he grinned at me. I still see him when I close my eyes. And even after I ran screaming, you still denied it. You maintained that you were alone. That no one else was in the house. You lied to me, right to my face.

Don't try to reach me. I don't know if you even would, but Mother and I are going away for a while. She thinks it would be best for me, and I can hardly argue. I don't want to be reminded of you, or of us. Or at least who we used to be, together. You broke my heart, Phillip. Do you even care? Somehow I doubt it.

I don't wish you ill. I just don't want to see you again. Not ever again. I also wish you would get some kind of help. Help I simply cannot provide. Consorting with vile people. Engaging in who knows what at all hours of the night. Spending hours buried in your weird books. Living in filth (I saw all the bugs). Who or what have you become?

Perhaps you need to ask yourself that question. Will you like the answer? I doubt it.

Marjorie

mymcg.info/tdh-longcorridor-show-remnant16

REMNANT 17
In Section, the Backrooms (and Beyond), Discoveries in the Backrooms (page 119)

[An undated, handwritten journal page, in some different handwriting]

We entered this house (?) days ago. Maybe weeks.

I really don't know how the passage of time works here. We have no way of knowing whether or not it's night or day. And sometimes, what seems like a day goes by . . . too fast? And other times very slowly. Does time speed up or slow down here, or is it just our perception of it? Or perhaps there's no difference between time and our perception of time. Maybe time is only our perception, and nothing more. If that's really true, then I wish I could speed it up to the point when we find our way out of here.

Some of us grow despondent. We don't know how to get out of this place. We've heard tell of a Doorman that provides a way out. And some "mystic tools" as well, but how it all works, we don't know.

We've also heard the name Phillip Harlock a few times, and found some journal pages that I now assume are his. Were his. For someone who supposedly owned the house, he didn't seem to know much about it. It makes me think that the house changed. Perhaps Phillip and the house changed together. Did he go mad? Did the house? That's my theory.

~~Nights~~ The times we stop to sleep, I don't know if they're nights, are the worst. The nightmares are terrible. But last "night" I thought I could hear the ocean. It didn't give me comfort. It sounded cold.

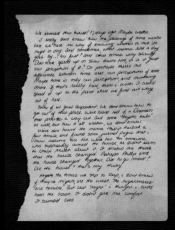

mymcg.info/tdh-backrooms-show-remnant17

REMNANT 18
In Soror, the Music Room, Instruments (page 222)

[On a sheet of music (Marchenbilder, Op.113 - Viola and Piano Score, Viola and Violin Parts), handwriting matching that of the majority of the journal entries]

Oh dearest sister, your love of all things secret and forbidden will be the end of you someday. Some things are unknown because they should stay unknown. What darkness do you get up to in that hidden chapel deep within the house, I wonder?

mymcg.info/tdh-musicroom-show-remnant18

[A handwritten page, appearing like it's torn from a journal]

May 1

There are new rooms in the house I haven't seen before. And perhaps some that I've lost, but I can't remember them. It's as though as the house changes, so too does my mind. Maybe this has been happening for a while now, and I've just forgotten.

At this point, it's far beyond me wondering if the house is haunted. But I do wonder if the new rooms already existed somewhere else before, and if the house chose them because they already had their own hauntings. Because who are were these people?

May 3

I've lost my ring. I actually lost it a few days ago, I believe, and last night I dreamt that the reason I couldn't find it was that it was stolen by a wolf. My dreams have been so odd lately. I should probably record them here more often. Perhaps make some sense out of them.

Strangely, though, it feels almost that I have already done that, but forgotten it. Well, all the more reason to write them down, I suppose.

May 4

The house has eyes. And the eyes have teeth. There is a hole in the parlor. Not sure the house always had a parlor. In any event, there's a hole. In the wall. I think something lives in there. At first, I thought it was some animal that had made its nest or home there, crawled in from some outside hole. I seem to remember hearing some scratching in there a few months back. Honestly, I haven't been outside in so long, I wouldn't even know where to guess such a hole might be.

A thought just occurred to me: is the outside of the house growing and changing too? It seems like no, but some mornings, when I awaken and look out the window, just for a moment, it's as though I'm looking out into another town, in another land.

In any event. The hole. I suppose I am stalling. I don't really wish to write about it. There's something disturbing in the hole. And it watches me. But more than that. I could hear a gnashing of teeth. Grinding.

May 5

I went back to examine the hole in the parlor again. There was, without question, something or someone watching me from that blackness. It wants something of me. I can't say that I'll be going back in there again. That would have been an impossible claim before, but now, with new chambers and passages in the house, I don't think it will be hard to avoid a single specific room.

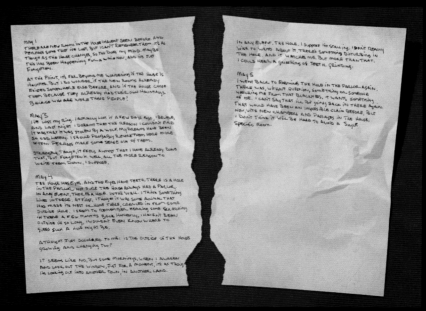

[An oil-stained page that appears to be torn from a journal]

May 28

Today for the first time I became well and truly lost in my own home. I wandered into a large chamber, as cold as the hand of a dead lover. Dimly lit, I couldn't see the other side. I walked and walked and found no far wall. The chilling thought that there was no far wall was more than I can bear. Then I remembered the funny old mantlepiece clock in the living room. The one with the two faces that tell different times. I wandered in this dark room until I could hear its absurdly loud ticking. Following that sound, I found my way back to a room I knew. I remember my parents telling me about it, and how they bought it in a second-hand store as a joke because they could never agree on the time, and it could have the time for both of them. Comforted by it, I swore then and there that if I ever lost my way again, the thought of that fine pewter piece would see me home again. It's as tied to this old house as I am.

June 3

I placed my grandmother's diamond pin in the trunk in the attic. I wanted to keep it safe, and safe isn't really a word I would use lightly here in the house anymore. I don't believe the attic to be safe just because the hidden staircase to reach it in the dining room is cleverly concealed, it's more that it seems . . . well, I'll just say, "out of reach." Somehow, the attic seems to be unchanged, unlike almost the entire rest of the house. I don't know why that would be.

Curiously, while I was up there, I had a memory of little girls playing games, burning candles and calling out strange names. While in the attic, the memory was quite vivid. I could see the girls, I even knew their names. One seemed close to me, like a sister.

But I never had a sister.

It's like something was missing. Or perhaps it would be better to describe it as something added that doesn't belong. Perhaps what's happening to the house is clearly happening to my mind as well. Or it's all the same thing and I'm just utterly mad.

mymcg.info/tdh-drippingroom-show-remnant20

[A handwritten page, appearing like it's torn from a journal]

June 19

Thinking of the strange memories I had of the attic, I found a book with similarly attached unfamiliar memories. A book of some importance to my father, I think. It seems very familiar in that way, even though there's a distinct part of my mind that says I'd never laid eyes upon it before.

I couldn't read it, for some reason. The letters swam before my eyes. I considered that it was simply eyestrain, so I went into the library and pulled a few other books off the shelf. Vilhouse's excellent Eyes on the Skies? Read it just fine. Same with Arul's Spirit Guide and The Tooth and the Claw. But this book—perhaps my father's book?—unreadable. So it wasn't my eyes, it was the book.

Of course, my father frequently kept journals of his own, which I've never found, even after his passing. I presume that in them he took notes on his so-called Great Work. But he never shared them with me. After a while, I just assumed that he burned all those journals. Could this be his? I honestly can't even see it clearly enough to determine if it's handwritten or not, let alone in his hand. (Would I even recognize it anymore if I did see it?)

That doesn't seem quite right though. I have an old magnifying glass in my study that had been his. I wonder if that would help bring this into focus? Perhaps I'll try that.

June 20

I was putting away some old junk in the basement when I found . . . something. An odd sort of freestanding structure with a metallic tripod stand. It seems multifaceted, but strange as it sounds, I couldn't tell you its shape. It brought to mind geometries that would have driven poor Euclid quite mad. That fiction writer with the odd ideas and the preoccupation with sea life mentioned the concept once or twice. Perhaps I should research such things to see if they are real.

June 21

I met someone today in the house. He looked, well, very much like me. Like an old uncle that I had never met, although he assured me that was not the case. He called himself the Antinomy, which I found strange. It's a relatively obscure word for incompatible contradictions and paradoxes. While he was reticent to talk about himself or his past—or perhaps of just as much importance, what he was doing in my house—he seemed quite willing to discuss the house. Unfortunately, very little of what he told me made any sense at all. He spoke of backrooms that seeped down into something or other. Of people that never lived in this house as far as I know. And a thing he called the aeolotropic structure, which I eventually determined was a reference to the thing in the basement. It seemed a fitting enough name, I suppose, as it does seem to have qualities that seem to change depending on how it might be measured. I think I will find a better name for it, though, once I know more about it.

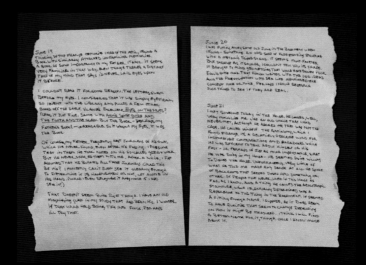

REMNANT 22
In Amator, Master Bedroom, Folded Paper (page 238)

[A handwritten letter, in a hand we have not yet seen]

Object of My Heart's Empty Grasp,

I should not write this. I should let you be, so you can live your life free from me and the worry and stress I likely cause. But I just cannot. I need to have some kind of connection to you, even if it is just through the mail.

I know that I am not supposed to love you. I am committed to another, and so are you. You have your life, and I mine, and they could not be farther apart, in every sense of the phrase. And yet, I feel such a longing to talk to you, and share some part of my life with you. It's wrong, I know. So wrong.

Love is meant to be blissful and joyous. To me, it is neither. To me, love is pain and denial. Love spurs me toward wrongness—deceit, betrayal, and more. And it wants me to pull you into my schemes as well.

To the poets who speak of the goodness inherent in love, I scoff. I spit. Love ushers me only into dark corners where I dream of all the things I should not do.

I should not have written this. But I was compelled as surely as if there was a blade at my throat. Love's eager blade.

Your Forbidden But Ever True Love

mymcg.info/tdh-masterbedroom-show-remnant22

REMNANT 23
In Amator, Meditation Chamber, Books (page 234)

[A handwritten page, appearing like it's torn from a journal]

December 3
Feeling good, despite the cold. Finished my re-read of Eyes of the Child. Always reminds me of a painting I saw once in a gallery somewhere back in the city where I used to live.

December 4
It's been quite a while since I've seen Marjorie. I miss her. I must keep to my studies.

December 6
I had the strangest dream last night. I was lost in this huge house. It seemed to go on forever. Some of the rooms were familiar, but others were very strange. I encountered odd beings like something out of one of my books. But then I found myself in a sort of vestibule, I suppose you'd call it. Curving staircases and—perhaps most notably—orchids. Orchids in vases, just like my mother used to adore. I spoke the mother's name and was returned safely home.

December 7
I swear that last night I had the same dream—or perhaps a very similar one—as the night before. I was lost in a maze of a house, rooms and corridors extending forever it seemed, but I was able to escape by speaking mother's name into some orchids. But there was more this time. There was a strange angular structure in the basement. And a man, or at least he wore the face of a man—familiar, but not—was down there with it.

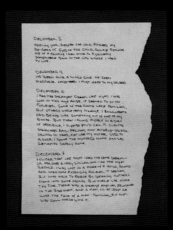

mymcg.info/tdh-meditationroom-show-remnant23

[A handwritten page, almost like a note or letter, in the same hand as most of the journal pages]

The King of Anger. The Curator. The Lost One. The Monarch of Pain. So many entities. So many realms beyond our own, filled with impossible beings utterly unlike us. But aware of us—more than we are of them. Just at the edge of the fire's light. Watching us. Each seemingly taking on some role, but I think there's much more to them than that. The role is just something it's just what we can understand of them. The stag in the woods only knows of us what it can see and understand—hunters and loggers amid the trees. Houses in the distance, away from the forest. To the stag, that's all we are. It's how we fit into their life. There's so much about us that the stag could never begin to comprehend, and frankly, so little about us that it would even be interested in.

[There is a large section blacked out here, unreadable.]

How did they all get here? I suppose that's not really the question. The question is why? Why this house? It's tempting to think of a parasitic relationship, but who's truly the parasite here?

It's tempting to think that the house is about hate. The house hates me. It hates you, if you're reading this. But the house is actually about love. Twisted, perverted love. Love corrupted into something terrible: jealousy, loneliness, selfishness, possessiveness, bitterness, longing. Love as understood by the unloved.

There are five sections to the house. That much is clear. And each seems to express itself as a family member as someone who loves you. Mother, father, sister, brother. Lover. Different kinds of love. But in this case, the manifestations are twisted versions of that love, and those roles.

Of the five, the Lover seems most hidden and hardest to reach. But through that part of the house, one can reach the Lacuna and its capture of the original house in space and time. Like how a photo would capture a scene and hold it in an unchanging stasis, forever. It is truly the last piece of the puzzle. In more ways than one.

Replace the missing piece, and seal the door forever. Cut off the house. Free your world from its clutches. Have your own happy family.

Do you understand me, reader? I don't know who you are but I know how you got here. I can't say for certain if you're reading this in the future or in the past. I suspect it could be either. Regardless, go, free yourself and your world if you're brave enough and strong enough. Look for the house within the house. Within the house. Into infinity. You can't save infinity, but you can save your little part of it. You can make sure no one you love ever falls into the clutches of the house ever again.

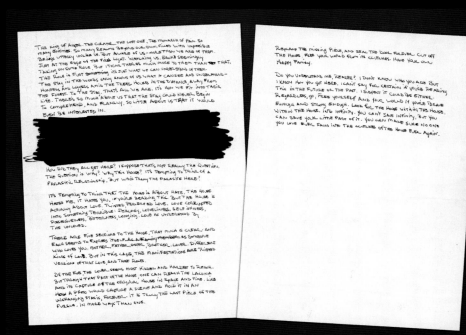

REMNANT 25
in Amator, the Prisoner,
Notebook (page 252)

[Several small, handwritten notebook pages, in a hand that's different from the others we've seen]

Prisoner won't relate her name.
Never seen snow. Never even heard of it.
Has a daughter.
Looking for the Book of Names. Asking about the attic.

X
  X
 X X
   X

~~Claims~~ they knew Phillip Harlock. Or sister.

[Page break]

No prisoner
Alone

XXXX

[Page break]

Probably not human.
strange manner of speaking
Cloudy eyes
No idea where they are. Confused. Mentioned Jerusalem. Wandered the courtyard.
Theory—Bedroom consumed by house while sleeping.

[Page break]

Prisoner male Caucasian
      dark hair   darting eyes
Found near the elevator in the Great Hall.
Trying to convince the Host to take him to the party.
Smells like something from a swamp.
Takes medication
Lost dog
Shouts
Sleeps

[Page break]

New prisoner.
Says there are witches in my beard. That I am from hell.

Nyaar

Real name Nick Fuller

[Check mark] Devious

[Check mark] Hostile

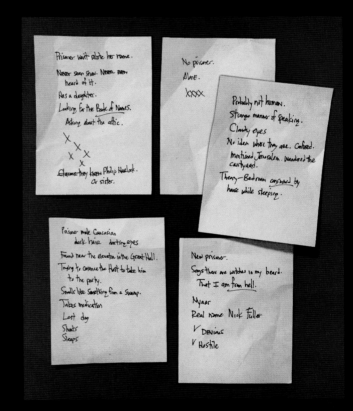

mymcg.info/tdh-prisoner-show-remnant25

[A handwritten note. Looks like the same handwriting from most of the journal pages. It's intentionally unfinished.]

[There's a hand-drawn circle around the word "rooms" in the sentence "Even the rooms of the house that I'm fairly certain weren't there originally have a certain feeling for me." Then a line that goes down with an arrow to the following paragraph.]

Trying to write everything down. I keep forgetting things. Keep losing track of time. Are things happening in the right order?

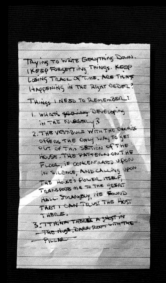

Things I need to remember:

1. What's ~~growing~~ developing in the nursery?

2. The vestibule with the orchids offers the only way to get out of this section of the house. The pattern on the floor, if concentrated upon in silence, and calling upon the house's power itself, transports me to the Great Hall. Strangely, I've found that I can trust the Host there.

3. ~~I think there's a ghost in the huge, dark room with the pillar.~~

4. Not sure I can abide that chapel or temple or whatever it is deep under the house. I don't trust it. I don't feel any connection to it. Even the rooms of the house that I'm fairly certain weren't there originally have a certain feeling for me. Like I belong. But not there.

5. That damned hole in the attic. I know that's important. But why? I've not found anything that would fit it. The shape of it, it reminds me of something particular, though. Something from when I was young.

Except for those rooms with the yellow wallpaper. Those are strange, sort of liminal spaces that have no meaning to me. And yet I'm afraid of them. I think I'll have to gather my courage and explore them eventually. First, though, I need to remember where I put my bag.

6. I keep

mymcg.info/tdh-privatestudy-show-remnant26

REMNANT 27
In Amator, the Vestibule,
Phillip's Bag (page 245)

[A handwritten page, appearing like it's torn from a journal. At the top, in angular text (with the same handwriting, but in a different color), it says, "Found this on the kitchen floor. Dated at the end of the month. Looks like what I would write, or maybe will write. Definitely torn from my journal. But I hold that intact journal in my hands. Makes no sense."]

August 31

I feel like I'm forgetting something. Something about the orchids. I think I wrote myself a note about it, but where did I put the damn note?

Well, I know how to leave the house, now. I know there's a man who stands at the threshold. Or rather, he is the threshold. He is the lock and the door. A key that I've found opens up his chest and will let me out. The key is behind the bar in the ballroom. He let me create a second lock in his head that takes me to the secret room in my study.

None of these rooms are what I remember them to be. It's all just so odd. And the people that live here now. The entities. I thought I lived alone and now it seems the house is actually quite crowded. I've made note of some of them here and there. Not sure where I put those notes now. Maybe they're with the other notes I'm missing. I honestly cannot remember.

Yesterday, I entered the Lacuna. I saw the creation of the house, or rather, how my house fused with something that already existed. And now my house—the house, the Darkest House—has always existed. But it's also other houses, ones that were never mine. It's hard to pull it all together. So many pieces. Now I know if I can just get back there . . . I can figure things

out. Except I can't. Today, I can't find any of the familiar rooms. Not even my real bedroom—just the new, larger one I've been using for a few weeks now. I can't figure out how to get back down into the basement.

I need to start writing things down so I don't forget goddamned everything.

There's a stop that the elevator makes—not all the way at the bottom. That's not the basement. I don't know what that thing down there is, although it clearly knows me. That seems significant somehow. But nothing will get me to ever go back down there. Just before the elevator reaches the bottom, though, there's a series of rooms. I think I shall explore them. Perhaps there I will find a way back to the familiar rooms of the house. I can leave the house, but when I come back in, things quickly become unfamiliar.

Where is the kitchen? The sitting room? I can't find them anymore. If I can just get to the basement the real basement, I can find the Lacuna and maybe even the Antinomy.

mymcg.info/tdh-vestibule-show-remnant27

REMNANT 28
In Amator, the Vestibule,
Phillip's Bag (page 245)

Remnant 28 (in the Vestibule)

[A simple business card with an artistic flourish]

Phillip Harlock
Esoteric Specialist and Occult Consultant
237 Carpenter Lane
Clive,
Flanagan 42A1B

mymcg.info/tdh-vestibule-show-remnant2...

The Wheel of Blood Turns
We kill. We eat. The blood nourishes us.
From that blood comes new life.
We are the Wheel of Blood. The house
has five occupants, but one is secret.
Each has their portion of the house.
The Wheel of Blood, and the names
of the four, lead you to the secret fifth.

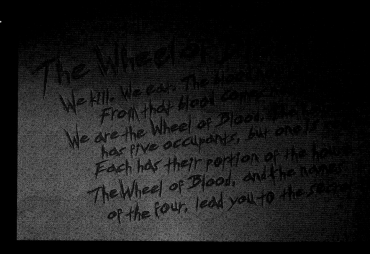

mymcg.info/tdh-foyer-show-remnant29

RESEARCHING THE HOUSE RESULTS

You find two references to the house, both quite contradictory.

One is about the supposed original owner of the house, a man named Phillip Harlock. Apparently, long ago, he went a bit mad and would never leave the house, telling friends—all of whom he eventually pushed away, one by one, over the course of a year or two—that there were "always more rooms in the house to see. Always more halls to walk." Eventually, he disappeared altogether. Other owners took possession and moved in over the years. All reported that the house was haunted. Various exorcists and experts were called in. The first three failed. The fourth died. The last owner claimed "it's not even a house anymore," before disappearing mysteriously. No one has lived there in a very long time, and it's been cordoned off for years. Occasionally, foolish thrill-seekers manage to get inside. Some report terrifying stories. Most won't talk about it or are never seen again. People began referring to it as the Darkest House.

The other, more esoteric, source says that the house has always existed, stretching between every layer of reality (whatever that means), filling in the cracks and seeping into whatever metaphysical pits it can find. This reference also mentions Phillip Harlock, but seems to suggest that he wasn't the first owner at all and that he inherited it from a distant relative and moved it to its current location somehow. But mostly this source just goes on about how the house is more a dark, fundamental force of the universe that takes on the appearance of a house than an actual house, like an animal that uses a part of its own body to lure in prey (it specifically references the spider-tailed horned viper). It also says that the house's outward appearance looks different in the other locations that it extends into, fitting in with local context. To top it all off, someone has written in that section of the book, scrawled over the print itself, "THE HOUSE HATES YOU."

http://mymcg.info/tdh-Researching-Results

Character Sheets

mymcg.info/tdh-Character-Sheets

Crossing the Threshold Player PDF

mymcg.info/tdh-Crossing-the-Threshold

GM Reference Sheet

mymcg.info/tdh-GM-Reference-Sheet

House Diagram

mymcg.info/tdh-house-diagram

Journal of Phillip Harlock

mymcg.info/tdh-Journal-of-Phillip-Harlock

Key Guide

mymcg.info/tdh-Key-Guide

**The House System
Reference for Players**

mymcg.info/tdh-the-house-system-reference-
for-players

ROOMS INDEX

This inhuman place
makes human monsters.

~Stephen King,
The Shining

RECOMMENDED MEDIA

IN THE BEGINNING . . .

When it was originally designed and subsequently released, *The Darkest House* lived as a web application, so that it could be easily used while gaming online. Because, well, pandemic. That's why all the art, maps, and remnants exist as online resources. All the secret messages were meant to be texts or DMs. There were a lot of suggestions for how to best portray the creepiness and horror over the internet.

It all turned out so beautifully, that one day when Monte was using it, he realized it also really needed to be a big, wonderful, terrifying book, which you now hold in your hands. Every aspect of the product has been reconfigured for you to use in a traditional game played in person. You have all the content here. You're not missing anything.

The app is still available, though, and pretty nifty. We just wanted to give you the choice to visit the Darkest House in whatever way you ~~dare~~ wish.

`The Darkest House`
`App   View   Navigate`

THE DARKEST HOUSE

If you're reading this, you've entered the Darkest House already and it's too late to warn you off. So you might as well discover the house's secrets.

This app presents the rooms of the Darkest House, a house that could be located in any (or every?) world. It's a house with a mind of its own, and a deep, dark hatred for anything and everything that has to do with people. But the app is only a part of all the information and material we've prepared for you to make running the Darkest House adventure as easy and fun as possible.

Take a look at the House Diagram, a flowchart that shows how all the rooms in the house connect (a conventional map would never work because the house doesn't exist within conventional space or worry about trivialities like geometry). Visit the rooms of the house and start reading (we recommend that you start in the Living Room, as that's where the front door is). But to really get started, you probably want to review some of the The Darkest House PDFs. Start with *Secrets of the House*—it's pretty much everything the GM needs to know. *Crossing the Threshold* is meant to be given to your players, as are the different character sheets (there are four different versions) as well as The House System Reference for Players.

You'll want not only *Secrets of the House* with you as you go through the rooms and as you run the adventure, but also the GM's Reference Sheet, which is form-fillable so you can track the house's actions. Plus don't forget the Key Guide, another form-fillable sheet that lets you track the keys that are important to the navigation through the house, as well as which keys the characters have found. Lastly, you can take a look at the *Journal of Phillip Harlock*. Players can find the scattered pages of the journal to see Phillip's descent into madness within the house, but that file offers all the text of the journals in order, so you can get the clearest possible understanding of something that's not at all clear and beyond mortal understanding.

LINKS

ROOM INDEX

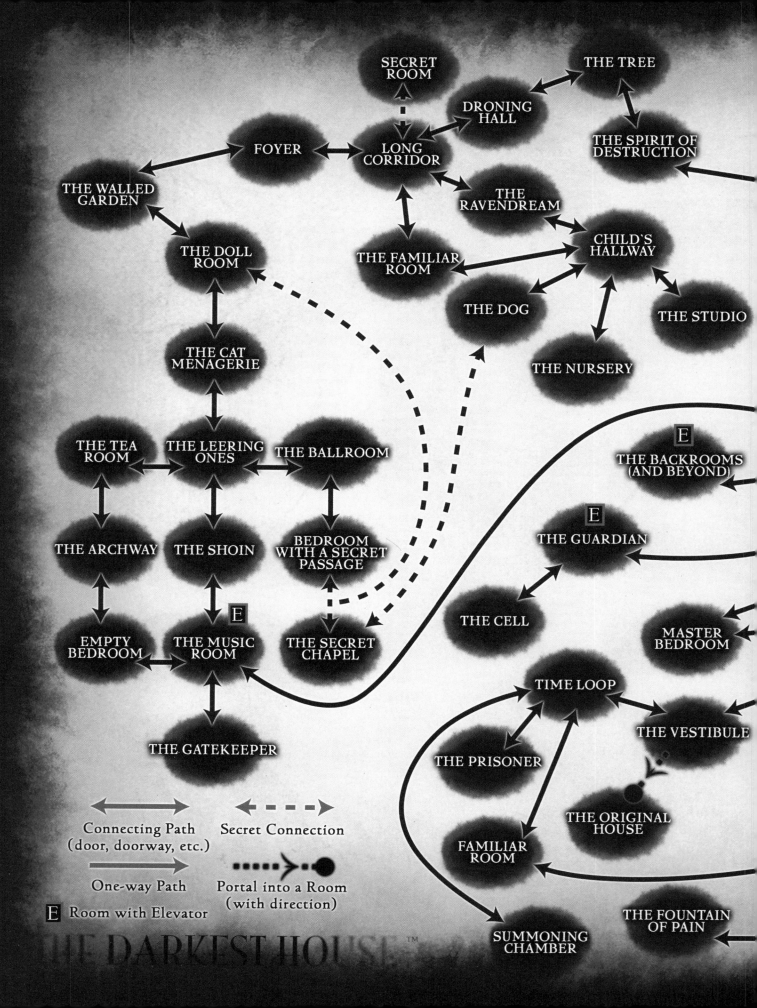

SECRET ROOM

THE TREE

DRONING HALL

THE SPIRIT OF DESTRUCTION

FOYER

LONG CORRIDOR

THE WALLED GARDEN

THE RAVENDREAM

CHILD'S HALLWAY

THE DOLL ROOM

THE FAMILIAR ROOM

THE DOG

THE STUDIO

THE CAT MENAGERIE

THE NURSERY

THE TEA ROOM

THE LEERING ONES

THE BALLROOM

E THE BACKROOMS (AND BEYOND)

THE ARCHWAY

THE SHOIN

BEDROOM WITH A SECRET PASSAGE

E THE GUARDIAN

THE CELL

MASTER BEDROOM

EMPTY BEDROOM

E THE MUSIC ROOM

THE SECRET CHAPEL

TIME LOOP

THE VESTIBULE

THE GATEKEEPER

THE PRISONER

THE ORIGINAL HOUSE

FAMILIAR ROOM

THE FOUNTAIN OF PAIN

SUMMONING CHAMBER

Connecting Path (door, doorway, etc.)

Secret Connection

One-way Path

Portal into a Room (with direction)

E Room with Elevator

THE DARKEST HOUSE ™